EGYPT IN THE ARAB WORLD

Egypt in the Arab World
The Elements of Foreign Policy

A. I. DAWISHA
Lecturer in International Politics
University of Lancaster

A HALSTED PRESS BOOK

JOHN WILEY & SONS
New York

First published in the United Kingdom 1976 by
THE MACMILLAN PRESS LTD
London and Basingstoke

Published in the U.S.A.
by Halsted Press, a Division
of John Wiley & Sons, Inc.
New York.

Printed in Great Britain

Library of Congress Cataloging in Publication Data

Dawisha, A I
    Egypt in the Arab world.

    Bibliography: p.
    1. Arab countries – Foreign relations – Egypt.
2. Egypt – Foreign relations – Arab countries.
I. Title.
DS63.2.E3D38   1976   327.62'017'4927   76-7517
ISBN 0-470-19960-1

For My Father and Mother
Isam and Najma

Contents

List of Tables

List of Figures

Preface

The emergence of the charismatic authority of Gamal Abd al-Nasser in the mid-fifties had a profound impact not only on Egypt's domestic politics, but also on her relations with the rest of the Arab world. By mobilising Egypt's human and material resources, President Nasser pursued an activist Arab policy which consolidated Egypt's primacy in the Arab world. Although Egypt under President Sadat has been increasingly preoccupied with domestic rather than foreign policy, Egypt still sees herself, and is still perceived by the other Arab states, as a central actor in the Middle East regional system. Egypt's involvement in the Arab world, therefore, continues to have a major influence on the configuration of forces in the area.

This book attempts to describe Egypt's foreign policy towards the states of the Arab Middle East. It is divided into two parts. Through the utilisation of a historical analysis, Part One describes the development of Egypt's relations with the other Arab states during the period 1952–70. The second part which forms the major portion of the book explores the setting, the actors, the attitudes and the processes of Egypt's foreign policy. It begins with a methodological chapter setting out a simplified model (a framework of analysis) which involves the identification of the underlying elements of a state's foreign policy and their classification under a series of specified categories. These categories are then explored in detail in successive chapters of the book. They include the capabilities of, and the constraints on, the country's foreign policy, the institutions and processes of policy-making, the values and images of the decision-makers, the political and economic objectives pursued by the policy-makers, and the instruments with which these objectives are implemented. The last chapter then brings the analysis up to date through a detailed application of the model to the Sadat period.

The book, both in content and style, owes much to the intellectual influence of two men. First and foremost, I must thank Professor Geoffrey Goodwin of the London School of Economics for meticulously guiding this work in its initial form as a PhD thesis. Professor Goodwin's advice and criticisms were particularly valuable in matters of methodology, and as such his ideas, as much as those of the author, have helped to shape the book's basic assumptions about the analysis of foreign policy behaviour. In a less specific context, I owe a major intellectual debt to Professor Philip Reynolds of the University of Lancaster, who first introduced me to the rigours and rewards of conceptual analysis in the study of international relations. First as a teacher then as a colleague, his impact on my intellectual development has been considerable.

My thanks also go to Mr David Smidman and Mr David Hemming of Twickenham College of Technology for recognising early in my studies that I was more intellectually suited to the social sciences than to engineering. I also wish to thank Miss Lesley Hoyle, Miss Christine Basset and Mrs Wendy Hópfl for typing the manuscript. Finally, I owe a debt to my wife and colleague, Dr Karen Dawisha of the University of Southampton, whose contribution differs from that traditionally associated with the wife of an academic. Since we have neither children nor a home, I cannot say that she sacrificed her time and energy to shelter me from the traumas of family life. Rather, our frequent discussions and criticisms of each other's work have helped to shape and clarify many of the ideas in this book. Consequently, in this age of equality, she as much as I should be given credit not only for any of the book's virtues but also for its defects.

University of Lancaster   A. I. DAWISHA
January 1976

Acknowledgements

The author and publishers wish to thank the following who have kindly given permission for the use of copyright material: Oxford University Press, Oxford, for Fig. 2 from *The Foreign Policy System of Israel* by M. Brecher; Prentice-Hall, Inc., for Fig. 1 from *International Politics*: A Framework for Analysis, © 1967. Reprinted by permission of the publishers; The State University of New York Press for Table 9 and Fig. 4 from *Egypt Under Nasir* by R. Hrair Dekmejian.

1 The Historical Setting

Egypt occupies a unique position in the Arab world. It constitutes the north-eastern part of Africa and is linked to the Asian continent by the Sinai peninsula. Consequently, Egypt forms a natural bridge between the western and eastern sectors of the Arab world. To the west and south of Egypt lie the African Arab states of Libya, Tunisia, Algeria, Morocco and Sudan. Across Sinai and the Red Sea, Egypt has easy access to the Asian Arab states of Syria, Lebanon, Jordan, Iraq, Saudi Arabia, the two Yemen republics and the Gulf states of Kuwait, Bahrain, Qatar and the United Arab Emirates. Probably more than anything else, it is this geo-strategic position of centrality which explains the traditional persistent Egyptian interest in the area throughout history.

In the African continent, the Egyptian rulers have always perceived the area constituting present day Sudan as vital to Egypt's strategic and economic interests. As early as 1365 BC the area had become culturally and economically incorporated into Egypt.[1] To her west, too, Egypt had experienced continuous interaction with Libya. The great conquests of Pharoah Remsis III owed much to the Libyan mercenaries and slaves in his army. Indeed, around the year 945 BC, the northern Libyans conquered Egypt while the southern Libyans wrested the Sudanese areas from Egyptian control and established an independent monarchy.

Egypt's involvement in Asia is similarly rooted in ancient history. It can be traced back to Thutmose III (1502–1448 BC) who extended Egypt's rule as far east as the banks of the Euphrates in Mesopotamia. Indeed, the earliest known treaty between two sovereigns was that signed by Pharoah Remsis II and the Hitti King in the year 1278 BC.[2] This pact recognised north Syria as Hittite and south Syria as Egyptian and was meant to usher 'peace and good brotherhood between the contending parties for ever'.[3]

As stated above, it was primarily the factor of geographic proximity which contributed to the continuing political, economic and strategic interaction between Egypt and her neighbours in the two continents throughout ancient history. Yet the cultural marriage of the two regions did not occur until the year AD 642 when the Moslem Arabs, emanating from the Arabian Peninsula and having already conquered Iraq, Palestine and Syria, defeated the numerically superior Byzantine forces and entered Alexandria to herald the Arabisation and Islamisation of Egypt. Within the next twenty-eight years Libya and Tunisia were added to the Arab empire, and by AD 710 the entire lands of North Africa had come under the control of the Arabs. It was this series of successful campaigns which set the seal on the cultural character of the area we now call the 'Arab world'.

Egypt's primacy in the Arab world was first initiated during the Fatimid Caliphate (AD 909–1171). During this period, Cairo became the capital, and Egypt the base, of a magnificent civilisation that extended to Syria, Yemen and Hejaz, including the holy cities of Mecca and Medina. The country's primacy was sustained and reinforced through the ascendency of the Ayyubid (1169–1252) and Mamluk (1252–1517) dynasties who, centred in Egypt, went on to control vast segments of the Arab world and were responsible for the final expulsion of the Crusader armies from Palestine. Thus, for over 600 years, until the Ottomans defeated the Mamluks in 1517, Cairo was the centre of gravity in the Arabic and Islamic world.

This historical primacy was not lost on the young army officer who was appointed by the Ottoman Sultan as Viceroy of Egypt in 1805. Albanian by birth, Muhammed Ali Pasha utilised Egypt's supremacy in the Arab world for the purpose of furthering his own irredentist ambitions in the area. In his quest for an Arab empire independent of the Ottoman Sultan and under Egypt's hegemony, Muhammed Ali complemented the method of military conquest with an emphasis on the Arab character of Egypt and the traditional and existing cultural affinities between Egypt and the rest of the Arab world in Asia and Africa.

The Pasha first tried to achieve Egypt's domination of the area with a campaign against the Wahabis of Arabia in 1811. Initially undertaken at the request of the Ottoman Sultan, by 1818 the Arabian War had brought the Arabian Peninsula under Muhammed Ali's control. His next exploit in the Arab east was directed against Syria, which had always figured prominently in the expansionist ambitions of Egyptian rulers. The Pharoahs, the Fatimids, the Ayyubids and the Mamluks had all endeavoured, at one time or another, to extend their political control to Syria. Thus, when Muhammed Ali made a request to Constantinople in 1827 for the addition of Syria to his viceroyship, he was only following in the footsteps of his erstwhile predecessors. The request, however, was rejected by the Ottoman Sultan, who was becoming suspicious of the Viceroy's increasing power in the area. However, Muhammed Ali ignored the Sultan's orders, and in a series of brilliant military campaigns, the Egyptians, under Muhammed Ali's son, Ibrahim Pasha, routed the Turkish armies in 1832 and established total control over Syria. Only the interference of the European powers, particularly Russia, prevented the Egyptians from entering

Constantinople.[4] Between 1832 and 1840, Muhammed Ali was in actual control of a vast segment of the Arab east which included the cities of Mecca, Medina, Jerusalem and Damascus.[5] During these years, both Muhammed Ali and his son advocated and publicised the Arabic character of Egypt as a means of rendering Syria and the Arab east more susceptible to the idea of an exclusive Arab state ruled by Muhammed Ali and his dynasty.[6] However, wary of the Pasha's increasing powers in the area and fearing for her own interests, England in 1840–1, through a combination of diplomatic, military and subversive action, forced Muhammed Ali to abandon all his acquisitions in the Arab east, leaving him with only Egypt and the Sudan.[7]

The incorporation of Sudan into Egypt had been completed by 1839 when after nineteen years of military campaigns, the Egyptian southern thrust reached a point near the present Sudanese–Ugandan border. However, not until the reign of Khedive Ismael in 1866 did the Ottoman Sultan officially recognise Egypt's hereditary control over Sudan. This concession was an acknowledgement on the part of the Sultan of Ismael's vigorous pursuit of Muhammed Ali's goal to restore Egypt's ancient Sudanic empire. By the end of Ismael's rule, the boundaries of Egypt had extended

southwards to the equator, including the Lakes of Albert and Victoria with the territory lying between them. The eastern boundaries reached the shores of the Red Sea and the Gulf of Aden, while the Sudan, on its southeastern boundary, touched the Indian Ocean, thus including Swakin, Mosawah, Teila, Barbara, Harar, and the northern coasts of Somaliland. All the western shores of the Red Sea from Suez in the north to Bab El-Mandab in the south were parts of Egypt. Egypt's dominion also extended to the shores of the Gulf of Aden from Bab El-Mandab to Cape Cordafwi 'Guardafui' and to Cape Hafoun. The Egyptian Empire extended westwards to the Kingdom of Wadai which lay to the west of Darfour.[8]

While this imperial expansion extended Egypt's political control and influence, it weighed heavily on the country's fragile economy, especially after the collapse of cotton prices following the termination of the American Civil War. This was aggravated by the Khedive's own personal extravagance. For example, to celebrate the opening of the Suez Canal in 1869, he entertained European royalty at a cost of 2 million Egyptian pounds. The accumulation of personal and national debts to European financiers forced Ismael to sell his shares in the canal company to the British government, and to allow Egypt to be placed under the financial control of Britain and France. These were the first steps in a tragic process that was to eventually lead to the occupation of Egypt by Britain in 1882.

The period of British rule in Egypt coincided with the rise of nationalist aspirations among the Arabic-speaking regions of the Ottoman empire. Paradoxically, this period witnessed an increase in cultural linkages between Egypt and the other Arab regions. Egypt under Lord Cromer became an intellectual haven for the Arab nationalists who, persecuted in their own countries by the Ottoman authorities, found in Egypt a measure of freedom in which they channelled their anti-Turkish nationalist sentiment. However, in the ensuing nationalist drive for independence, there was an important point of departure between the Arab nationalists and the Egyptians. While the former utilised the concept of 'Arab nationalism' in their fight against the 'Turkish' Ottoman Empire, the Egyptians were increasingly resorting to 'Egyptian nationalism' as the major ideological motivation for their anti-British independence struggle.[9] The Egyptian nationalist leaders did not conceive of their anti-British campaign as constituting a part of the general Arab struggle for independence. For example, the term 'Arab' was completely absent from the memorandum on 'Egypt's national claims' which the Egyptian nationalist leader, Saad Zaghloul Pasha, presented to the Geneva Peace Conference in 1919.[10] In short, the Egyptian nationalist leaders saw their struggle purely as a fight to assert Egyptian sovereignty and integrity over Egyptian soil.

It was not until the end of the Second World War that efforts at political co-operation between the various independent Arab states were operationalised through the establishment of the 'Arab League'. The creation of the League was basically the result of competition for the political leadership of the Arab world between the rulers of Iraq and Egypt, Nuri al-Said and Mustafa Nahas Pasha.[11] In 1943, Nuri al-Said circulated his famous 'blue book' which called for the immediate federation of Syria, Palestine, Jordan and Lebanon. This was to be followed by the establishment of an 'Arab League' which would initially comprise Iraq and the newly federated state. Other Arab governments would then be encouraged to join the League.[12] Nahas Pasha, suspicious of any unity move designed to create a strong and united Hashemite entity to the east of the canal, immediately initiated his own counter-moves. In a series of bilateral talks with the Arab leaders, he presented the idea of a 'League of Sovereign Arab States' as a counter-proposal to Nuri's plan. As a result of these extended negotiations, the leaders of Egypt, Syria, Iraq and Trans-Jordan met in Alexandria in September 1944 and produced the 'Alexandria Protocol' which provided for the future convocation of a 'General Arab Congress' in order to institute a 'League of Arab States'. The Congress duly convened in March 1945 and established the League, whose aims were to strengthen relations between the independent Arab states, to co-ordinate their policies, and to work for the general interests of the Arab countries.[13]

It seems clear, therefore, that Egypt's interaction with the Arab world had tended historically to assume a political and strategic rather than an ideological character. Thus, Muhammed Ali's involvement in the Arabian Peninsula and Syria was primarily the result of irredentist ambitions. The cultural affinity existing between the two regions was used as a convenient instrument for facilitating such ambitions. Considerations of regional and domestic power politics on the part of some Egyptian decision-makers were more important factors in the establishment of the Arab League than a clear-cut ideological Arab orientation. In short, as the movement for 'independence' in the area clearly shows, Egypt seems to have been little inspired or motivated by an 'Arab sentiment'.[14]

PART I

The Relations of Egypt with the Arab World, 1952-70

2 Pre-Union Involvement, 1952-8

On July 23, 1952, a number of army officers carried out a coup against the existing regime in Egypt. They abolished the monarchy and proclaimed the advent of the Egyptian Republic. The officers were nominally led by General Muhammed Nagib. Real power, however, rested with an eleven-man committee of junior officers known as the Revolutionary Command Council whose acknowledged leader was Colonel Gamal Abd al-Nasser. General Nagib had been hastily recruited on the night of the coup to add a semblance of legitimacy and respectability to the new order.

During the initial period of the revolution, the new military rulers saw themselves mainly as Egyptian nationalists with a mission to implement social reform domestically, and to expel the 'imperialist' forces from Egyptian soil. As such, they tended to reflect the ideological orientations of the earlier generation of Egyptian nationalists in so far as their priorities lay primarily with Egyptian, rather than Arab affairs. Their paramount foreign policy objective, therefore, was to resolve the dispute with Britain over Sudan. As we have seen, Sudan had been officially regarded as an indivisible part of Egypt since the reign of Khedive Ismael. However, real control of the territory passed on to Britain after the latter's occupation of Egypt. British control over the Sudan was later legitimised through the 1899 accord with Egypt, in which the Egyptians recognised Britain's seniority in the condominium of Sudan.

Like all of their predecessors, the new rulers of Egypt adhered to and vigorously pursued Egypt's irredentic aspirations in the African continent, namely the 'unity of the Nile valley'. To achieve this goal, however, the Egyptian leadership had to first eliminate British control over Sudan. To this end, General Nagib opened negotiations with Abd al-Rahman al-Mahdi, leader of the pro-British Umma party in Sudan, which carried the main opposition to unity with Egypt. On the basis of these talks, Egypt and Britain later reached an agreement on February 12, 1953, which signalled the end of British rule and gave the Sudanese the option to choose between independence and unity with Egypt.

Immediately, the Egyptian junta set out to influence Sudanese public opinion in favour of union with Egypt. Large sums of money were spent and intense propaganda utilised to reorient Sudanese per-

9

ceptions northwards towards Egypt. Initially, these efforts were rewarded when the Umma party was defeated in the first parliamentary elections and the pro-Egypt National Union Party (NUP) formed Sudan's first national government under Ismael al-Azhari in early 1954.

Egypt responded with understandable satisfaction. It was felt that Egypt's aspiration of uniting the Nile valley had become realisable with the NUP's success in Sudan. Consequently, Egyptian propaganda under the direction of Major Salah Salem was intensified. General Nagib, himself half Sudanese, made a number of visits to Sudan and so did other important officers and officials of Sudanese origin.

Egypt's high hopes, however, were not destined to last for very long. It soon became apparent that the Sudanese were as hostile to future Egyptian domination as they were to existing British control. The growing anti-union feeling among the Sudanese was soon reflected in the political orientation of the NUP and its leader, al-Azhari, who were beginning to favour total independence. The Egyptians were alarmed but still hopeful. In an interview in July 1955, Nasser agreed that there had been some change of attitude among the National Unionists, but he was sure that the party still stood for some form of link with Egypt. He, nevertheless, admitted that if the Sudanese were to opt out for complete independence, it would be 'a great personal tragedy'.[1] These fears were soon justified when on January 1, 1956 on the recommendation of the Sudanese parliament, al-Azhari declared the independence of the Sudan. The Egyptians stoically concealed their obvious frustration and hastened to commend the declaration. Egypt's long-standing and traditional foreign policy goal in Africa of promoting the unity of the Nile valley had come to an abrupt and disappointing end.

Apart from the Sudanese involvement, the initial years after the revolution witnessed minimal Egyptian participation in Arab affairs. In fact, this period saw the almost complete isolation of Egypt from the Arab world, as the new leaders channelled their energies to Anglo-Egyptian relations and to the consolidation and legitimisation of their political control within Egypt. Yet by 1958, 'every Arab revolutionary [had come] to regard himself as a Nasserite irrespective of his willingness to relinquish his sovereign status in favour of Egyptian domination'.[2] In other words, in less than five years, a radical change had occurred in the orientations of the policy-making elite, transforming them from Egyptian patriots to proclaimed Arab nationalists and elevating Nasser to the leadership of the 'Arab Nationalist Movement'.

The root of this change could probably be traced to May 1953 when John Foster Dulles, the United States Secretary of State, visited Cairo to muster support for his plan for a Western defence alliance to counter the perceived Communist threat to the region. Responding to Dulles's

proposals, the Egyptian leaders stressed that as far as they were concerned, the only possible communist threat would.emanate from within
the region itself rather than from the Soviet Union, 'whose forces were
five thousand miles away'.[3] To the Egyptians, strengthening the already
existing Arab Collective Security Pact would be the most effective
deterrent to any potential takeover by indigenous Communist
elements.[4]

Nasser's lukewarm reception of Dulles's plan lay in his scepticism
over the nature of 'Western' alliances. Ideologically, Nasser perceived
such alliances as renewed manifestations of 'imperialist' forces in the
region, the very forces he and his colleagues had promised to eradicate.
The new leaders, therefore, showed little inclination for joining any
'Western-controlled' alliance. This course of action, however, would
have inevitably led to a further problem: if the other Arab states were
to join, Egypt would then find herself politically and strategically
isolated from the rest of the region. Thus, the policy of the Egyptian
leaders was not only to boycott these pacts, but also actively discourage other Arab states from joining as well.

Egypt, therefore, had to break out from her self-imposed isolation
and to pursue a more active Arab policy. More emphasis was laid on
concepts such as 'Arab unity' and 'Arab brotherhood'. In July 1953,
the 'Voice of the Arabs' started its radio transmissions to the Arab
world. In January 1954, its transmission time was trebled, and it
declared that 'the Voice of the Arabs speaks for the Arabs, struggles for
them and expresses their unity.'[5] During the same month, an official
communique pronounced the establishment of an Arab bloc free from
imperialist influences to be a principle of Egypt's foreign policy.[6]
On July 23, 1954 in a major address, Premier Nasser declared that the
'aim of the revolutionary government is for the Arabs to become one
nation . . . the weight of the defence of the Arab states falls first and
foremost on the Arabs and they are worthy of undertaking it.'[7] That
same month, the transmission time of the Voice of the Arabs was
increased by four hours daily.

Egypt's wholehearted entry into regional Arab politics, however, did
not fully emerge until January 1955. It was mainly a response to the
sudden announcement by Nuri al-Said of the Iraqi–Turkish Treaty.
Most analysts agree that the Treaty (later to be known as the Baghdad
Pact) was the single most important variable in regional power politics
which served to change the entire configuration of forces in the region,
thus giving rise to new power alignments and constellations. It compelled Nasser and Egypt fully to enter, participate in, and then
dominate the regional politics of the Arab Middle East.

The Egyptian leaders waited for only four days after the announcement of the Baghdad Pact before starting their own counter-attack.
On January 16, Egypt launched its first radio and press campaign

against Western alliances in general and the Baghdad Pact in particular. In the meantime, the Egyptian leaders endeavoured to strengthen and secure Egypt's diplomatic position in the region. In early March, Nasser formed an alliance with Syria which was endorsed by Saudi Arabia and the Yemen. It was proclaimed that the alliance was to be the beginning of a wider integration of the Arab World.[8] These moves were cemented later in the year when, in the name of 'Pan-Arabism', Egypt signed the Egyptian–Syrian Mutual Defence Pact, followed a week later, on October 27, by another pact with Saudi Arabia which the Yemen joined. In a sense, these alliances were Egypt's practical answer to Nuri's proclamation that the Arab countries had no other alternative but to rely on the West for their security. These pacts may not have had much military significance; however, their importance lay in their psychological effect on the Arab populations by their exhibition of the seeming independence of the Arab states. They also highlighted Egypt's central and leading position in the Arab world.

Egypt's prestige was further enhanced through Nasser's participation in the Bandung conference of the non-aligned states in April 1955. In the conference, Nasser was treated as an Arab, rather than just an Egyptian leader. He had important meetings with major neutralist statesmen such as Tito, Nehru and Sukarno, as well as Chou En-Lai. He thus emerged from the conference, and was perceived by many Arabs, as a major figure in the emerging Third World neutralist camp. This contributed to a considerable elevation of Nasser's image in the Arab world. Consequently, the attention of the Arabs were being increasingly drawn to the Cairo radio stations, whose propaganda had, by now, 'shifted its focus from earlier attacks on Egypt's evil past to an offensive against reaction and dependence upon imperialism in the Arab world as a whole.'[9]

Another event which contributed to the enhancement of Egyptian prestige in the Arab world was the conclusion of the Czech arms deal in September 1955, which, in Arab eyes, further endorsed Egypt's proclaimed independence from 'Western influence'. The reasons for the deal could probably be traced directly to February 28, 1955, when the Israelis launched a massive raid on Gaza, destroying the Egyptian headquarters there, killing thirty-eight soldiers and wounding thirty-one. Whatever the reasons for this attack,[10] its impact on Egypt and the Arabs was considerable. It exhibited the near-impotence of the Egyptian armed forces and intensified the external and domestic pressures on Nasser. Externally, the Arab populations who had given him their support were now bound to question the viability of an Arab security alliance. Domestically, Nasser came under pressure from the army. He admitted that his soldiers had been ineffective and that his officers had accused him of spending too much on Egypt's social services and too little on her defence.

Nasser had, in fact, been willing to spend more on his armed forces. He had consistently asked Britain and the United States for more arms, but these requests were either refused or held in abeyance by bureaucratic or Congressional procrastinations. Although some Centurion tanks had been delivered by the British, these were no match for the substantial arms deliveries the Israelis were beginning to receive from the French.[11] In January 1955, Nasser informed the American and British ambassadors that he was prepared to acquire arms from any source if their governments' intransigence continued. In February the United States refused a $27 million arms request from Nasser on the grounds that Egypt was unable to pay for them in hard currency.[12] During the following months, while British and American refusal to satisfy Nasser's arms request persisted, he received and communicated to the West a Russian offer of military and industrial assistance. However, the reaction from the United States and Britain remained negative.[13]

Meanwhile, the border tensions between Egypt and Israel had increased. The Egyptian Fedayeen (the Egyptian guerrilla force) had become more active, and Israel retaliated by intensifying her military activity in the area. Between August 22 and September 21, Israel initiated four major military operations – attacking Gaza and Khan Yunis, shelling the town of Gaza on a market day, and invading and occupying the Al-Auja triangle, a demilitarised zone under the 1949 armistice agreement. The Egyptian army could do nothing to prevent Israel's incursions into Egyptian territory or to check her undoubted military superiority, and consequently there was a danger that Nasser's insistence on Egyptian and Arab strength would begin to lose credibility among the Arabs. It was, thus, imperative that he should strengthen his army. On September 27, 1955, he announced the Czech arms deal.

The arms deal contributed immensely to enhancing Nasser's popularity and esteem in the Arab world. His paramount position as a neutral and independent leader had been reinforced. Politically conscious Arabs saw in the arms deal an elimination of the Western arms monopoly and an emphatic assertion of Arab independence. The enthusiasm for the arms deal by Arabs was such that it even compelled the staunch pro-Western Nuri al-Said to pledge his own support of the deal. Nevertheless, the power configuration in the Arab Middle East had become polarised into the pro-Nasser and the anti-Nasser camps. As a result, diplomatic channels experienced an inevitable strain. In fact diplomatic communication had been nearly severed since the creation of the Baghdad Pact, which led to the emergence of propaganda as the major instrument of Egypt's foreign policy in the Arab World. The Egyptian leadership used the radio to impose, through pressure of public opinion, considerable constraints on the governments of the other Arab states. For example, Charles Cremeans argues that

> Nasser's outpouring of propaganda . . . and particularly his empha-
> sis upon Pan-Arabism and the importance of Arab solidarity against
> 'imperialism' and Israel, soon began to affect Arab public opinion,
> undermining any inclination the Arab leaders in other states might
> have had to support Iraq.[14]

The above argument can be well illustrated by Jordan's ultimate
refusal to join the Baghdad Pact. Britain and Turkey had tried to
persuade Lebanon and Jordan to join the Pact, but the Lebanese
indicated that they would wait for the Jordanian decision first. The
Jordanian Prime Minister, Habis al-Majali, had already declared his
intention to join, and a formal request for membership was handed to
the British ambassador on November 16, 1955. In December, Sir
Gerald Templer, the British Chief of Staff, arrived in Amman seemingly to discuss Baghdad Pact membership. Egypt immediately unleashed
a violent propaganda campaign against the Templer mission, and the
country witnessed, throughout his visit, a wave of strikes, demonstrations and riots which was instrumental in bringing two governments
down. The Templer mission failed, and both Jordan and Lebanon
shied away from the Pact, never to contemplate joining it again.

Although 'Radio Cairo' and 'The Voice of the Arabs' were instrumental in encouraging riots and demonstrations against the Pact, it is
erroneous to cite radio propaganda as the sole cause for the demonstrations. The Pact, from its inception, was met with hostility from the
majority of the politically aware Arabs. The role of the Egyptian radio,
therefore, was to crystallise and encourage already existing attitudes
and beliefs which proved to be susceptible and sympathetic to Cairo's
message.

The end of 1955, therefore, saw the ascendency of Egypt over its
political antagonists in the Arab world. Syria, Saudi Arabia and the
Yemen were allies, the pro-Western Lebanon and Hashemite Jordan
had refused to join the Baghdad Pact, and Iraq was successfully isolated
from the main current of Arab politics. Egypt had now firmly moved
from the periphery to the core of the Middle-Eastern international
system and as such had become the focus not only of the Arab political
situation, but also, and perhaps more importantly, of its major ideological manifestation, the 'Arab nationalist movement'. This new role
for Egypt was legitimised by Nasser when for the first time in Egypt's
history, the first article of the 1956 constitution declared that 'Egypt
is a sovereign, independent *Arab* state . . . and the Egyptian people
are an integral part of the *Arab* nation [my italics].'[15]

Domestically, the junta's pursuit of support-winning measures concentrated on the construction of the Aswan High Dam, presented as
the symbol of the new, dynamic, industrialised Egypt. The Aswan Dam

had been, since the first year of the revolution, the major development scheme planned by the officers for Egypt. As it was conceived, it would extend continuous irrigation to Upper Egypt, thus enabling another 125 million acres of land to be cultivated. Moreover, it would also provide electric power for the envisaged industrialisation programme. In December 1955, the United States, Britain and the World Bank offered to assist Egypt in building the dam. This offer, however, was accompanied by several conditions, including the supervision of Egypt's budget and her balance of payments. Nasser hesitated at such stipulations which amounted, in his opinion, to foreign control of the Egyptian economy. The United States and Britain, on the other hand, had already decided that Nasser's reaction to the offer and the conditions attached would be an important factor in assessing future prospects for his co-operation with the West.[16] As such, Nasser's hesitation was interpreted by Eden and Dulles as a surreptitious effort to negotiate a separate deal with the Soviet Union. Dulles, therefore, publicly announced on July 18, 1956 that the United States had decided to withdraw its offer of assistance to Egypt mainly because 'the ability of Egypt to devote adequate resources to assure the project's success has become more uncertain than at the time the offer was made.'[17] Nasser retaliated quickly and decisively. In a major speech a week later, he declared that since the Western powers refused to finance the dam, Egypt was compelled to raise her own money. This it could only achieve by nationalising the Suez Canal Company.

The British and French response to the nationalisation was the tripartite attack on Egypt, the primary objective of which was to topple Nasser and restore the international character of the canal. It began with the Israeli invasion of Sinai on October 29, 1956, and on November 5, as prearranged, British and French paratroopers were dropped on Port Said.[18] However, the Allied initiative slowly came to a halt, mainly because urgently needed American support was not forthcoming, and consequently a run on sterling, among other reasons, finally forced Eden and Mollet to capitulate. At midnight on November 6, a cease-fire was announced.

Although the Egyptian leaders had lost part of their army and air-force, and their revenues from the canal and the oil of Sinai, the final outcome was a victory for Egypt. The British and French had failed to topple Nasser, and the canal remained under Egyptian control. Suez, in fact, gave Nasser 'almost unlimited credit in his own country and throughout the Arab world'.[19] It bestowed upon him the aura of a hero who dared to defy the might of the tripartite powers, and win.

The support from the majority of Arab public opinion received by the Egyptian leadership throughout the Suez crisis was considerable. The pro-British Iraqi government was compelled through pressure of public opinion to condemn Anglo-French action as a flagrant collusion with Israel. The Iraqis refused to sit with Britain in a Baghdad Pact meeting, and diplomatic relations with France were severed. Syria and Saudi Arabia broke relations with both countries, and the Jordanian Arab Legion seized some of the British army stores in Amman. Thus, at the end of a crisis designed to affect his demise from the Arab political scene, Nasser emerged as the prime manipulator of Arab politics.

At the end of 1956, President Nasser's influence in the Arab world had become more conspicuous. In Jordan, a nationalist government headed by Suleiman Nabulsi had been elected on October 21, 1956 and had promptly joined Syria and Egypt in a military pact which placed Jordanian and Syrian forces under an Egyptian commander-in-chief. In January 1957, the 'Treaty of Arab Solidarity' was concluded among Egypt, Saudi Arabia, Syria and Jordan for a period of ten years.

This was Nasser's high tide. Throughout the Arab world he was supported by the majority of the populations and many of their governments. In order to make this leading role credible, an Arab orientation began to replace the domestically oriented policies of the pre-1955 period. This new orientation was gradually utilised as the paramount reason for explaining actions of, and decisions taken by, the Egyptian leadership. Even the coup of 1952 was now being explained in terms of Arab nationalism. In an article in *Al-Ahram* in March 1957, Anwar al-Sadat, an important member of the leadership, declared:

> there was nothing behind our coup other than Arab nationalism . . . which awakened a new historical development . . . We must nurture this link between the peoples of the Arab nation . . . for when the revolution occurred in Egypt, it rendered the Arab nation one nation, sharing one history and claiming one destiny.[20]

Nevertheless, the full emergence of an Arab dimension to Nasser's policies and his utilisation of radio propaganda in appealing to mass opinion over the heads of their governments, gradually forced the hands of his allies who had become suspicious of what his popularity and his revolutionary use of the concept of 'Arab nationalism' could do to their positions within their own states. What precipitated the break was a sustained American initiative, epitomised by the Eisenhower Doctrine announced in January 1957, which pledged American assistance including the dispatch of armed forces to nations requesting American help 'against overt armed aggression from any nation controlled by international communism'.[21]

That same month Saud visited the United States. Erskine Childers claims that the visit was arranged by ARAMCO in the hope that Saud would be made into 'the rallying figurehead for anti-Nasser and anti-neutralist forces'.[22] The fact that after his return Saud did change his pro-Nasser stance must be regarded as a vital coup for the American government; for it must be remembered that throughout the intra-Arab conflict over the Baghdad Pact, the debate over the Czech arms deal, and the crisis of Suez, Saudi Arabia was Egypt's staunchest ally. Indeed, its Arab policy followed that of Egypt so closely that, according to one observer, Saudi Arabia seemed to be 'on the way of becoming Egypt's most valuable colony'.[23] However, during 1957, Saud gradually shifted his policies away from the Egyptian line. This change was first noticed when he sent troops to help his old enemy the Hashemite Hussein against the pro-Nasser Nabulsi, and culminated on March 5, 1958 with Nasser's disclosure that Saud had attempted to assassinate him in order to stop the union between Egypt and Syria.

The next erosion of Nasser's influence in the Arab World occurred in Jordan in early 1957. The popular nationalist policies of Nabulsi had been approved by King Hussein, and both leaders had been eulogised by Cairo radio as the heroes of 'Arab nationalism'. However, Hussein began to perceive Nabulsi's popularity as an indication of the Egyptian potential to infiltrate and subsequently dominate Jordan. He therefore dismissed Nabulsi on April 10 and requested military help from Iraq and Saudi Arabia. For the next fortnight massive civil disturbances plagued the country, and Hussein allegedly survived two 'coups' against him from the Nabulsi followers.

The rioters were urged on by Egyptian radio which accused 'imperialist forces' within the palace of trying to ally Jordan with the Baghdad Pact. On April 23, Dulles, in a statement to the press, made a pointed invitation to Hussein to ask for American help. This encouraged Hussein to call a press conference the next day in which he accused Egypt of being behind the riots and the two abortive coups. He then declared martial law and embarked on a mass arrest of pro-Nabulsi elements. The United States followed this action with military and economic aid worth $70 million.[24] 'In Washington, a State Department spokesman coolly called attention to the obvious connection between the Hussein press conference, the Dulles statement and the Eisenhower Doctrine.'[25] The Egyptian leaders retorted by unleashing a propaganda campaign against Hussein, so violent in tone and content that it led to Jordan breaking diplomatic relations with Egypt in June.

Consequently, in the summer of 1957 Nasser had only one ally left: Syria. In six short months, he had witnessed the gradual disintegration of the alliance system he had built around him. Saudi Arabia no longer toed the Egyptian line; Jordan had severed her diplomatic relations with Egypt; the Lebanese Prime Minister, Camille Chamoun, had publicly accepted the Eisenhower Doctrine; and Iraq was counteracting Cairo's propaganda with a corresponding propaganda campaign of her own. Thus, although Nasser was still the most influential

Arab leader, the diplomatic ascendancy over Iraq that cemented his popular image had, by the summer of 1957, been thoroughly eroded. Only Syria remained a faithful ally, and she was in the midst of an international crisis.

The Syrian Defence Minister, Khalid al-Azm, a wealthy landowner of vague pro-Soviet leanings had led, in August 1957, a high-level delegation to Moscow and concluded a major agreement for military and economic aid. On his return he replaced the Syrian Chief of Staff with an officer of perceived Communist sympathies. Reports emanating primarily from Baghdad and Beirut exaggerated the gravity of the situation and convinced the Americans of an impending Communist takeover. On August 24, Mr Loy Henderson, Deputy Under-Secretary of State for Administration, arrived in Ankara to confer with allies and members of the Baghdad Pact. After discussing the situation with the leaders of Iraq, Jordan, Turkey and Lebanon, it seems that the emerging consensus of opinion was that 'the present regime in Syria had to go; otherwise the take-over by the Communists would soon be complete.'[26] Turkish troops moved along the Syrian borders in September, and the Turkish government hinted that it may take action if the Communists came to power in Syria.

A fortnight of tension ensued. Cairo unleashed a barrage of propaganda against the United States and its 'stooges' in the Arab world. It accused the Eisenhower administration of plotting against Syria and alleged that the United States was inciting Syria's neighbours against her in the hope that this would facilitate the invocation of the Eisenhower Doctrine. This propaganda was instrumental in increasing the hostility of many Arabs against American policy in the Middle East, which in turn exerted immense pressure on those Arab leaders sympathetic to the United States. Thus, far from increasing their capabilities, those leaders found that their identification with the Eisenhower Doctrine, by virtue of its extreme unpopularity with their public, was proving to be a substantial constraint on their actions. Consequently, by the first week of September, it had become clear that any interference in Syrian affairs by another Arab country would bring considerable unrest and domestic upheaval in that country. One by one, those leaders who had originally favoured taking some form of action against Syria, began to disengage. The Jordanian Foreign Minister declared that Jordan had no intention of interfering in Syria's domestic affairs; the Iraqi Premier announced 'complete understanding with the Syrian President';[27] and King Saud sent a message to Eisenhower urging moderation towards Syria.

As the crisis gradually subsided, the pro-unionist forces inside Syria embarked upon a concerted effort of campaigning for unity with Egypt. At the head of these forces was the pan-Arab Baath Party, which by 1957 had become an important political force in Syria. Dominated by two intellectuals, Michel Aflaq and Salah Bitar, and a tough politician, Akram Hourani, they commanded considerable support among the urban professional classes and intellegentsia. They had many sympathisers within the army ranks and they possessed a pivotal role in the Syrian Cabinet with the ministries of Economy and Foreign Affairs.

The main theme of the Baath agitation was the call for the unity of all the Arabs, but the Baath's perception of 'Arab Unity' was different from that envisaged by Nasser. While Nasser sought the establishment of a common front amongst the Arab states in the face of perceived foreign interference, the Baath conceived of unity 'as the urgently needed liberation of an already existing "Arab Nation" from political interference and pseudo-national divisions imposed on it by foreign interests'.[28] This perceptual difference did not come to the surface until after unity had taken place. However, in the years immediately preceding the union, the Baath identified itself and its policies fully with Nasser and acknowledged Egypt's central position in the Arab world. They needed, and waited for, the opportunity to compel Egypt to unite.

In the autumn of 1957, there was a near paralysis of political life in Syria. The crisis of the summer had subsided but had left in its wake three forces competing against each other: the conservative, feudalist and financial classes; the Baathists and their nationalist allies; and the Communists. This conflict was also reflected in the army where there was now almost complete diffusion of power which prevented the usual practice of a prominent group taking over and restoring stability among the warring political factions. As this political stalemate persisted, attention turned to Cairo. A solution to the deadlock had to be found to prevent a complete disintegration of political life. On January 12, 1958, the Chief of Staff led a delegation of fourteen officers to Cairo to try to persuade Nasser to accept some form of unity with Syria and a week later, Salah Bitar, the Baathist Foreign Minister, joined the officers for the talks with Nasser.[29]

The Syrians, encouraged by the Baathists among them, surprised Nasser by demanding more than the expected federal union. They argued that federal union would be neither strong enough nor popular enough to combat Communist and conservative pressures. Sensing Nasser's reluctance, they proceeded to limit his options by appealing to his declared role as the 'Leader of Arab Nationalism'. The Baathists were the main driving force behind and architects of these demands, for they were the only party to benefit from the union. If the union were to be achieved, then they hoped to form the ideological base for the new united state. They would thus be able to utilise Nasser's prestige as the means to achieve their own objectives. In short, it was hoped that the Baath would formulate the ideology and Nasser would verbalise it. As Salah Bitar put it, 'We, in the Baath, always hoped that a union would foster in Egypt the same nationalist sentiments that fired us.'[30]

Nasser, his options limited and under pressure, reacted swiftly. He argued that if federal union was not a viable proposition, then union should be total and this meant the complete and organic merger of Syria and Egypt, with the condition that the Syrian political system should follow that of Egypt. In other words, all political parties had to be dissolved; the Syrian army had to withdraw from politics; the two economies had to be blended; and state control and agricultural reform had to be extended to Syria.

The Baathists were obviously caught by surprise. The last thing they wanted was the dissolution of their own party, but they had already committed themselves, and they could not back down now, not while Nasser was ostensibly offering them their maximum objective. In any case, they reasoned that they would still be a dynamic political force within the National Union (Nasser's sole political organisation) which they might eventually be able to dominate. On this basis, the United Arab Republic, under the presidency of Gamal Abd al-Nasser, was announced on February 1, 1958.

3   The UAR and the Arab World, 1958-61

Three weeks after the announcement heralding the creation of the United Arab Republic, a plebiscite approved the merger under Nasser's presidency by a vote of over 99.8 per cent in both Syria and Egypt, which became the Northern and Southern Regions, respectively, of the UAR. A new provisional constitution was promulgated on March 5, 1958 in which the President of the unified republic was given sweeping powers. He could appoint and dismiss ministers and vice-presidents; he could initiate and veto legislation; he was given the authority to convoke and dissolve the National Assembly; and he was made responsible for the formulation and implementation of foreign policy.[1]

As befits Nasser's style, he quickly moved to augment these legalistic measures with effective means of political enforcement. He immediately dispatched hand-picked security men to Syria, and he started the process of unifying the foreign services. Soon after, Field Marshall Abd al-Hakim Amer, Nasser's heir-apparent, was appointed Commander-in-Chief of the combined armed forces, and one of his first actions was the dismissal of thirteen pro-Soviet officers, including the Chief of Staff, from the Syrian command.

The news of the union was greeted with almost universal enthusiasm by Arab public opinion throughout the Arab world. No more so than in Syria, which gave Nasser a tumultuous welcome on his first visit there as its President. Only three weeks earlier, he had, in a speech to the Egyptian National Assembly, struck a note of caution advising the Egyptians not to be swept by the excitement of the present into underestimating the inevitable problems lying ahead.[2] But in Syria, he himself was swept by the emotions generated by the adulating crowd and was led to declare his hopes for a wider unity of all the Arab people.[3]

The changes precipitated by the newly found union affected the images of the other Arab leaders who perceived the infant republic, in its capacity as a symbol for the aspirations of their own indigenous populations, as a direct threat to their own political positions. This necessitated new alignments and power clusters among various states. Thus, the two Hashemite kings of Iraq and Jordan announced on February 12, 1958 the formation of the 'Arab Union Federation' and asked Nuri al-Said to become its first Prime Minister. The union's primary purpose was to consolidate the Hashemite alliance in the face

21

of the initial upsurge of nationalist, anti-Western (and consequently, anti-Hashemite) sentiment engendered by the birth of the new republic. Furthermore, within the traditional context of Egyptian–Iraqi rivalry over Syria,[4] the creation of the UAR meant a political and strategic incursion into Iraq's role in the configuration of forces in the area. Fadhil al-Jamali, the Iraqi Foreign Minister, fiercely attacked the UAR, calling it 'an artificial creation based on propaganda and personal interests'. He added that 'the truth which should be grasped by every Arab who claims to be a nationalist is that isolation of Syria from Iraq is against the [Arab] national interest.'[5]

In the Lebanon, the impact of the formation of the UAR on the strictly confessional and sectarian society was the direct cause of the disintegration of domestic national cohesion.[6] The Lebanese political structure was, and remains, based on the 'Pact of 1943' which divided governmental responsibilities between Christians and Moslems. The pact was designed to orient Lebanese domestic politics towards a compromise situation between two communities. However, an ideological schism between those communities had existed since before 1943; for while the majority of the Christians advocated the preservation of Lebanon's independence as the primary goal of Lebanese politics and feared the perceived expansionist tendencies of 'Arab nationalism', the majority of the Moslems' national identification stretched beyond Lebanon's political boundaries to the wider ideological frontiers of the 'Arab nation'.

The announcement of the UAR's formation acted as a catalyst for the further polarisation of an already potentially explosive societal structure. Consequently, in the days immediately following the UAR announcement, many of the Moslem schools closed down in Lebanon for the purpose of celebrations, and demonstrations were held throughout the country despite governmental bans. Delegation after delegation crossed over to Syria to congratulate its leaders on the 'historic decision' and were told by President Quwatly of Syria that the Lebanon was invited to join whenever she so desired. The Christian community, however, was simultaneously and feverishly reiterating its faith in, and hopes for, the continuation of Lebanon's sovereignty. Both Camille Chamoun and Charles Malik, Lebanon's President and Foreign Minister, respectively, insisted that Lebanon's independence and national integrity had to be maintained at all costs. The increasing polarisation between the two communities was to erupt into a civil war in May 1958, which the Lebanese government blamed entirely on the UAR.

Taking the matter to the United Nations, Dr Malik, in a bitter speech to the Security Council, accused the UAR of massive interference in Lebanon's domestic affairs which, according to the Foreign Minister, was conducted through a large supply of arms to the rebels, the training of subversive elements in Syria, the participation of UAR nationals in the civil war, and the employment of hostile press and radio campaigns against the Lebanon.[7] These allegations were, however, completely rejected by the Egyptian delegate, who insisted that the UAR had no wish to interfere in Lebanon's internal affairs.[8] The Security Council subsequently adopted a Swedish compromise resolution which established the United Nations Observation Group in Lebanon (UNOGIL). During the five months from June until November 1958 in which the group operated, five reports were submitted to the Security Council on the situation.

An analysis of these reports indicates that the Lebanese accusations of the alleged UAR supply of arms and the supposed massive infiltration of men from Syria were largely unfounded. By July 30, the observers had in no case 'been able to detect the presence of persons who have indubitably entered from across the borders for the purpose of fighting'.[9] In the case of arms smuggling, the group concluded that 'while there may have been a limited importation of arms into some areas prior to the Presidential elections on July 31, any such movement has since markedly diminished.'[10] As such, it seems that there was minimal, if any, infiltration of men or smuggling of arms. Nevertheless, it must be remembered that geographical conditions epitomised by an exceedingly difficult and mountainous terrain, in addition to the organisational, financial, and material difficulties encountered by the group, served to limit its effectiveness, and hence the absolute credibility of their reports are open to question.

It is abundantly evident, on the other hand, that the Lebanese allegations concerning the UAR's hostile press and radio campaigns were justified. A thorough study of the various UAR newspapers and journals, and the broadcasts of 'Radio Cairo', 'Radio Damascus' and 'The Voice of the Arabs', fully support the Lebanese accusations. Consequently, any physical involvement in the Lebanese civil war seems to have been minimal, since the UAR leaders appear to have preferred to rely primarily on the propaganda instrument to achieve their objective – the ascendency of the unionist forces over the isolationist elements in Lebanon.

This objective was a direct derivative from the general Egyptian policy during the period. The upsurge of nationalist sentiment in the wake of the formation of the UAR was naturally expected to generate an ideological momentum and a political climate in which it would be logical to expect the resultant ascendency of the unionist forces in the Arab world. It was no doubt realised that this, in itself, might not have led to comprehensive unity engulfing the rest of the Arab states. However, whether it did or not, an upsurge in unionist ideological orientations would have certainly represented a political 'gain' for the UAR leadership. A condition of 'falling dominoes', inevitably leading to constitutional and comprehensive unity, would represent the maximum dimension of this gain. The minimum aspect would be manifested in the obvious limitations a pro-UAR ideological orientation would place on the policy options available to alternative Arab leaders. This policy, therefore, was vigorously pursued by the leaders of the UAR through intensive propaganda campaigns directed at nourishing and encouraging this ideological trend.

The success of this policy soon became evident in a number of Arab countries, nowhere more dramatically than in oil-rich Iraq. This acknowledged leader of the anti-UAR forces in the Arab world had adopted an intensely activist and hawkish policy towards Nasser and his 'disruptive' influence in the Arab world and particularly, at that time, in Lebanon. The avowedly pro-British Prime Minister, Nuri al-Said, had ordered two army brigades to move into northern Jordan and 'await further orders' there. Instead, the two brigades occupied Baghdad, and with the collaboration of other army units, they proclaimed the demise of the Hashemite Kingdom and the birth of the Iraqi Republic. It was soon apparent that the coup and its two main personalities, Brigadier Abd al-Karim Kassem and Colonel Abd al-Salam Aref, were well disposed towards the leaders of the UAR.

As a result of the Iraqi coup, the positions of the Lebanese and Jordanian governments became desperate. In their conflicts with the UAR and President Nasser, they had relied heavily on the support of Nuri al-Said. Now that Nuri had been eliminated and Western influence generally had suffered a massive setback, both governments were in a state of near collapse and consequently appealed for urgent Western help. On their part, Western leaders had already decided that 'without vigorous response on our part [the Iraqi coup would] result in the complete elimination of Western influence in the Middle East.'[11] Thus, American marines landed in Beirut on July 15 to be followed two days later by British paratroopers in Amman.

The initial period of the Iraqi coup clearly indicated a dramatic reversal of the earlier Egyptian–Iraqi bilateral relations. The new Iraqi government promptly recognised the UAR, and Nasser reciprocated by declaring his country's resolve to resist any aggression against the infant republic. True to his words, he supplied the Iraqis, during the first week of the coup, with quantities of arms, ammunition, airplanes and radar equipment. On July 19, a delegation led by Colonel Abd al-Salam Aref arrived in Damascus and signed with Nasser the UAR–Iraqi Mutual Aid Pact which initiated provisions for co-operation between the two countries in various fields. At the beginning of October, a UAR air force detachment arrived at Habbaniya air base, near Baghdad, as a gesture of military co-operation, and on October 28, an agreement was signed by Kamal al-Din Hussein, the UAR's Minister of Education, for the co-ordination of the educational systems of the two countries. Moreover, during this period Colonel Aref, who was the Iraqi Deputy Prime Minister, Deputy Commander-in-Chief of the armed forces and Acting Minister of the Interior, increasingly expressed views in support of President Nasser. In a succession of addresses to mass rallies throughout Iraq, he referred to Nasser as 'our senior brother', 'our beloved leader', 'the champion of Arabism', and so forth. As a consequence, he emerged, and was perceived by the Egyptian elites, as the leader of the 'unity now' forces in Iraq.[12]

In the Lebanon, the political developments which followed the July events resulted in an indirect 'gain' for the UAR and its President. The pro-Western and anti-Nasser Chamoun was successfully prevented from running for another term of office: instead, General Shihab, the universally respected Chief of Staff of the army was elected to the presidency. Rashid Karami, one of the nationalist leaders, became Prime Minister and all but one of the new cabinet were drawn from the nationalist forces. It soon became clear that the new cabinet, and consequently Lebanon's foreign policy, would be well disposed towards President Nasser and the UAR.

In the wake of the Iraqi coup and the Lebanese civil war, Nasser's prestige in the Arab world naturally soared. He was now in complete control of Syria; Rashid Karami's new government in Lebanon finally normalised relations with the UAR; after the death of Nuri al-Said, Iraq emerged as a radical and anti-Western republic following policies of close co-operation with the UAR; the Americans duly withdrew from Lebanon in October, followed soon after by the British from Amman; and although the British had been instrumental in preventing Hussein's overthrow, nevertheless the King's credibility as an alternative leader of 'Arab nationalism' had been seriously undermined.

Yet as in 1956, the dominance of Nasser in the Arab world during the autumn of 1958 was not destined to last for very long. The first Arab leader to undermine this ascendency was Tunisia's Habib Bourguiba. Together with Morocco, Tunisia had gained independence in March 1956. But, in contrast to the cordial relations which existed between Nasser and King Muhammed V of Morocco, Egyptian–Tunisian relations were plagued with persistent difficulties. From the very beginning the two leaders developed an intense personal antipathy towards each other. This was not helped by the clear divergence in their views on relations with the West, particularly as the emergence of a pronounced pro-West orientation in Tunisia's policies occurred at the height of Nasser's 'anti-Western' crusade. Relations were further aggravated by the Tunisian belief that Nasser was sheltering and supporting Bourguiba's prominent political rival, Salah Ben Yousif. Consequently, in their first Arab League meeting in September 1958, the Tunisians vehemently attacked Nasser's alleged domination and manipulation of the League, and a month later they severed relations with Egypt. This was the first erosion of Nasser's primacy in the Arab world since the formation of the UAR.

The next and far greater setback occurred in the Arab east, when during October–November 1958 the earlier hopes for Iraq joining the UAR were slowly diminishing as a result of a developing power struggle between the two leaders of the Iraqi coup. Brigadier Kassem had begun to resent Aref's agitation for immediate unity with the UAR. In fact, the conflict between the two leaders merely reflected the growing political polarisation in the country as a whole between the 'unity now' forces and the 'Iraq first' elements.[13] Foremost amongst the latter group were the Communists who were particularly strong in Iraq, as they had for many years been extremely active in the underground opposition to Nuri's rule. The advent of the republic increased their strength considerably, for under the new regime they succeeded in acquiring a number of key posts in the army and the bureaucracy. They also created an armed militia called the Popular Resistance Front and proceeded to organise farmers, workers, teachers, students and professional men on a national basis. Indeed, by late 1958, they had become the single most influential force in the country. This particular configuration of power among the political forces in the country was reflected in the conflict within the leadership. On September 30, Colonel Aref was relieved of all his cabinet and military functions and appointed ambassador in Bonn. On November 4, an announcement on Radio Baghdad declared that due to the unauthorised return of Aref to Iraq, he had been arrested and would stand trial 'on the charge of plotting against the safety of the homeland'.[14]

The UAR leaders observed the developing influence of the Communists and the arrest of their faithful ally Aref with increasing alarm. It was becoming clear to the Egyptians that Kassem, the Communists, and other 'Iraq first' groups (e.g. the Kurds, the National Democratic Party, and the al-Ahali group) had no intention of acknowledging Egyptian centrality in the 'common struggle against imperialism'. On the contrary, a conspicuous shift from 'unity' toward Iraqi 'sovereignty' had coloured the recent policy utterances of Iraqi leaders. As a result, the relations between the two states began to experience progressive strain. Nevertheless, the Egyptian leadership still hoped for the eventual normalisation of relations. As late as the end of November 1958, *al-Ahram* attacked 'the imperialists' for trying to aggravate differences between the UAR and the Iraqi Republic.[15] Nasser himself dispatched four letters to Kassem requesting a meeting to settle these incipient differences, but no response from the Iraqi leader was forthcoming.[16] It is important to note here that Kassem's cool reaction to Nasser's overtures probably related to the recently uncovered plot by Rashid Ali al-Gaylani, the old popular and nationalist leader, in which the UAR embassy in Baghdad was conclusively implicated.[17]

It is clear, therefore, that during this period the UAR was conducting its relations with Iraq on two levels. On the one hand, it was trying, through diplomatic channels, to normalise relations with Iraq in order to attain a measure of solidarity and co-operation. On the other hand, through clandestine activity, it was aiding unionist, anti-Kassem forces in Iraq to affect a change in the leadership which would reorient Iraq towards its earlier sympathies with the UAR's goals and aspirations. However, on both levels, the objective remained the same: to bring back Iraq into the fold of the pro-UAR 'Arab nationalist' forces in the Arab Middle East.

The concern of the UAR's leadership with the developing events in Iraq had a domestic manifestation as well. This related to the potential ability of the Iraqi Communists to influence events in Syria, specifically by reviving the pre-union, Communist strength. Consequently, when Khalid Bakdash, the Secretary-General of the banned Communist Party called for more 'democracy' in Syria and 'closer links' with Iraq,[18] the UAR leadership retaliated quickly and decisively. On December 23, 1958, in a major address, Nasser attacked the Syrian Communists as separatists who worked against Arab nationalism,[19] and followed this verbal assault with a wave of mass arrests of Syrian Communists which reached is climax on New Year's Day 1959. On January 20, Muhammed Hasneen Heikal, the influential editor of the semi-official *al-Ahram*, addressed an open letter to Kassem entitled 'Your Excellency the Sole Leader' in which he expressed his astonishment at Kassem's seeming nonchalance in the face of Communist activity which, according to Heikal, was not being restricted to Baghdad but was intentionally directed at Damascus.[20] This growing mistrust between the two countries and their leaders did not lead to an immediate break in relations. A tenuous interaction, characterised by concealed recriminations and verbal accusations and counter-accusations, persisted until March 9, 1959, when the Shawaf revolt in Iraq triggered the complete severance of relations between the two states that was to last until Kassem's death in February 1963.

The UAR was again actively involved in the Shawaf revolt. It had transferred arms, ammunition and a radio station to Mosul, the northern Iraqi city where Shawaf's headquarters were located. Syrian officials had concurred with tribal shcikhs who were hostile towards the Baghdad government, particularly after it had announced its agrarian reform law. They had also been in contact with a number of anti-Communist army officers who intended to carry out a coup backed by a tribal insurrection. However, the coup suffered from various handicaps. It was badly conceived and poorly executed; it was ill-timed at the height of the Communist drive and it suffered from a serious fragmentation within the ranks of its leadership. Thus, the revolt disintegrated almost immediately and Shawaf was killed the next day by one of his own soldiers. The entire affair had lasted just over twenty-four hours.

The reciprocal battery of accusations, recriminations and insults followed almost instantaneously. Colonel Majid Amin, the pro-Communist public prosecutor of the notorious 'People's Court', attacked Nasser bitterly, calling him a 'pharoah' and accusing him of bearing direct responsibility for the coup.[21] Nasser countered this attack by reprimanding Kassem for his Communist, anti-Arab leanings and labelling him 'the divider of Iraq'.[22] He also belittled Kassem's role in the Iraqi coup and insinuated that it was Aref who was the real leader of the Iraqi revolution.[23] In retaliating to this, the Iraqi leadership, through Colonel Mahdawi, declared 'openly and firmly that Syria and Egypt . . . must be liberated from Nasserite fascist rule'.[24] Kassem did not personally get involved in this slanging match until April 1, when he declared that 'the forward progress of our republic has shown the Arabs, particularly the Syrians, that our revolution responds to the needs of the people. Our democratic rule has disproved the allegation of Egypt's ruler that democracy is not in the interest of the people.'[25] Later on that year, he developed this theme further by revising Nuri al-Said's original 'Fertile Crescent' plan, which advocated the merger of Iraq and Syria and as such constituted a direct challenge to the sovereignty of the UAR. Kassem agreed that this project might have been a 'reactionary' scheme under Nuri, but now that Iraq had been 'liberated' it did no longer constitute a danger.[26]

Such mutual enmity and reciprocal personal animosity underlined this new political polarisation between the two sets of leadership. The acrimony that characterised the press and radio propaganda between the two countries reached a level of personal vindictiveness that overshadowed the earlier pre-republic conflict between Nasser and Nuri. The bitterness of the Iraqi leadership could be directly related to their own domestic insecurity. The attacks on Nasser were mainly a reflection of their own struggle against the indigenous unionist forces. As such, their verbal onslaught in the foreign policy sector simply mirrored the actual political acrimony which characterised Iraqi domestic politics of the period. In the case of the UAR, the unprecedented viciousness of the leadership's attacks on the Iraqi rulers was probably the result of two main causes. In the first place, it merely exhibited the leaders' frustration at their inability to employ the usual propaganda methods of accusing Arab leaders who did not conform to their own views and aspirations of being 'reactionary' rulers in the service of 'Western imperialism'. Kassem, unlike Nuri, Saud, Hussein or Chamoun, was no 'reactionary' but a 'revolutionary' in his own right who enjoyed, especially in the early years of his rule, considerable domestic support, particularly among the peasants and the slum-dwellers of Baghdad. He was the enemy of the 'imperialists' and the friend of Nasser's mentors, the Soviet Union. Secondly, Kassem and the rest of the Iraqi left-wing, non-unionist leadership presented a direct threat to the credibility of the UAR. The main tenet of this particular phase of Egypt's policy-making was a conviction in the ultimate unity of the Arab world once the Arab states had succeeded in delivering themselves from 'imperialism'. Implicit in this perception was the UAR's central role in the struggle for unity. As such, if 'emancipated' and 'revolutionary' Iraq were to steer an independent, even contradictory course from Nasser's policy prescriptions, then the Syrians might begin to question them as well, thus undermining both Nasser's leadership and the internal cohesion of the UAR. Hence, Kassem had to be fought at all costs and in every possible way.

A natural corollary to this state of affairs was the gradual decline in the utilisation of diplomatic communication which characterised the earlier phase of the Iraqi revolution. The worsening of relations between the two states tended to have an adverse effect on diplomatic channels and agencies. In the aftermath of the Mosul revolt nine members of the UAR embassy in Baghdad were asked to leave Iraq within twenty-four hours. In Cairo, the Iraqi ambassador defected to Egypt, claiming that Iraq was ruled by a 'red clique'.[27] This was treated in Cairo as a diplomatic coup, but it only served to heighten the paralysis of diplomatic channels. A further erosion into diplomatic communications came with Iraq's refusal to attend the Arab League meetings because, the Iraqis claimed, the organisation was dominated by Egyptians. Iraq also refused to attend the first Arab oil conference, held in April, for no other reason than that it met in Cairo. The Egyptians, on their part, expelled the assistant cultural attaché in the Iraqi embassy from Egypt, and so by May 1959, an almost complete breakdown in diplomacy between the UAR and the Iraqi Republic had been effected.

In Syria, too, the Egyptian leadership was beginning to encounter multiple difficulties. Unlike their Egyptian 'brethren', the Syrians have been traditionally politically divided and were accustomed to expressing their diverse political views regularly and vociferously. Thus, the integration of Syria's various political parties into the monolithic and centrally controlled National Union removed from the Syrians what to them was a very essential facet of the political life: the need for active involvement in the 'body politic'.

Moreover, the Baathists' earlier hopes for sharing power with Nasser had, by mid-1959, considerably diminished. As Salah Bitar later explained, Nasser 'failed to accept a necessary association of other Arab progressive leaders in the management of the Arab cause and its policies'.[28] The first ominous sign for the Baathist leadership appeared as early as October 1958, with Nasser's announcement of his first UAR cabinet. This included only fourteen Syrians among the thirty-four members, with all the key posts going to the Egyptians. During 1959, the Baathists frequently complained of being decreasingly consulted by the Egyptians and that an effort was made to cut them off from their political base in Syria.[29] In the elections for the Syrian National Union in July 1959, the Baath Party could only manage 5 per cent of the seats and then subsequently accused the Egyptian leadership and its supporters in Syria of rigging the elections against them. By December, the conflict between them and Nasser had become irreconcilable, and leading Baathists resigned from the central and regional cabinets of the UAR. During 1960–1, the Baath became one of the primary critics of Nasser's rule in Syria.

More generally, the Syrian resentment grew at what they perceived to be an effort to Egyptianise Syria; for in order to bring the Syrian administrative, legislative, bureaucratic and military systems in line with Egypt's, Egyptians seemed to be gradually filling most of the important domestic posts in Syria at the expense of the Syrians themselves. Ex-President Quwatly later said that 'the Nasserite system relegated the majority of the population to the rank of traitors, governing by terror and trampling on the honour and dignity of citizens.'[30] Economically, too, there were difficulties. The earlier nebulous slogan of social justice had been gradually replaced by the crisper notion of a 'socialist, co-operative and democratic society', which entailed intensive socialist measures. The Syrians, however, used to a free-market economy, could not accept as readily as their Egyptian counterparts Nasser's economic restrictions. An official statement put out on Damascus Radio immediately after the secession declared that 'the major bones of contention was that 'the Syrian economy . . . had developed through the efforts of individual activity.'[31] Furthermore, the Agrarian Reform Law promulgated in September 1958 alienated the powerful land-owning class in Syria, and the situation was not helped by a succession of bad harvests which resulted in severe shortages of basic commodities.

The worsening situation, both in the domestic and international arenas, compelled the UAR leadership to redefine their policy objectives in the Arab Middle East. The result was an abandonment of the earlier efforts for comprehensive unity and the espousal of a much more moderate and pragmatic objective of Arab solidarity. Lacking in ideological rigidity, this new orientation did not insist on 'constitutional unification'; merely on co-operation among sovereign Arab states. It allowed the Egyptian leaders to improve relations with other Arab countries, thus isolating Iraq, the UAR's most 'dangerous' adversary. Secondly, the new objective's minimal need for political activism in the inter-Arab environment would afford the UAR leaders more time to devote to the ever increasing domestic problems of Syria.

On the other side of the spectrum, the other Arab leaders, too, found the tenets of the new objective to be more accommodating than the previous goal. Arab solidarity allowed them publicly to espouse the cause of 'Arab nationalism', thus profiting from the prestige it carried with it, without having to compromise their own domestic positions. Thus in July 1959, the borders were opened between Syria and Jordan, and diplomatic relations severed since the Iraqi coup were re-established in August. In September, King Saud was received in Cairo for a state visit which normalised relations between the UAR and Saudi Arabia. Furthermore, although the alleged assassination of the Jordanian Prime Minister, Huzah al-Majali, by UAR agents (vigorously denied by the UAR) strained relations to the extent that Hussein felt compelled to recognise the Iraqi regime, relations were soon back to normal as a result of an exchange of letters between Nasser and Hussein in which Nasser expressed his hopes that the two leaders would face their differences 'in a spirit of fraternal forgiveness'.[32]

However, as has been noted, this spirit of conciliation was not extended to the Iraqi leaders. On the contrary, the conflict between the two states and their respective leaderships reached new heights in June and July of 1961 when Kassem claimed that the newly independent state of Kuwait formed 'an indivisible part of Iraq'.[33] Small, rich and ruled by a despotic and feudalist order, Kuwait was all that the UAR professed to fight against. However, because of their hostility to the Iraqi leaders, the UAR policy-making elite declared that Kuwait's independence and her right to self-determination had to be safeguarded. Later, the UAR leaders were faced with a clear dilemma in their policy orientation when British forces landed in Kuwait. It meant that 'while supporting the Kuwaiti people against Kassem's stupidity, [the Egyptians] also supported the Iraqi people against the British concentrations near them.'[34] However, deciding that British evacuation was the highest priority objective in this case, the UAR agreed to participate in a mixed military force with the Jordanians and the Saudis. This decision served two favourable purposes. On the one hand, it replaced the British presence in Kuwait, and on the other, it defended Kuwait against Iraq's ambitions. On both accounts, the UAR leaders succeeded. The British duly withdrew and Kuwait was soon accepted as a full member of the Arab League.

Apart from the Kuwaiti incident, the relative calm which characterised inter-Arab political interaction afforded Nasser the opportunity to accelerate the level of social reform domestically. In June, the whole of the cotton trade was taken over and all import–export firms were brought under public control. In July, he nationalised all banks, insurance companies, heavy industries and most medium-sized and light industries. Maximum land ownership was halved to a hundred feddans, and no income in any organisation was allowed to exceed $14,350.

These measures were met with extreme hostility by the very powerful financial and landowning class in Syria. By this time, the alienation of Syria from Nasser's political, social and economic order was almost complete. Whereas Nasser formulated policies designed for long-term planning, the Syrians could only see and feel their immediate adverse effects. As such, the new restrictive measures only served to precipitate the final breach. On September 28, the Syrian army carried out a successful coup against those 'who humiliated Syria and degraded her army'.[35] Jordan immediately recognised the new regime and was followed ten days later by Iraq. Thus with the failure of the first experiment in modern Arab history to operationalise the ideal of Arab unity, the configuration of forces in the Arab world had once more become polarised between the UAR and the other 'non-unionist' forces.

4 Post-Union Involvement, 1961-7

The Syrian coup came as a considerable shock to the Egyptian policy-making elite. On the morning of September 29, 1961, the day after the Syrian coup, Nasser went on the air to inform the Egyptian public that units of the Syrian army had rebelled but that loyal army units were on their way to crush the mutiny, as no attempt to sever Syria from the UAR could be tolerated. He added that such an attempt constituted a more dangerous attack on 'Arab nationalism' than the tripartite attack on Suez five years earlier.[1]

The report that the army garrisons at the two northern cities of Aleppo and Latakia were still resisting the new regime encouraged the Egyptian leadership to dispatch Egyptian paratroopers to the two areas, and they followed this move by ordering the UAR navy, loaded with troop reinforcements, to steam toward Latakia. However, during the following day, when it was confirmed that the two garrisons had joined the rebels, Nasser immediately ordered the ships to return and the 120 paratroopers who had already been dropped on Latakia to surrender. He explained that he did not want the union to degenerate into a bloodbath.[2] On October 5, a week after the secession, President Nasser in a major address, finally acknowledged the break-up of the union and said that he would not oppose Syrian application for renewed membership of the Arab League and the United Nations.[3] He ended the speech with a moving gesture, when he told the bitter multitude: 'Fellow citizens, I pray that God may help beloved Syria, lead her to the right path and bless her people.'[4]

As has already been explained, the reasons for the secession were as complex as they were varied. Later, in a series of articles, Heikal attributed the failure of the UAR to the Egyptians' non-readiness for Arab unity, to the geographic division between the two countries, and to the inability to overcome regional chauvinisms. Furthermore, 'there was no solid economic and social foundation on which the experiment could be based and firmly depend.'[5] Finally, he identified the excessively repressive police system created by Abd al-Hamid Saraj as a major reason for the secession. In Heikal's words, the police machinery of Nasser's protégé was taking 'the form of a severe and destructive cancer'.[6] However, the initial Egyptian response was to blame the rebellion on reactionary and separatist elements within Syria.[7] Four days after the secession, Nasser emphasised the role of 'reaction' in the

33

separation movement and pointed out its ultimate dangers. It was a mistake, he declared, to coexist with the forces of 'reaction' because they are the internal enemies of 'Arab nationalism'.[8] Indeed, this particular image progressively came to shape the perceptions of the Egyptian elite throughout the world.

Nasser's identification of reaction as the cause of the secession was by no means an exaggerated claim. Many of the leaders of the army coup were generally of a conservative background in alliance with civilian politicians associated with the wealthy business class, particularly the 'Khamssiya Group' (a consortium of five wealthy families influential in the fields of banking, finance and industry). The prominent figure in the army coup, Lt Colonel Haider al-Khuzbari, and the interim President, Dr Ma'moun al-Khuzbari, both belonged to one of Damascus's wealthiest families. Early in 1962, most of Nasser's nationalisation decrees were repealed by the new regime, and the Agrarian Reform Law was drastically amended. Moreover, the newly elected members of parliament immediately voted themselves a 333 per cent rise in salary.

The Egyptian leadership, therefore, perceived the Syrian secession primarily as a counter-movement undertaken by the Syrian capitalist and feudalist classes against the socialist measures (particularly the nationalisation measures of June and July 1961) enacted by the regime. It was thought that this privileged minority had successfully manipulated the grievances of the Syrian people to its own advantage and for its own self-interest. Consequently, the Egyptian leadership reasoned that the fault rested in the fact that not enough was done to restrict privileges and to limit the power and influence of these classes. Thus in quick systematic blows, the regime attacked the remainder of the capitalist classes in Egypt. Many 'reactionaries' were arrested, and scores of 'capitalists' had their funds and property sequestered.

The leadership's assault on reaction went beyond the arrest of the 'reactionaries' and the confiscation of their fortunes. The leadership promised a radical reorganisation of the political system, in which a National Charter,[9] designed to define the regime's political, social and economic goals, would be submitted to an elected Congress of Popular Forces. The Congress would ensure the representation of peasants, workers, students, teachers, women and professional people, but would exclude landowners and those arrested on charges of working against the state.

Accordingly, the National Charter was presented to the National Congress of Popular Forces on May 21, 1962. In the domestic political field, the charter's main contention was that progress would be achieved only when a complete reorientation had been affected in the political culture of the society.[10] The charter declared that in the past 'the domination of feudalism in collusion with the exploiting capital over the economy of the land . . . enabled them to dominate the political activities in all their forms. [Consequently] democracy on this basis was merely the dictatorship of reaction.'[11] In order to combat exploitation and affirm true democracy, therefore, 'the new constitution must ensure that its farmers and workmen will get half the seats in political and popular organisations at all levels.'[12]

In the economic field, the charter required that the basic infrastructure of the economy – including railways, ports, air, land and sea transport, public services, and banks and insurance companies – should be placed under state ownership. Land ownership had to be kept within strict limits so as to prevent the re-emergence of the 'exploiting' feudalist class.

On 'Arabism', the charter reaffirmed the Arab character of Egypt. It argued that Egypt had always formed a vital part of the region and put the blame for the failure of the 1919 revolution in Egypt on its inward-oriented leaders who 'were incapable of deducing from history the fact that there is no conflict whatsoever between Egyptian patriotism and Arab nationalism'.[13] This oversight was not only instrumental in the failure of the 1919 revolution in Egypt, but it also deprived the Arab struggle 'of the Egyptian revolutionary energy at one of the gravest moments of its crisis'.[14] Hence, it was concluded:

> The United Arab Republic, firmly convinced that she is an integral part of the Arab Nation, must propagate her call for unity and the principles it embodies, so that it would be at the disposal of every Arab citizen, without hesitating for one moment before the outworn argument that this would be considered an interference in the affairs of others.[15]

This radicalisation of Egyptian domestic and Arab politics translated itself into an ideological assault on 'reaction' throughout the Arab world. It was carried through beyond Syria to the 'backers of the Syrian separatists' in the Arab world, particularly Hussein and Saud.[16] The Egyptian troops were promptly withdrawn from Kuwait, since it was no longer possible to co-operate with the reactionary monarchs, and the propaganda war against them, which had subsided over the last two years, was reinstituted with added ferocity. To the Egyptian leadership, the Kings were beginning to extend their 'reactionary' policies beyond their borders to attack 'Arab socialism' and Egypt's 'egalitarian' state.

Another monarch who had rejoiced at Syria's secession was the Imam Ahmad of the Yemen, whose own country was federated to the UAR. The Yemeni leadership had initially requested the federation for the purpose of cementing its own domestic political position. However, the Syrian coup had illustrated to the Imam that he no longer needed an association with Nasser. He thus broadcast a poem ridiculing

Nasser's socialism and declaring it to be incompatible with Islam. Nasser, on his part, was finding that the Yemen's affiliation to the UAR was becoming increasingly more embarrassing; for no one epitomised the image of reaction against which Nasser was supposedly fighting more than the despotic and medieval Imam with whom Nasser was federated. Moreover, even if the federation had served, in 1958, a psychological function by highlighting the appeal and potential of 'Arab unity' to the other Arab monarchs, its utility had long expired as it had become progressively apparent that it was no more than a paper agreement. Seizing on the Imam's attacks on Egyptian socialism, therefore, Nasser in December, 1961, retaliated by denouncing the Yemeni leadership and announcing Egypt's unilateral dissolution of the Federation of Arab States.

The advent of 1962, therefore, coincided with an increasing Egyptian militancy against the 'reactionary' Arab states. Egypt had broken diplomatic relations with Jordan, attacked the corrupt and backward social and political structure of Saudi Arabia, refused to recognise the new Syrian regime, and resumed its pre-federation attacks on the Yemen.

This intransigence against 'reaction' necessitated an ideological reappraisal of the nature and meaning of Arab unity. In a speech on February 22, 1962, Nasser reaffirmed his faith in Arab unity, which was an 'irreversible process of nature'. However, since reactionary monarchs and leaders, acting for foreign interests, persisted in undermining and sabotaging this process, no actual unity could be achieved in the present situation. Endeavouring to unify Arab states with contrasting social systems was not a viable proposition, as it was impossible to close ranks with reactionaries. Thus, the process of unity had to begin with social revolutions in the backward Arab states in order to bring them to the level of Egypt's social 'enlightenment'. It thus transpired that unity of aim was more important and had to precede the unity of ranks.[17] Consequently, the tranquility of the phase of 'Arab solidarity' was abandoned and replaced by this new, more activist, more revolutionary objective.

The reaction of the Arab monarchs to Egypt's new activism did not lack bitterness. Hussein and Saud intensified their own campaign against Nasser's socialism and proceeded to undermine Egypt's central position in the Arab world. With the help of Egypt's other adversaries (Iraq, Syria, Tunisia and Yemen), they challenged Egypt's dominance in the Arab League by demanding that Cairo should cease to be the permanent headquarters of the League. Saud, moreover, presented the Islamic Charter, which was meant to be an alternative to Egypt's National Charter and 'which by criticising fake nationalism based on atheistic doctrine, implied condemnation of Nasser's policy'.[18] In actual fact, the year 1962 witnessed a vehemently bitter interaction between

Egypt and Saudi Arabia in which radio propaganda was most effectively utilised. The Saudi authorities also used the holy shrines of Mecca as an instrument of their foreign policy. In one instance, they demanded that Egyptian pilgrims should pay in hard currency of which Egypt, as they well knew, was very short; and in another instance, they refused to accept the Kiswa (the cover for the holy Ka'aba) which Egypt had traditionally provided during the annual pilgrimages. In the latter case, the Saudis attributed their refusal to the poor quality of the Egyptian offering.

Egypt's relations with Syria and Iraq were no better. The Egyptian leadership was particularly suspicious of the close relations Iraq was developing with Syria after the latter's secession. In November, 1961, visas were abolished between the two 'Fertile Crescent' countries, and this was followed in March of the following year with the Military Co-operation Agreement. In December, Kassem declared that he was ready to co-operate with the Syrians for the purpose of unifying the two countries. The Egyptian leaders, like all the pre-1952 governments, viewed any attempted unity between Iraq and Syria as a challenge to Egyptian centrality within the Arab world and as an effort to isolate Egypt strategically and politically from the Arab east. Egypt, thus, increased its propaganda to the Syrian people, inciting them against their government and its 'reactionary' domestic and foreign policies.

Egypt's activity in Syria did not limit itself to propaganda warfare. In August 1962, the Egyptian military attaché in the Lebanon defected to Syria and supplied the Syrians with a list of Egyptian agents working against the Syrian government. The Syrian government promptly called for a meeting of the Arab League which was duly held in Shtoura in the Lebanon. Once assembled, the Egyptians were accused of interfering in Syria's domestic affairs and endeavouring to undermine her security. The Syrians were, naturally, strongly supported by the Saudi and Jordanian delegations. After a violent meeting which necessitated the intervention of the Lebanese police, the Egyptian delegation walked out of the meeting, and for the next year Egypt snubbed the Arab League. As a result, the summer of 1962 saw the almost complete political isolation of Egypt from the Arab world.

In the midst of this depressing isolation, a revolution in one of the most backward of Arab countries thrust Egypt yet again into the mainstream of Arab politics. On September 26, 1962, a group of army officers seized power in Sana' shortly after the death of Imam Ahmad and proclaimed the birth of the Yemeni Republic. However, after the first uncertain hours, it later transpired that the coup was only partially successful. Imam Badr (Ahmad's son) escaped to the mountains of the Yemen, gathered support from amongst the northern tribes, and was promised money and arms by Saudi Arabia. The army officers immediately asked for help from Nasser, and he responded by committing the Egyptian army to a war that was to last for five inconclusive years and which was to effect a severe strain on Egypt's structurally fragile economy. There is little doubt that the Egyptian leaders did not foresee the burden they were undertaking when they dispatched the Egyptian troops to help the republicans against the Imam's loyal tribes and his Saudi backers. Nasser later admitted that the Yemeni venture was a 'miscalculation'.[19] He had thought that only limited help on his part would be adequate to defeat the Imam and establish a secure and permanent pro-UAR republican order.

In this respect, it seems certain that the Egyptian leadership's appreciation of the geographic, political, social and military situation in the Yemen was inadequate. The Yemeni population was basically divided between the urban Shafei plainsmen and the predominantly tribal Zaidis who inhabited the northern mountains and the western deserts. Once the news of the new Imam's escape became known, it was expected that the majority of the Zaidi tribes would give their allegiance to the Zaidi Imam, who was the religious as well as the political leader. The tribal Zaidis were the more warlike of the two clans, and the mountainous terrain they inhabited made it especially difficult for an enemy to defeat them. In short, it needed much more than the limited assistance the Egyptians thought was adequate to defeat the Imam and his tribes.

This fundamental miscalculation may have had its roots in the Egyptian perception that the coup was enjoying immediate and universal support.[20] Given this image, the Egyptian leadership deemed it inconceivable that King Saud and the 'reactionary' forces would allow the Yemenis to exercise their 'free will', and thus within only twenty-four hours of the coup, it had become evident to President Nasser 'that King Saud would not keep quiet.'[21] This suspicion was confirmed when three Saudi pilots defected to Egypt with a plane-load of arms destined for the Imam and his supporters. Finally, it is also probable that the coup was seen in Cairo in the context of previous coups in other Arab states, where the control of the major urban areas meant almost certainly the success of the coup.

On September 30, the Egyptian leaders decided to dispatch trainers, advisers and military equipment to aid the army officers. However, as it became clear that the military capability of the Imam's forces, which was uncompromisingly sustained by Saudi Arabia, was in fact grossly underestimated by the Egyptian leadership, Egypt's involvement in the civil war increased. Within two months, the number of Egyptian troops increased from 100 to an estimated 8,000; and it soon became evident that the main brunt of the war would have to be borne by the Egyptian army. In 1963, the number of Egyptian troops in the Yemen rose to 20,000; then it increased to 40,000 in 1964 and reached a staggering 70,000 in 1965.

Even allowing for Nasser's 'miscalculation', the decision to involve the Egyptian army, even on the most limited scale, constituted a very grave step. It must be remembered that the Yemen was the first Arab country in whose domestic affairs the Egyptian leadership had militarily intervened. The question thus arises as to why the Egyptian leaders so readily and so quickly committed their armed forces to the republican cause. David Holden offered a plausible explanation when he wrote:

> It was a foregone conclusion that he [Nasser] would agree to help them, not only because his agents and his propaganda had openly encouraged them beforehand, thereby morally committing Nasser to their cause, but also because he simply dare not leave them at the mercy of King Saud. To have done so would have betrayed the vague hopes of social justice that Nasser had aroused among the Arabs, and would have seriously diminished his stature as an Arab leader.[22]

While this interesting explanation highlights two very important variables that determine a decisional situation, namely the prestige of the decision-makers and the various environmental constraints acting upon them, it certainly offers only a limited evaluation of the multiplicity of factors which, in their totality, determined Egypt's decision to intervene in the Yemen. Strategically, Egypt's commitment to the Yemeni republicans provided for an actual Egyptian presence contiguous to an area dominated by Britain, the perceived 'imperialist' power. Moreover, the strategic proximity of the Yemen to Saudi Arabia constituted a further impetus for Egyptian involvement. Particularly significant was the potential danger of this proximity to the internal security of Saudi Arabia. This was soon evident when, shortly after the coup, the republican leaders began to express hope for the establishment of a 'Republic of the Arabian Peninsula'.[23] Ideologically, the Yemeni coup was perceived by the Egyptian leadership as a progressive revolution dedicated to the liberation of the country from reactionary and corrupt rule.[24] As such, the image of the crusading young army officers fighting for social justice fitted neatly within the ideological and perceptual prisms of the Egyptian elites. One must also remember that the conservative forces in the Arab world had been gathering strength since Syria's secession. This led to the Egyptian perception that the defence of the Yemeni Republic constituted a defence of Egypt itself. Within this context Nasser rhetorically asked, 'shall we keep quiet and watch while reactionism destroys the revolution in the Yemen, and after that reactionism would turn toward us and decide to transfer the battle against socialism and progress and against the people in Cairo.'[25] Heikal voiced the same fears when he wrote that 'we did not go to the Yemen to start a war but to prevent a conflict.'[26] Indeed, the Egyptian army had been dispatched to the Yemen 'to defend Cairo in the heart of the Arabian Peninsula'.[27]

It seems that the conservative monarchs' evaluation of the situation followed similar lines. They, too, felt that a victory for Egypt in the Yemen constituted a direct threat to their own political order. On October 1, King Hussein of Jordan sent a military mission headed by his Chief of Staff to Jeddah in Saudi Arabia to establish contact with Prince Hassan, the uncle of the deposed Imam, and followed this move by signing a military alliance with Saudi Arabia on November 4. In Saudi Arabia, the King was compelled to appoint his more rational brother Faisal as Prime Minister in order to confront the new threat. After an Egyptian air raid on the Saudi border which was meant to neutralise the source of aid to the royalists, Prince Faisal severed diplomatic relations with Egypt, obtained arms for the royalists from Pakistan, enlisted the support of Iran, and asked the United States Air Force to carry out a display of strength over Jeddah – all of which contributed to the Egyptians' perception of an 'imperialist plot' engineered by CENTO against them.

By the beginning of 1963, the military situation in the Yemen had become clearer. There were approximately 15,000 Egyptian troops supported by tanks, heavy artillery, and some 200 combat aircraft.[28] They were in control of the coastal plains including the three major cities of Sana', Hodeida and Taiz, whereas the royalists were mainly concentrated in the northern mountains and the eastern desert. After a visit by Field Marshal Amer to the Yemen in February, the Egyptian army launched a major offensive designed to achieve an early and decisive victory. However, after an initial period of isolated successes, the offensive eventually petered out and the two sides returned more or less to their earlier positions. Thus, by the summer and autumn of 1963, it had become evident that the war had reached a stalemate and that Egyptian presence was the primary factor preventing the collapse of the republican regime, where factionalism and political in-fighting had started to beset the leadership.

The cost of the Yemen war to Egypt in human and material terms was nevertheless somewhat offset by Egypt's prestige in the Arab world as a result of its uncompromising stand against 'reaction'. For a revolutionary leader like Nasser, the pursuit of the objective of 'Arab solidarity' naturally led to a certain loss of credibility. Thus, a reversion to a 'revolutionary', 'anti-reactionary' posture invariably restored his standing and regained the initiative for him. His ascendency among the Arabs was highlighted when four Saudi princes and seven air force pilots followed by the Commander-in-Chief of the Jordanian air force and two of his officers defected to Cairo. This process was crowned in February and March of 1963 when military coups in Baghdad and

Damascus eliminated two hostile governments and brought in Baathist leaderships who, eager for Nasser's blessings and support, took the initiative in approaching him to discuss plans for some form of tripartite unity amongst Egypt, Syria and Iraq.

On March 14, talks on the possible unity of the three countries started in Cairo. It was obvious that the talks were far more important to the Baathist leaders than to the Egyptians. To the Baath leadership, unity was 'the biggest political action [they] could present to the people'.[29] The Egyptians, however, approached these talks with the utmost suspicion. The Egyptian negotiators were worried that the Baathists' real motive for a tripartite unity was to place Egypt between a hammer and an anvil.[30] Their mistrust of the Baath dated back to the collective resignation of the Baathist ministers from the UAR cabinet in December 1959; to the endorsement by both Bitar and Hourani in 1961 of the declaration of secession by the Syrian parliament; and to alleged Baathist activities in the Egyptian army aimed at creating an anti-Nasser movement. Nasser, thus, unequivocally insisted:

> If the Baath party is ruling Syria and unity is to be with the party, then, I, definitely am not prepared to hold any discussion . . . The Baath Party, in my opinion, [was] one of the forces that facilitated the secession. And as if this was not enough, it tried to influence the situation in Egypt itself in the delicate period that followed the secession and I consider this to be a crime.[31]

During the talks, it was evident that Nasser's willingness to negotiate depended on the Baathists' acceptance of Egypt's central position in any union that might be formed. Particularly important to the Egyptian decision-makers was the role of the political leaderships in such a union. To the Egyptians the 'unity of states [was] not enough; the unity of the political leaderships [was] more important.'[32] Thus, Nasser insisted on a definite agreement on the nature of the proposed collective leadership. The Baathists endeavoured to reassure him by proposing that the leadership should include one member from each country with Nasser as the chairman, making four members altogether. In this way 'the problem of being caught between the hammer and the anvil . . . would not arise.'[33] Yet Nasser's mistrust of the Syrians, which stemmed from his past dealing with the Baathists, remained the dominant obstacle to any constructive move towards unity. He even suspected that the Syrians would 'try to turn the Iraqis against us',[34] and he predicted that as a result of inevitable future disagreements with the Syrian Baathists 'Egypt will withdraw from the unity before four months had elapsed.'[35]

It was thus becoming evident from the mistrust and suspicion that pervaded the meeting and from Nasser's personal dislike of the Baath, that only a hollow agreement could be reached. Consequently, a declaration was announced on April 17 proclaiming a transitory period of two years of loose unity and close co-operation, at the end of which, a federal constitution would be promulgated and elections held.

Almost immediately, the differences between the parties began to be publicly apparent. During May and June, pro-Nasser elements were purged from the army and the political leadership in Syria, and a move toward closer co-operation with Iraq followed. In May, Heikal declared that the UAR's co-operation and coexistence with the Baath leadership in Syria was no longer possible.[36] On July 18, General Amin Hafez, Syria's Baathist strongman, crushed a pro-Nasser coup in Syria and executed twenty-seven of the plotters. This precipitated the final break. In a speech on July 22, Nasser declared that Egypt was no longer 'bound to the present fascist regime in Syria by any common aim [because the Syrian regime was] built on fraud and treachery, [was] non-unionist and non-socialist, [and because it was] secessionist, inhuman and immoral.'[37]

Nasser's assault on the Syrian Baath triggered off a vicious campaign by the Egyptian propaganda machine which continued throughout the summer and autumn of 1963. This particularly effective policy instrument contributed to an incipient power struggle between the 'left' and 'right' factions of the Iraqi Baathist leadership. As this fragmentation increased, reaching almost anarchic dimensions, the army under Abd al-Salam Aref (who had fully demonstrated his wholehearted devotion to Nasser in 1958) took control of the situation in November 1963 and expelled the warring Baathist leaders. Cairo immediately and enthusiastically recognised the new regime and cautioned the Syrians against any military operation directed at Iraq.

Egypt's activism in the area did not restrict itself to the Arab east. During the autumn of 1963, Nasser became embroiled in a conflict which had erupted in the Arab Maghreb. In September, serious border clashes occurred between Morocco and Algeria, during which the Algerian leaders urgently appealed to Egypt for political support and military aid. Nasser's response was immediate, unequivocal and clearly partisan. He publicly identified the Moroccans as the aggressors, called on the Arab League to stop the fighting and mediate between the two antagonists, and quickly dispatched several shipments of tanks to the poorly equipped Algerian army. While this action cemented Nasser's already warm friendship with the Algerian revolutionary leader, Ahmad Ben Bella, it also poisoned Egyptian–Moroccan relations. In the wake of Nasser's intervention, the Moroccan King, Hassan II, recalled his ambassador from Cairo, expelled some 350 Egyptians from his country, and accused the Arab League of being a puppet of Egypt.

Thus, as the end of 1963 approached, Egypt was involved in inter-

Arab conflicts conducted on a number of fronts. The Arab Middle East was about to embark on yet another period of political deadlock when quite suddenly and dramatically the situation changed. Enmity made way for cordiality, and suspicion was replaced by tolerance. The catalyst for this change was Israel; the perceived common enemy of all Arab states, be they monarchies or republics, traditional or revolutionary.

During the last months of 1963, while the Arab states were engaged in their various quarrels, Israel was approaching the completion of its project to divert the headwaters of the river Jordan from the Sea of Galilee. The Arabs had, in the past, frequently declared that such a diversion would be regarded as an act of aggression by Israel and as such would have to be met by force. However, as in many earlier instances, Arab action did not match Arab rhetoric; and Israel was allowed to continue work on the project unhampered. But now that the work was nearly completed, and in order to safeguard his credibility as an Arab leader, Nasser had to act. However, he could not go to war with Israel when nearly 35,000 of his troops were engaged in the Yemen. He was thus particularly anxious not to be dragged into hostilities through the precipitous action of another state, especially Syria and her demagogic Baathist leadership. Moreover, an assessment of the objective capabilities of the two disputants convinced the Egyptian elites that Israel should not be militarily engaged except by the forces of all Arab states, using all elements of their power, operating under a unified command, and executing a concerted and predetermined plan.[38] Thus on December 23, 1963, in a major speech, Nasser declared:

> In order to confront Israel, which challenged us last week when its Chief-of-Staff stood up and said, 'we shall divert the water against the will of the Arabs, and the Arabs can do what they want', a meeting between Arab Kings and Heads of State must take place as soon as possible, regardless of the conflicts and differences between them. Those with whom we are in conflict, we are prepared to meet; those with whom we have a quarrel, we are ready, for the sake of Palestine, so sit with. . .[39]

Obviously, the motivation for Nasser's conciliatory speech did not lie solely within the domain of Arab–Israeli relations. While not overtly concerned about the developments in the Yemen, Nasser must have hoped that a normalisation of inter-Arab relations would lead to a rapprochement with Saudi Arabia over the Yemeni war, which was proving to be a ruinous burden on the weak Egyptian economy. For all the above reasons, therefore, Nasser convened the first 'Arab Summit Conference' in Cairo in January 1964. For the next two and one-half years, the Arab world was to experience a period of peaceful coexistence and inter-state co-operation.

The results of this new policy were quickly apparent. An all-round improvement in Egypt's relations with the other Arab states was achieved. Diplomatic ties with Jordan were immediately restored, and relations between Nasser and King Hussein became openly cordial. Consequently, in the Cairo summit, the King raised no objections to the creation of the Palestine Liberation Organisation (PLO) or to the establishment of an Egyptian-dominated Arab Military Command. He was even persuaded by the Egyptian leadership in July 1964 to recognise the republican regime in the Yemen at the expense of the royalists. Indeed, his friendship with Nasser became so close that he made four highly publicised visits to Egypt during 1964. Similarly, Iraqi–Egyptian relations improved to the extent that in May 1964, Nasser and President Abd al-Salam Aref signed an accord creating a joint Presidential Council and a unified military command. The two presidents agreed that these institutions were to form the basis for a constitutional union between the two countries within two years. While the initiative for unity emanated primarily from the Iraqis, and although Nasser remained sceptical about its eventual viability, the accord served to emphasise and highlight the new spirit of the period. In addition to Jordan and Iraq, Egypt's relations were also markedly improved with Syria, Tunisia and Morocco.

To the Egyptian leaders, the most important consequence of the new policy was their reconciliation with the Saudi rulers. The Cairo summit afforded Nasser the opportunity to establish a dialogue with King Saud which led to the resumption of diplomatic relations between the two countries in March 1964. By September, relations between the two countries were sufficiently improved to allow Nasser and Prince Faisal, the Prime Minister of Saudi Arabia, to reach an agreement over the Yemen. The two leaders pledged their co-operation in order to 'help the people of Yemen towards stability, security and freedom'.[40]

The September agreement led to a peace conference between the two Yemeni factions who agreed on a ceasefire to take effect on November 8 and on the convocation of a national congress by November 23. However, although both Egypt and Saudi Arabia genuinely, even anxiously, desired some sort of a formula which would allow them to disengage from their conflict, their protégés were finding it somewhat difficult to abide by their own agreement. The two years of continuous conflict had created a deep schism between the two Yemeni sides, and consequently, it was not much of a surprise when the projected national congress was never held, or when the royalists broke the ceasefire agreement in the first week of December. Thus, for the first time in the Yemeni war, the two clients assumed independent attitudes and proceeded to impose various constraints on their patrons' policies.

The failure of the peace conference, therefore, can in no way be attributed to a lack of genuine desire for peace on the part of Egypt or Saudi Arabia. The efforts of both governments to reconcile their differences and reach a compromise solution to the Yemeni deadlock reflected their current attitudes towards intra-Arab politics in general. Indeed, this conciliatory orientation was simply a manifestation of the general environment of co-operation which pervaded the Arab world during this period. Certainly, the years 1964 and 1965 provided the most harmonious period of inter-state relations in the Arab Middle East since Egypt had activated its Arab policy a decade ago. Only the Tunisian President managed to disturb this tranquil atmosphere. In the spring of 1965, Bourguiba toured the Arab world to assess for himself the problems facing Arab–Israeli relations. Admirably frank, yet with a clear lack of political prudence, Bourguiba publicly suggested that the Arabs should accept the *status quo* situation existing in Arab–Israeli relations. Furthermore, he urged the Arab leaders to enter into negotiations with Israel with the view to concluding a lasting peace. Considering the ideological impasse in Arab–Israeli relations operative at the time, these untimely policy prescriptions were met with universal condemnation throughout the Arab world. They naturally drew a swift and immediate retort from Nasser, who accused Bourguiba of being an agent of Israel. Nor was Egypt prepared to allow the controversy to subside. In a major speech nearly four months after the incident, Nasser declared: 'I consider Habib Bourguiba an Arab setback. He has finally appeared, and has been discovered by the Arab masses, as an agent for imperialism and Zionism.'[41] This exchange marked the sharp deterioration in Egyptian–Tunisian relations which eventually led to Bourguiba's boycott of the September summit conference in Casablanca.

It must be remembered, however, that in the context of the Arab world as a whole, Egyptian–Tunisian enmity ran contrary to the mainstream of intra-Arab politics of the period. As noted above, the years spanning the Arab summit conferences witnessed a genuine desire on the part of most Arab leaders to pursue policies of co-operation instead of confrontation. This orientation was clearly exhibited by Nasser's repeated efforts to reach a settlement with Saudi Arabia over the Yemen. Thus in July 1965, Nasser announced that Egypt had formulated a peace plan which, if accepted by Saudi Arabia, would facilitate the complete evacuation of Egyptian troops from the Yemen in six months. He went on to declare that Egypt 'sincerely wished to arrive at a peaceful solution'.[42]

To this end, Nasser met Faisal (who through a palace coup had succeeded his brother to the throne) in Jeddah on August 22, where an agreement was quickly reached, providing for an immediate ceasefire and the convocation of a conference to determine the future of the

Yemen. It was decided that the conference, to be held in the Yemeni town of Harad on November 23, would consist of fifty representatives of various Yemeni interest groups. The object of the conference was to decide on a transitional government until a national plebiscite could be held, no later than November 3, 1966.[43] Backing this diplomatic initiative, the Egyptians announced that beginning on December 1, Egypt would recall 10,000 troops every month for seven months, allowing her to withdraw completely by June 1966.[44]

Yet neither Egypt nor Saudi Arabia had bargained for the intransigent attitudes and entrenched interests of their respective clients. After three years of conflict, little effort at compromise was forthcoming from either side, and the Harad conference became deadlocked on the issues of the transitional government, the Egyptian withdrawal, and the timing of the plebiscite.[45] Efforts by the two patron states to break the deadlock and save the conference were futile in the face of the ideological and political polarisation of the two Yemeni parties. Thus, the conference recessed on December 24 but was scheduled to reconvene on February 20, 1966. In the meantime, the two parties agreed that the existing armistice was to be observed and the propaganda war was to remain inoperative.

However, the conference was not destined to meet again. By February 1966, neither the Yemeni clients nor their patrons were exhibiting much enthusiasm for a compromise solution. In fact, on February 22, 1966, Nasser declared in a major speech that Egypt 'can stay in the Yemen for one year or two, three, four or five years'.[46] The intra-Arab politics of conciliation and co-operation which characterised the preceding two years were giving way to intransigence, dogmatism and political entrenchment. Thus, the move towards confrontation among the various Arab states gradually gathered momentum, reaching its climax with the collapse of the Algiers summit conference scheduled to meet in September 1966. By this time, the period of 'Arab solidarity' and 'Arab coexistence' had come to an end.

The demise of the era of conciliation can be attributed to a number of causes. To begin with, King Faisal, on a state visit to Iran in December 1965, had joined with the Shah in calling for an Islamic conference. In what seemed to be a pointed reference to Nasser's 'Arab socialism', Faisal proposed that Iran and Saudi Arabia should unite in fighting elements and ideas alien to Islam.[47] In January 1966, he visited Jordan and repeated the call for an Islamic summit to be held in Mecca later in the year.[48] These proposals were treated with the utmost suspicion and hostility by the Egyptian leaders. Particularly suspicious to the Egyptians was Iran's role in the proposed Islamic alliance, since the Shah was a pivotal member of the Central Treaty Organisation, a major supplier of oil to Israel, and an active supporter of the Yemeni royalists. Consequently, the Egyptian leadership perceived the Islamic conference as a renewed conservative drive aimed at isolating Egypt and the other progressive forces in the Middle East. Thus, in a major speech on February 22, 1966, Nasser declared:

> We are against all suspicious and reactionary movements . . . We are against the Islamic Pact or the Islamic Conference just like we were against the Baghdad Pact and the Eisenhower Doctrine and all other imperialist and reactionary movements that have sprung up in this region from the beginning of the Revolution until now.[49]

The fear of a 'conservative' drive against 'progressive' Arab forces acquired an extra-regional dimension when, in December 1965, Britain and the United States announced the conclusion of a big arms deal with Saudi Arabia worth $350 million. British and American firms were contracted to supply Saudi Arabia with Lightning jet fighters, radar equipment, and surface-to-air missiles.[50] To the Egyptians, the almost simultaneous timing of the arms deal with Faisal's overtures to the Shah of Iran was a clear indication of an international, 'anti-progressive' conspiracy. Thus, in an interview with Moscow's *Izvestia*, Nasser contended:

> The forces of colonialism and reaction inside and outside the Arab world [were] launching a new offensive, and, therefore, all progressive forces inside and outside the Arab world should close their ranks, solidify their unity and redouble their vigilance, and thus become effective.[51]

The perception of an international campaign against 'progressive' forces was reinforced a few months later, when in quick succession the International Monetary Fund refused to grant Egypt a loan of $70 million and the United States deferred negotiations on an Egyptian request for $150 million worth of surplus food.[52] In both cases, alleged dissatisfaction with the economic performance of Egypt and its costly commitment in the Yemen were forwarded as the primary reasons for witholding aid. The Egyptians, however, perceived these measures and activities as clear manifestations of a new 'imperialist and reactionary onslaught against the national revolutions in Asia, Africa and Latin America'.[53] Meanwhile, the ouster of Ghana's President Nkrumah and Indonesia's President Sukarno by pro-Western, right-wing regimes, only served to reinforce the Egyptian perception of a world-wide 'anti-progressive' offensive. It was, therefore, in such a setting that the period of 'peaceful coexistence' officially came to an end. In a major address on July 22, 1966, Nasser violently denounced the 'pro-West', Arab 'reactionaries' and categorically declared that because co-operation with these forces had become impossible, Egypt would not be attending the forthcoming Algiers summit meeting scheduled for September.[54]

A further factor contributing to the demise of the era of conciliation was the February coup in Syria which installed a Marxist-oriented neo-Baathist leadership, intent on improving relations with Egypt on the one hand, and on carrying out a 'revolutionary struggle' against Israel and the 'Arab reactionaries' on the other. The new Syrian leaders advocated the 'liberation of Palestine' as the first and necessary step towards their ultimate goal of forging a new social and political order in the Arab world. This goal was to be achieved through a revolutionary struggle on the Vietnam model. Consequently, the Syrians extended their wholehearted support to the infant Palestinian guerrilla groups. As a result of increasing guerrilla activity, the level of violence on the borders with Israel steadily rose throughout 1966. Although based in Syria, the Palestinian guerrillas often crossed into Israel through northern Jordan thus inviting heavy Israeli reprisals against the villages of the West Bank. Hussein's response to the new Syrian activism was, naturally, hostile. Commando operations in Jordan only served to expose Jordanian vulnerability to superior Israeli military power. Moreover, Hussein feared that the growing prestige of the guerrillas might have a disruptive influence on the sizeable Palestinian community resident in Jordan. Nor could he be particularly sympathetic to the anti-monarchic orientations of the Syrians. The Jordanian King, therefore, embarked upon extricating himself from his earlier commitment to co-operate with the PLO by accusing the organisation of subversive activities in Jordan. He followed this move by cementing his relations with Saudi Arabia in order to counteract the growing rapport between Syrian and Egyptian leaders.

Syrian activism was, therefore, a contributing agent to the situation of confrontation in intra-Arab politics existing in the latter half of 1966. The all too familiar environment of reciprocal accusations, recriminations and insults was once again a feature of the political interactions between the 'radical' and 'conservative' camps. Within such an atmosphere any increase in inter-camp hostilities was bound to result in a corresponding reinforcement of intra-camp solidarity against the perceived external threat. This was particularly the case with Egyptian–Syrian relations, where fears of an impending 'plot' against the Syrian regime caused much anxiety in Egyptian quarters. In August, Heikal emphatically stated that 'Damascus does not stand alone in its fight against imperialist plots',[55] and on November 4, Egypt signed a defence alliance with Syria which asserted that aggression against either state would be regarded as an attack on the other. The way was now open for the chain of events destined to lead to the most disastrous confrontation of Nasser's entire career in June 1967.

The beginning of this chain can be traced to November 13, 1966, when an Israeli armoured brigade backed by the Israeli air force, systematically demolished the Jordanian village of Samu, killing eighteen Jordanians and wounding fifty-four. Officially, the Israelis insisted that the attack was in reprisal for repeated guerrilla incursions into Israel. However, the magnitude, target and timing of the action suggests that it was meant either to deter Hussein from joining the Egyptian–Syrian alliance or, conversely, to highlight the impotence of the alliance to the Arab public, thus diminishing the stature of Nasser and driving a deeper wedge between the two opposing camps in the Arab world. Subsequent events suggest that the Israeli objective was achieved on both accounts. Referring to the inactivity of the Unified Arab Command during the Israeli operation, the Jordanians, vigorously backed by the Saudis, attacked the Egyptians and the Syrians for refusing to come to Jordan's aid in her hour of need. They derisively emphasised the apparent contrast between declaration and performance in Nasser's policy towards Israel. The Egyptian and Syrian leaders counteracted with a violent campaign, in which they incited the Jordanians to overthrow their 'reactionary' King. Hussein retaliated in February 1967 by recalling his ambassador from Cairo and withdrawing his recognition of the republican regime in Sana'.

These events reinforced the state of political polarisation existing in the Arab world and led to an increase of ideological militancy in the 'radical' camp, and particularly in Syria. This radicalisation manifested itself in the escalation of Syrian-backed guerrilla operations in Israel. This time, Israeli retaliation came in the form of an air battle in which six Syrian jet fighters were shot down, and Damascus was subjected to the indignity of an impromptu air parade staged by the victorious Israelis. By now, an ongoing process of action–response–reaction had been set in motion, which was to eventually lead to the devastating Israeli air strikes against Egyptian, Syrian, Jordanian and Iraqi airfields in the early morning of Monday, June 5, 1967.[56]

5   The June War and After

By June 8, 1967, after only four days of fighting, Egypt had suffered the most crushing military defeat of its modern history. Its frequently praised air force lay devastated on the ground, and its army, the perceived 'guardian of the Arab nation', had been dealt a humiliating blow by the mobile, superbly equipped and brilliantly led Israeli forces. Nasser later admitted that during the four days of fighting on the Egyptian front, his armed forces had lost 10,000 men and 1500 officers, in addition to the 5000 men and 500 officers taken prisoner by the Israelis.[1] In equipment, the losses of the Egyptian armed forces were estimated at 600 tanks and 340 combat aircraft.[2] Heikal attributed this remarkably swift and massive Israeli victory to

> three fundamental and indisputable facts. Fact one is that we are facing an enemy in receipt of exceptional aid. Fact two is that this enemy has utilized the resources he received with exceptional skill. Fact three is that in tackling him with our own resources – which were not inconsiderable – we acted with exceptional ineptitude.[3]

The combination of these factors facilitated the occupation by the Israeli forces of Jordan's West Bank, the Golan Heights in Syria and the entire Sinai Peninsula, bringing Israeli soldiers to the Suez Canal.

Nasser, the 'revolutionary' leader of his people, could not but accept responsibility for Egypt's 'disaster'. On June 9, in a moving television and radio address, Nasser announced that he had resigned his official posts and that he had asked Zakariya Mohyddin to take over the presidency of the republic. He told the stunned multitude not to despair but to embark on the task of eradicating the consequences of 'Israeli aggression'. He reminded them of the lasting achievements of the 'Egyptian Revolution', and urged them not to relinquish the fight against 'imperialism'. Observers in Cairo at the time have confirmed that in a spontaneous emotional outburst of loyalty to the fallen leader, the people of Cairo immediately filled the streets of their city demanding that he withdraw his resignation. To most Egyptians, it had become inconceivable that the country could function, let alone survive its present predicament, without the towering figure of 'al-Rais'. A decade of charismatic authority had established Nasser as an intrinsic part of the social fabric of the country. He had come to be perceived as the embodiment of Egypt's national dignity, the symbol of its regional

50

leadership, and the essence of its international prestige. His resignation therefore would have been synonymous with the defeat of 'Egyptian socialism' and 'Arab nationalism' by the forces of 'imperialism' and 'international Zionism'. This was unthinkable to the Egyptians, and indeed to the majority of Arabs, who, along with Nasser's colleagues, including Mohyddin, categorically rejected Nasser's resignation. Reportedly surprised by such a response, Nasser reconsidered his decision and withdrew his resignation. The entire episode had lasted less than twenty-four hours.

The immediate aftermath of the war found Egypt in an almost hopeless position. Apart from the nearly total decimation of her armed forces, Egypt's economy was in a desperate condition. The Suez Canal was closed; the oil-fields in Sinai were under Israeli control; and a massive migration to an overpopulated Cairo from the canal cities of Suez, Ismailia and other towns was beginning to gather momentum. These domestic liabilities, plus the humiliating presence of Israeli troops on Eygptian soil, necessitated a change in Nasser's global policies. He was forced finally to abandon the policy of 'non-alignment' and to turn almost exclusively to the Soviet Union for military and economic aid. In fact, his need was so urgent that he was prepared to sacrifice the hitherto sacrosanct ideal of Egyptian sovereignty by offering the Soviet Union military and naval facilities in Egypt.[4]

The only positive result of Egypt's defeat was that it stimulated a vigorous public debate concerned with analysing the causes of the 'disaster' through a critical evaluation of basic Arab values and attitudes. In the forefront of this wave of 'self-criticism' was Heikal and *al-Ahram*, which suggests that the campaign was conducted with Nasser's blessings and encouragement. Thus, three weeks after the end of the war, Heikal attributed the Arab defeat to four basic mistakes:

> Firstly, we often say more than we actually mean; thus the calls to crush, kill etc. can deny us international support because such rhetoric transforms our glorious struggle into a mere bloodbath. . . Secondly, the Arab cause was not convincingly presented to the outside world. We believed that the legitimacy of our cause, which was obvious to us, was enough to convince others . . . Thirdly, we have tended to establish relations on the basis of black and white without any regard to other colours. We must understand that only God can face his servants with two alternatives – Paradise or Hell . . . Finally, we have not tried to maintain direct and effective contact with the outside world except in times of stress, consequently, our foreign policy is often perceived by others as spasmodic and non-rational.[5]

These 'mistakes' were analysed within the broader context of certain basic 'shortcomings' in the Arab 'nature'. This intellectual exercise

sought to examine such deficiencies in the Arab character as 'emo-
tionalism', 'fatalism' and, most frequently, 'self-righteousness'. The
Arabs were reminded that 'if others are guilty of the sins of the devils
it does not necessarily follow that we possess the infallibility of angels.'[6]
This process of 'self-criticism' contributed to modifications in Arab
perceptions in at least one important respect: it opened the way to a
more rational assessment of reality, which was to become evident in
future years. Moreover, the vigour with which the debate was conducted in the post-war months indicated that the Arab public was
gradually recovering from the initial shock of the defeat.

This recovery was confirmed when the Arab heads of state met in
Khartoum on August 29, 1967 to discuss future Arab strategy towards
Israel. Given the prevalent balance of forces favouring the Israelis, the
bargaining position of the Arab leaders was one of obvious weakness.
The assembled heads of state realised that any Israeli concessions
regarding the new situation would depend primarily on the latter's
magnanimity, since the Arab leaders possessed little capability for
inducing Israel to make the kind of compromises needed to placate an
angry Arab public convinced of Israel's innate 'expansionism' and
'aggressiveness'. Thus, only the promise of substantial territorial concessions by the Israelis would have succeeded in promoting a flexible
policy on the part of the Arab leaders. However, for a number of
reasons elaborated elsewhere,[7] the Israeli government had felt unable
to make these necessary compromises. On the contrary, its official
position, as defined by Prime Minister Levi Eshkol on June 12, 1967,
emphasised Israel's determination not to revert to the pre-war borders.
In a crucial passage which had an electrifying impact on Arab perceptions, and which later was to be frequently quoted by Arab leaders
and public alike as signifying Israeli 'intransigence', the Israeli Prime
Minister had declared

> to the nations of the world that they should not labour under the
> illusion that Israel is ready to return to the state of affairs that
> existed a week ago . . . The state of affairs that existed a week ago
> will not return. The hand of Israel will no longer be exposed to acts
> of sabotage and murder . . . A new situation has been created. It
> can serve as a starting point for direct negotiations for a peace
> settlement with the Arab states.[8]

Two weeks later, Arab perceptions of Israel's determination to hold on
to the occupied territories had received positive reinforcement when
the Knesset passed three draft bills by which East Jerusalem was
annexed to the State of Israel. The laws also introduced new administrative and judicial measures for the rest of the West Bank, which,
according to an Israeli newspaper, clearly indicated Israel's resolve
'to hold on to these areas for a long time'.[9]

Not only did they form effective external constraints on the likelihood of a more flexible policy being adopted by the Arab leaders assembled in Khartoum, but also through their impact on Arab perceptions, the Israeli measures and policy statements reinforced the domestic constraints operating on the Arab leaders against the possible adoption of such a policy. Thus, the policy options available to the Arab leaders in Khartoum, especially the moderate ones, were in effect extremely limited. Consequently, the summit produced a militant resolution which reiterated 'the main principles by which the Arab states abide, namely, no peace with Israel, no recognition of Israel, no negotiations with it, and insistence on the rights of the Palestinian people in their own country'.[10]

Nasser, Hussein and Faisal insisted, however, on utilising all possible instruments, including the 'political' and 'diplomatic' in the effort 'to eliminate the effects of aggression'.[11] In effect, while accepting the limitations imposed upon their policy objectives towards Israel, these leaders refused to accept any constraints on the instruments of this policy. It is within this context that Nasser's seemingly contradictory activities over the next three years can be understood. His endorsement of the Security Council Resolution No. 242, his efforts to establish a coherent eastern military front consisting of Jordan, Syria and Iraq, his participation in the peace missions undertaken by the United Nations Ambassador Jarring and the United States Secretary of State Rogers, his initiation of the war of attrition, and finally his acceptance of the ceasefire along the canal, were all measures consistent with the dictates of the Khartoum resolution.

In the realm of inter-Arab relations, the Arab leaders reached two important decisions. In the first place, Saudi Arabia, Kuwait and Libya agreed to extend annual grants of $280 million to Egypt and $100 million to Jordan to compensate them for the loss of land and revenue as a result of the June war. Secondly, an agreement was reached between Nasser and King Faisal of Saudi Arabia to disengage from the Yemeni conflict, with the date for complete Egyptian evacuation set for December 1967. Apart from finally extricating himself from his euphemistically termed 'Yemeni miscalculation', Nasser was obviously delighted to deploy the 50,000 troops operating in the Yemen along the defenceless west bank of the Canal.

The Khartoum conference, therefore, marked Egypt's readoption of the objective of 'Arab solidarity' within the Arab core of the Middle Eastern system. Nasser no longer possessed the capability or the motivation to pursue a revolutionary policy in the Arab world. Massive domestic problems, preoccupation with Israel, and economic dependence on other Arab states necessarily relegated Egypt's revolutionary ambitions in the Arab world to a secondary role within the overall policy priorities. Nasser's major regional objective became 'the eradication of the consequences of defeat', and all activities, including intra-Arab activities, were made completely dependent upon the achievement of this overriding objective. Thus, in a speech Nasser declared: 'Our attitude towards any Arab state depends on that state's attitude towards the battle.'[12] Such a policy necessitated the pursuit of harmonious inter-state relations with the other Arab states, irrespective of their political or social systems, in order to establish a coherent force capable of achieving the primary objective. However, Arab solidarity was to be severely tested as a result of the activities of an incipient movement which, gathering strength and prestige, was soon to establish itself as a vigorous non-state actor in the perennial Arab–Israeli struggle – the Palestine Liberation Organisation (PLO).

A coherent Palestinian movement began to emerge in 1964 when the second Arab summit in Alexandria decided to establish the PLO and the PLA – the Palestine Liberation Army. However, the institutionalised character of the organisation, and the fact that it was created by Arab governments, alienated many of the young Palestinians from the infant organisation. This new, highly politicised generation of Palestinians, many of whom had been brought up in refugee camps, had begun to despair of the Arab states' ability or willingness to 'liberate' their land for them. As a result, they advocated self-reliance and direct Palestinian action through guerrilla activity. Consequently and concurrently, a number of para-military organisations began to operate parallel to, but not necessarily in conflict with, the PLO and PLA. The most important of these new groups was al-Fat'h,[13] led by a Cairo-educated engineer called Yasir Arafat.

The defeat of the Arab states in the June War increased the prestige of the guerrillas in the Arab world, by reinforcing the guerrillas' claim that they alone were capable of realising Palestinian aspirations. However, the seminal event in the development of the guerrilla movement as a major political force in the Arab–Israeli confrontation occurred in March 1968 at Karameh in East Jordan, where Palestinian commandos inflicted heavy losses on a large Israeli force sent to destroy guerrilla bases in the town. In military terms, the Israeli operation was successful in that it achieved its basic objective of destroying the guerrilla base.[14] However, the commandos' ability to inflict heavy casualties on the 'invincible' Israelis was perceived, and indeed hailed, by the Arab public as a great victory. The 'battle of Karameh' (Karameh meaning 'dignity' in Arabic) became a cornerstone of Palestinian folklore and was the catalyst for the movement's rapid growth in both numbers and prestige. In May, al-Fat'h and other guerrilla groups, such as the Popular Front for the Liberation of Palestine (PFLP) officially joined and soon dominated the PLO; and in February 1969, Yasir Arafat was elected chairman of the Executive Committee of the Organisation.

The dramatic growth and increasing prestige of the guerrillas was bound to have major repercussions on the domestic situation of those Arab states, such as Jordan, within whose borders the guerrillas operated. Through an elaborate network of military, social, economic and administrative institutions within the areas of their operation, the guerrilla camps in Jordan became a state within a state. In fact, by the end of 1968, two largely independent political forces existed in Jordan: the Hashemite monarchy and the Palestinian commandos. Hussein's resentment of this state of affairs and his consequent efforts to confine the power and activity of the guerrillas led to increasing domestic tension. As the year drew to a close the domestic political situation became distinctly polarised between the two major, clearly antagonistic forces.

In all this, Nasser played the role of the mediator. He constantly urged both Hussein and Arafat to exercise caution and patience in dealing with each other since both were indispensable components of the overall Arab strategy. While sympathising with Hussein's protestations against the 'anarchic' activities of the guerrillas inside Jordan, Nasser nevertheless declared himself 'fully committed to offering all help to the Palestinian guerrilla action, [since] the emergence of the Palestinian struggle constituted a big transformation of the Arab situation.'[15] At the same time, he tried to convince Arafat that the guerrillas would be committing a costly mistake if they thought they were capable of defeating Israel on their own. The nub of this argument was elucidated by Heikal, who maintained that guerrilla action could not be decisive in Palestine where the terrain was open, where the 'oppressors' outnumbered the 'oppressed', and where, in contrast to Vietnam or Algeria, the guerrillas could not seek immunity from enemy action in friendly territory because Israel possessed the capability to strike at any place in the Arab world. Thus, the idea that defeating Israel could only be achieved through guerrilla action was no more than a myth propagated by ill-informed romantics. The task of defeating Israel, Heikal concluded, could only be accomplished by the entire forces of the Arab world, of which the Palestinian Resistance was an integral and important part.[16] In trying to convince Arafat of the validity of this argument, the Egyptian leadership hastened to impress upon the guerrilla leader the need for a situation of peaceful coexistence inside Jordan, so that rather than being expended in fighting each other, the capabilities of the Arab forces could be preserved and utilised against the enemy.

During this period, Egypt's strategy towards Israel focused on establishing a coherent command that would operationally link in the western front comprising Egypt with a projected eastern front of Jordan, Syria, Iraq and the Palestinian Resistance. As has been discussed, however, the eastern front was beset with dissensions amongst its ranks. In addition to the growing enmity between the Jordanians and Palestinians, relations between King Hussein and the left-wing Baath regime in Damascus were anything but harmonious. Only the Cairo-oriented government of General Abd al-Rahman Aref in Iraq was tolerated by all parties. Then in July 1968, a coup occurred in Baghdad which brought in the right-wing faction of the Baath party. Although the demise of the friendly Aref regime constituted a setback for Nasser, Egypt's initial reaction was guarded. Cairo radio simply expressed the hope that Iraq would continue to 'contribute positively to the defence of Arab rights'.[17] Yet soon afterwards, it became clear to the Egyptians that the Iraqi coup would only exacerbate the growing fragmentation of the eastern front. In describing the condition of the front in the wake of the Iraqi coup, Heikal noted that a unified front no longer existed because 'Amman is undecided about the two Baathist regimes in Iraq and Syria. Damascus is suspicious of the rightist wing of the Baath party which suddenly came to power in Iraq. Baghdad considers the leftist wing of the party in Damascus as usurpers who betrayed the party.'[18] In the face of these divisions, the Egyptians temporarily abandoned their efforts to establish an eastern front, concentrating their energies instead on reinforcing their own front with Israel.

By the end of the year, Egypt had rebuilt her forces sufficiently to allow Nasser to engage in a limited military action against the Israelis which, for nearly six months, took the form of intermittent artillery duels across the canal. In March 1969, however, Egypt suddenly increased the level of violence through intensive bombardment of the newly constructed 'Bar-Lev' defence line on the eastern bank of the canal. This was the beginning of Egypt's 'war of attrition' against Israel, in which the former's quantitative superiority and heavier concentration of artillery along the canal gave her an advantage over the smaller Israeli forces. Although the Israeli air force replied with repeated bombing of Egyptian positions, the 'war of attrition' was inflicting heavy losses on the Israelis. In October 1969, General Dayan admitted 'that while in the first and second year after the [June] war the monthly average of men killed on our side had been fifteen, we were now loosing an average of thirty killed monthly.'[19] It was obvious that Israeli public opinion could not tolerate such a casualty rate for much longer.

In an effort to present a unified front against the expected Israeli counter-offensive, Nasser tried to revitalise the conflict-ridden eastern front. When this particular endeavour came to nothing, Nasser, in November 1969, demanded the convocation of an Arab summit meeting to discuss the recent developments in the Arab–Israeli conflict. When the summit convened in Rabat a month later, Egypt submitted a detailed plan prepared by the War Minister, General Mahmoud

Fawzi, calling for various contributions in money and materials from the other Arab states. Nasser insisted on an immediate and blunt answer from the assembled heads of state as to whether they were prepared to participate in the 'battle'. According to Radio Cairo, when no satisfactory answer was forthcoming, Nasser walked out of the meeting declaring: 'it appears to me that the conference has not resulted in anything practical at all. Frankly, my opinion is that we should announce to the people in the joint communique that the conference has failed in order not to deceive the people and give them false hopes.'[20]

After the failure of the Rabat conference, Nasser returned to Cairo to face a worsening situation on the canal front. Israel's counter-offensive, spearheaded by its highly superior air force, had reached a devastating climax during the month of December. Almost daily, Israeli planes, including the newly acquired Phantom fighter-bombers, pounded Egyptian positions on the canal, so that by the end of the month the Egyptian front had almost ceased to exist. Like the encounter of 1967, the 'war of attrition' was lost to the Israeli air force.

The 'war of attrition' was immediately followed in January 1970 by a surprising decision on the part of the Israeli decision-makers to capitalise on Israel's complete air superiority by bombing targets deep inside Egypt. It is difficult to understand the reasoning behind the adoption by Israel's leaders of this strategic option. Having just neutralised Egypt's capacity to wage war, there was certainly very little strategic value in extending the bombing to the outskirts of Cairo. It seems, therefore, that 'deep penetration bombing' was pursued in order to achieve the psychological objective of weakening Egyptian morale and undermining Nasser's credibility with the Egyptian people.[21] If this was the objective, then subsequent events have clearly proved its failure and the short-sightedness of those decision-makers who adopted it. Neither Egyptian morale nor Nasser's credibility were undermined. In fact, the new policy proved to be completely counter-productive for Israel, since as a consequence of deep penetration bombing, Israel was suddenly faced with a new and dangerous situation. Because of Egypt's impotence to retaliate against the bombing, Nasser had no option but to ask for Soviet-manned surface-to-air missiles, the Sam 3's, and perhaps more crucially, Soviet pilots, who began to fly operationally in Egypt in the spring of 1970. The first admission by Nasser of this new level of Soviet commitment came in a speech on May 1, 1970, when he publicly thanked the Soviet Union for 'helping us safeguard our skies against the American-made Phantom raids'.[22] The introduction of this extra-regional element to what was until then an essentially local conflict, proved to be an effective constraint on Israel's freedom of manoeuvrability. Once a clash with Soviet pilots over Egypt became a possibility, Israel immediately halted its aerial operations in

Egypt, and the last Israeli attempt to penetrate deep into Egyptian air space occurred on the morning of April 18, 1970.[23] The policy of 'deep penetration bombing' is a good example of the tendency of decision-makers to pursue immediately attractive options, without fully evaluating their possible long-term consequences.

The failure of both Egypt's 'war of attrition' and Israel's 'deep penetration bombing' led to a period of relative calm and military stalemate on the Israeli–Egyptian front which was utilised by Secretary of State Rogers to announce an American proposal for peace in the area. This included a ninety-day cease fire; adherence by the conflicting parties to the Security Council Resolution 242; and their agreement to peace talks through Ambassador Jarring. Similar efforts earlier on in the year had been met with extreme Egyptian hostility. Rogers was accused of 'wanting to buy the Arab destiny with empty words'[24] and of 'proving that he possesses enormous talent for evading the truth'.[25] However, after the devastation of the Egyptian front, and Nasser's conviction after Rabat that his Arab neighbours' verbal bellicosity would not be matched by corresponding action, Egypt accepted the Rogers proposals on July 23, 1970. Heikal explained that four major reasons motivated Egypt's acceptance of the American plan:

> Firstly, to set the Middle East crisis in motion politically alongside the military action. Secondly, to test U.S. intentions after the awakening caused by the domestic and international dimensions of the crisis. Thirdly, the fact that the invitation was within the framework of Security Council Resolution 242. Fourthly, whether Israel accepted or rejected the plan, the result would be a great change which would not necessarily work against Arab aspiration.[26]

The Israeli leaders, surprised by Egypt's unexpected acceptance of the plan, had no alternative but to follow suit on July 30. Jordan soon emulated Egypt, and the proposals were endorsed by the Soviet Union, France and Britain.

The attitude of the Palestine guerrillas, however, was bitterly hostile. Suspicious of any American initiative, the various guerrilla organisations perceived the Rogers proposals as an offensive undertaken by the United States with the object of inducing the Arab states to freeze the conflict at the expense of Palestinian rights and interests. In the three years since the June war, regaining the occupied territories had gradually come to signify to the Arab states the end of the 'just struggle' against Israel. To the Palestinian guerrillas, this objective constituted only a step towards attaining the ultimate goal of 'a secular, democratic and multinational Palestine'.

Since the guerrillas were not strong enough to denounce Nasser directly,[27] they focused their anger on Hussein. With the resultant increase in tension, the dislocation of Jordan's fragile domestic structure became a distinct probability. In early September, clashes between the Jordanian army and the Palestinian guerrillas increased in frequency and intensity. Later, after a multiple hijacking operation by the Palestinians, the skirmishes between the guerrillas and the army developed into a bloody, full-scale civil war on September 16. The guerrillas with their light weapons had little chance against the heavy armour and the artillery power of the Jordanian army. Nasser, horrified at the ensuing massacre of the Palestinians, and fearing a possible American–Israeli intervention,[28] called for an emergency summit meeting to end the hostilities. After a stormy meeting, in which Nasser used all his diplomatic powers and his new prestige as the leading advocate of 'Arab solidarity and coexistence', an agreement was reached between the warring parties on September 27. The civil war had lasted eleven days, and had resulted in the death of 3000 Palestinian guerrillas and civilians and the final expulsion of the Palestinian Resistance Movement from Jordan.

The summit meeting in Cairo was destined to be Nasser's final activity in the Arab world. The emotional drain involved 'in racing with death to try and stop men, women and children dying',[29] and the enormous effort expended at negotiating an almost impossible agreement, left Nasser in a state of physical and mental exhaustion. On September 28, 1970, after twenty-eight years of leading Egypt's vigorous regional activity, Nasser suffered a fatal heart attack and died at his home at the age of fifty-two. No man in the modern history of the Arab world, and certainly no man since his demise, has succeeded in dominating Arab politics in the way Gamal Abd al-Nasser did.

PART II

The Foreign Policy of Egypt towards the Arab World, 1952-70

6　The Framework of Analysis

So far, this study has concentrated on the perspective of historical dynamics to explain the various interactions between Egypt and the other states of the Arab world. The analysis has attempted a chronological account of the development of these interactions between the years 1952 and 1970. Thus, through concentrating primarily on the nexus action–response–reaction over a specific time-span, an understanding of the dynamic nature of a state's external relations is facilitated. Within this context, foreign policy behaviour is postulated as a set of responses to stimuli which, in the main, are externally generated.

Such a treatment is, however, analytically limited and can offer only partial explanations for the formulation and conduct of foreign policy. Part II of this study, therefore, is meant to complement the analysis in Part I by identifying and explaining the general underlying factors which in their totality determine the specific nature of a state's foreign policy. The framework to be followed involves the identification of the elements of Egypt's foreign policy and their classification under a series of categories around which the analysis is structured and organised. Not only should these specified categories (or model) facilitate a more comprehensive understanding of the multiplicity of factors that determine the nature and conduct of Egypt's foreign policy, but they should also provide a framework for comparing Egypt's foreign policy with the foreign policies of other states. Before proceeding further, however, it would be appropriate to explore the conceptual boundary of the term 'foreign policy' as used by scholars and academics in the field of international relations.

The study of foreign policy, until recently, has lacked conceptual clarity. This has been the result of the failure to delineate the boundaries of foreign policy as a concept. Consequently, many professed studies of foreign *policy* have, in actual fact, been concerned with surveying the bilateral or multilateral *relations* of one state with other states in the international system (the approach adopted in Part I of this study). However, in the last two decades there has been an increasing tendency towards precise and orderly methods for analysing foreign policy in both its theoretical content and its operational aspects. This has led to a proliferation of theory-oriented studies concerned mainly with formulating explanatory theories of foreign policy behaviour.[1]

Much of the pioneering energy concentrated on defining foreign policy in an effort to separate it conceptually from foreign relations, K. J. Holsti defined foreign policy as the analysis of 'actions of a state toward the external environment and the conditions – usually domestic – under which these actions are formulated'.[2] Holsti, therefore, was concerned primarily with *actions* of a state and any study which was based on the *interactions* of two or more states was conceptualised, in Holsti's terminology, as international politics – defined as the government-sponsored aspects of a state's foreign relations (see Fig. 1).[3]

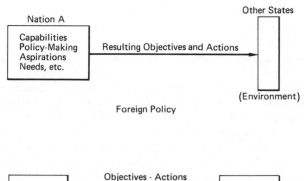

Foreign Policy

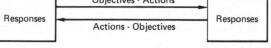

International Politics

FIG. 1 Foreign Policy and International Politics

Source: K. J. Holsti, International Politics: *A Framework for Analysis*, Englewood Cliffs, New Jersey: Prentice–Hall, Inc., 1967, p. 21.

Fred Sonderman agreed with this definition. To him, foreign policy was the study of 'activities of individuals and groups within states, and involving the governmental machinery of states, which are designed to have an impact on the policies of other states, or on individuals and groups within them'.[4] Joseph Frankel, too, defined foreign policy as the 'decisions and actions which involve to some appreciable degree relations between the state and other states'.[5] Here, again, a clear emphasis on *actions* rather than *actions and responses* emerged. In this, the three authors reflected the general tendency among the pioneering theory-oriented scholars to emphasise the primacy of the domestic variables at the expense of, and in reaction to, the earlier and more traditional preoccupation of the foreign relations scholars with external forces only.

Like in most extremes, both these poles have proved to be theoretically limited and empirically restrictive. Undoubtedly, a synthesis
incorporating the relevant variables of the two approaches should
provide the fullest and most meaningful analysis; for while domestic
variables explain the sources of decisions, external situational factors
affect the outcome of these decisions, thus influencing their subsequent
impact on the decision-making process of a state. As such, while it is
true to say that 'a state's situation conditions its policy and the outcome
of its policy may affect its situation',[6] it must be understood that the
statement refers to the state's situation both in its external and domestic
dimensions. Consequently, by attempting to minimise the effects of
external forces on state behaviour, many theory-oriented studies of
foreign policy offered the kind of analyses that were both limited and
static. In other words, it is only through exploring the external pressures on states that foreign policy analysis can acquire, through the
vital concept of 'feedback', the notion of dynamism.

The most sophisticated model to appear so far, which attempted to
incorporate the notion of 'dynamism' into the analysis of foreign policy,
was devised by Michael Brecher, Blema Steinberg and Janice Stein.[7]
The authors' conscious emphasis on 'feedback' and 'flow' was exhibited
by their criticism of earlier theory-oriented studies of foreign policy
behaviour. They found Frankel's model of foreign policy decision-
making limited because 'the crucial notion of circular feedback is
virtually unexplored, thus the construct remains essentially static'.[8]
Similarly, the Snyder, Bruck and Sapin study was criticised on account
of its 'indifference to feedback and ongoing process'.[9] The same criticism was levelled at other theorists such as Gabriel Almond and Roy
Macridis, and while they found James Rosenau's 'Pretheory'[10] 'highly
suggestive', the fact that it included neither 'the notion of an input–
output system nor of feedback'[11] was seen as a limit on its utility.

The Brecher, Steinberg and Stein model ('research design' in their
terminology) is partly derived from general systems theory and partly
from the input–output approach to foreign policy analysis. The main
premise of the model is that 'the concept of system is no less valid in
foreign policy analysis than in the study of domestic politics.'[12] The
foreign policy system consists of 'an environment or setting, a group of
actors, structures through which they initiate decisions and respond to
challenges, and processes which sustain or alter the flow of demands
and products of the system as a whole.[13] The boundaries of the foreign
policy system are essentially vertical in the sense that 'they encompass
all inputs and outputs which affect decisions whose contents and scope
lie essentially in the realm of inter-state relations.'[14] In other words,
these boundaries are not static but will tend to change from one issue
to another. The foreign policy system is likened to a flow into and out
of a number of structures and processes which produces decisions.

These, in turn, feed back into the system as inputs, thus achieving a dynamic circular flow (see Fig. 2).

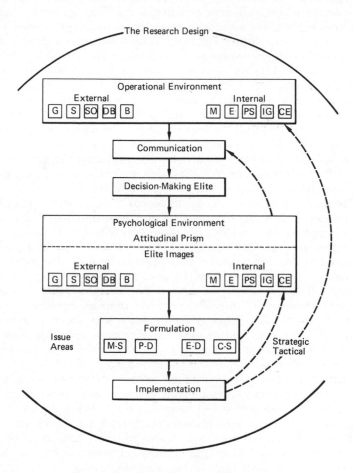

Fɪɢ. 2 Brecher's Research Design

G=Global System; S=Subordinate System; SO=Subordinate Other; B=Bilateral; DB=Dominant Bilateral. M=Military Capability; E=Economic Capability; PS=Political Structure; IG=Interest Groups; CE=Competing Elites. M–S=Military Security; P–D= Political–Diplomatic; E–D=Economic–Developmental; C–S=Cultural–Status.

Source: M. Brecher, *The Foreign Policy System of Israel: Setting, Images, Process*, London: Oxford University Press, 1972, p. 4.

The primary utility of the model lies in its schematic provision for observable, and even more significantly, researchable factors and categories which allow a rigorous and systematic study of a state's foreign policy. Yet it is probably this quest for rigour which has prevented the model from achieving the authors' claim of a 'dynamic, circular flow'; for while the multiplicity of variables provides a comprehensive tool for analysing one specific decision, the model, when applied to a state's *foreign policy over time*, fails to highlight the homeostatic capability a foreign policy system must possess in order to endure the action–response–reaction process embodied in inter-state relations. This is because by concentrating on the macro concept of 'policy' rather than on one foreign policy decision at a time the analyst sets himself the almost hopeless task of identifying and isolating numerous micro decisions and their corresponding feedback effects in order to ascertain their cumulative impact on the system's dynamism. In fact, this particular problem has proved to be the major obstacle to the development of empirically oriented theories of foreign policy behaviour. It is probably this inability which has spurred some theorists to question the utility of 'policy' as a dependent variable and to suggest alternatives such as 'decision' or 'undertaking'.[15] It is thus significant that when Brecher attempted to operationalise the model in a general study of Israel's foreign policy over a period of twenty years,[16] his analysis produced a static study of structures, institutions and processes which failed to incorporate the notion of feedback in terms of responses to decisions and actions. Brecher, himself, admits this limitation in his study. He asserts that the book is concerned mainly with the horizontal or macrodimensional aspects of Israel's foreign policy behaviour, that is, it endeavours to explain the various components of the operational and psychological environments and the policy process over the period 1948–68 without incorporating the notion of 'feedback'. The vertical or microdimensional aspect of Israel's foreign policy is analysed in a second volume, which concentrates on a number of specific challenges and decision responses that include the concept of circular feedback.[15] As has been discussed earlier, in such one-decision cases, the utilisation of the model fully and systematically explained, through the notion of feedback, the subsequent realignments of Israel's foreign policy in each particular case.

The analysis to be used in Part II of this study adheres to the premises of Brecher, Steinberg and Stein. The framework is an input–output model comprising a set of categories which should facilitate the orderly classification of data while emphasising the system's conversion process (see Fig. 3). The model will attempt to explore the setting, the actors, the attitudes and the processes of Egypt's foreign policy under Nasser. The categories that will be employed are the capabilities of, and the constraints on, Egypt's foreign policy, the institutions and

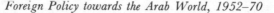

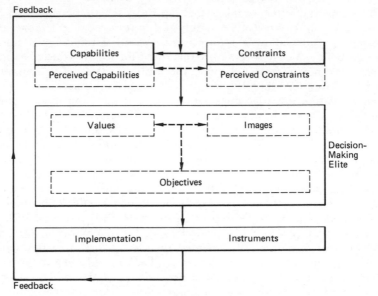

FIG. 3 The Foreign Policy Model

processes of Egyptian policy-making, the values and images of the decision-makers, the objectives pursued by the policy-makers, and the instruments with which these objectives were implemented. It is worth noting here that it is only for analytical purposes that these categories are analysed independently; in reality, they constitute interdependent elements of a 'foreign policy system' in which policy inputs (influences) are converted into policy outputs (decisions) through the process of policy formulation by the decision-making elite. In this study, the influences from the operational environment, conceptualised here as capabilities and constraints, comprise the inputs into the psychological environment of the decision-making elite, in which objectives are formulated according to a set of perceptions that the decision-makers hold of the environment, and the various values and principles to which they adhere. These objectives are implemented in the operational environment (outputs) and the resultant changes are then fed back into the system as inputs. Obviously, this particular model cannot claim to be as comprehensive as Brecher's 'research design'. This is primarily because many of Brecher's variables and categories were found to be either over-extensive and/or on the periphery of this particular study.

However, a major advantage of the model's structural simplicity is that it allows for more flexibility and a higher level of generalisation, a primary consequence of which is its ability, through the utilisation of a historical analysis in Chapter 10, to incorporate the concepts of 'feedback' into the general framework of Egypt's foreign policy towards the Arab states. In that chapter, the cluster of implementing (day-to-day) foreign policy decisions will be classified under three general headings termed the 'policy objectives'. These will be identified as a maximum objective of 'comprehensive unity', a minimum objective of 'Arab solidarity' and an intermediate objective of 'revolutionary change'. These objectives are deemed to have represented the major orientations in Egypt's foreign policy towards the Arab states during our period of study. The successive policy realignments inherent in the adoption of one objective instead of another occurred as a result of various influences and feedback effects emanating from the operational environment (whether international or domestic) and interacting with the images and values (the psychological environment) held by the decision-makers. It is precisely for the purpose of highlighting the continuing process of policy realignments and the consequent emphasis on the dynamic nature of the 'foreign policy system' that the above model is utilised.

7 Capabilities and Constraints

The term 'capability' can be defined as any real or perceived positive contribution to the achievement of the totality of a regime's foreign policy objectives. Capabilities usually act as an inducement for the pursuit of a dynamic foreign policy. A constraint can be defined as any real or perceived negative contribution to the achievement of the totality of a regime's foreign policy objectives. Constraints normally constitute a hindrance to the pursuit of a dynamic foreign policy. The influence of capabilities and constraints on foreign policy operates on two levels. On a general level, they are the primary determinants of the number of policy options available to the decision-makers. On a more specific level, once an option has been chosen, they determine the extent of the freedom of manoeuvrability decision-makers possess in the implementation of the chosen alternative. It is important to note here that the various capabilities, whether they emanate from the external or the domestic environment, will be examined in this study within the context of the operational and the psychological environments. In other words, not only will the objective elements of each capability be analysed but the way they were perceived by the decision-makers will also be scrutinised.

THE EXTERNAL ENVIRONMENT: THE GLOBAL SYSTEM

The main feature of the global system which existed during the fifties was the polarisation between two blocs loosely configurated around the United States and the Soviet Union. The awesome level of destructive capability attained by these two 'superpowers' plus their immense economic and technological power in relation to other states, made the United States and the Soviet Union the major actors in the global system. The ideological schism existing between the two blocs and their pursuit of conflicting strategic objectives gave the global system its polarised feature.[1]

During the first half of the fifties, the Middle East remained relatively free of superpower penetration.[2] In fact, the major intrusive[3] activity in the region continued to be monopolised by Britain and France, the two powers with a 'colonial tradition' in the area. The low level of involvement by the two superpowers in the Middle East was the result of a variety of factors. The leaders of the United States seemed content not to disturb the existing power configuration in the area which was heavily oriented in favour of its major bloc allies, Britain and France. On the other hand, Soviet leaders were preoccupied with internal reconsolidation following Stalin's death and were in any case, constrained from greater involvement by the ideological antipathy of the Middle Eastern governments towards the Soviet Union and its political system.[4] Moreover, the ideological and strategic conflict between the two blocs during this period was directed mainly at the European and East Asian sub-systems. This tended to shift the attention of both superpowers away from the Middle East. Finally, the polarity and the bitter ideological struggle of the early fifties induced both superpowers to allocate much of their resources to intra-bloc activity designed to strengthen their respective camps militarily and economically,[5] and to ensure the compliance of bloc members for the purpose of bloc cohesion and unity. This was clearly manifested by the United States' economic and diplomatic entry into the Italian election campaign of 1948,[6] and its military intervention in Guatemala in 1954, and by the Soviet leadership complicity in the 1948 coup in Czechoslovakia and its suppression of the East German uprising in 1953.

Notwithstanding the indirect and somewhat irresolute attempts at involvement in Middle Eastern politics, such as the United States' support for a Middle Eastern Defence Organisation in 1951 which drew an immediate verbal response from the Soviet Union,[7] and the visit by Secretary of State Dulles to the Middle East in 1953, direct and active participation by the super-powers in Middle Eastern affairs began only in the mid-fifties. Three factors appear to have facilitated this superpower penetration. In the first place, by correctly perceiving the competitive nature of the bipolar global system, the Egyptian leaders in the spring of 1955 began to advocate the policy of 'positive neutralism', which upheld the necessity of avoiding rigid alignments with the great powers by manipulating the conflict between the two blocs to the Arabs' advantage.[8] This policy obviously posed a threat to the *status quo* interests of France, Britain, and by implication the United States, especially as the latter two had been instrumental in the establishment of the recently announced Iraqi–Turkish pact in February 1955. This pact was designed to form the nucleus of a Middle East defence alliance directed against the Soviet Union. However, the pact was perceived by the Egyptian leaders as a Western effort to isolate the 'independently minded' leaders of Egypt politically and strategically from the region. For the first time, therefore, through the policy of positive neutralism and the creation of the Baghdad Pact, a convergence of interests between the Soviet Union and a Middle Eastern government occurred. This happened at a time when tensions between the blocs in the European and East Asian sub-systems had markedly subsided. The combination of all these factors contributed to the dramatic entry of the Soviet Union into Middle Eastern affairs in the form of an arms deal with Egypt, ostensibly conducted through Czechoslovakia, a subordinate intra-bloc member.

The Czech arms deal of September 1955 was the first direct threat to the hitherto monopolistic influence of the Western bloc in the Middle Eastern sub-system. The US response was delayed until the Suez expedition convinced the United States leaders that they could no longer depend on their bloc allies, Britain and France, to safeguard the region from the increasing Soviet influence. Consequently, in January 1957, the United States made her entry in Middle Eastern politics with the enunciation of the Eisenhower Doctrine, which pledged the assistance of the United States, including the dispatch of armed forces, to nations requesting American help 'against overt armed aggression from any nation controlled by international communism'.[9] Eighteen months later, the doctrine was operationalised through American and British interventions (bloc activity) in Lebanon and Jordan in July 1958.

During the late fifties and early sixties, however, the global system underwent gradual, yet marked structural and behavioural changes. Structurally, two factors contributed to this change. In the first place, aspiring units such as China, Japan and the infant EEC emerged from their earlier situations of economic and/or military dependence on the superpowers to positions of independent power and influence which, while not comparable to the two leading actors, nevertheless afforded them a higher status in the system. Secondly, the decolonisation process of the late fifties and early sixties created numerous independent units who tended to compensate for their lack of individual power by pursuing collectivist policies which were usually aimed at manipulating superpower rivalry. Consequently, such alignments as the African bloc, the non-aligned bloc, the Arab bloc, the Islamic bloc and so on, grew to be extremely influential in the system, particularly in international organisations such as the United Nations and its specialised agencies.

These structural changes in the global system occurred simultaneously with domestic changes in the Soviet Union and the United States. The consolidation of Khruschev's authority in the Soviet Union, and the advent of a new, less intransigent administration in the United States were the primary factors behind the perceptual transformation that led both parties to accept the maxim that ideological polarity need not produce military confrontation. Thus, Khrushchev's principle of 'peaceful coexistence', which advocated the elimination of the military option from US–USSR relations but which had been completely ignored by Dulles, was now positively received by the Kennedy administration. Consequently, the sixties witnessed increasing efforts by both parties to develop accepted criteria for behaviour in circumstances of ideological and political confrontation, thus decreasing the possibility of a suicidal military clash. The installation of a telephone hot-line between Washington and the Kremlin, the successful exercise of 'crisis-management' during the Cuban missile crisis and the Six-Day War, the test-ban treaty, and the numerous high-level summit conferences are all instances of the behavioural transformation which occurred in the global system during the sixties.

These changes produced one important modification in the structure of global relations in the Middle East. Both superpowers tacitly accepted that in pursuing their conflicting interests in the area they should stop short of actual military confrontation. An implicit understanding seems to have been reached, therefore, that regional conflicts will not be allowed to develop into global wars which might involve the two superpowers. However, apart from this modification, the intrusive activity of the global system into the regional sub-system during the sixties remained similar to that of the earlier decade. Superpower competition and rivalry were pursued with the same vigour on all levels, including the dispatch of huge amounts of sophisticated military equipment to conflicting states in the region. Nor could the newly emerging global powers match the economic and technological capabilities of the two superpowers, and as such their influence in the area remained minimal.

From 1955 until 1970, therefore, the Middle East was an arena of intense rivalry between the Soviet Union and the eastern camp on the one hand, and the United States and the western camp on the other hand. In other words the features of the global system were strictly translated into the Middle Eastern sub-system. This, in turn, tended to exert various pressures on, and present diverse opportunities for, the states of the Middle East. The following discussion will concentrate on briefly outlining these influences on the behaviour of Egypt in the Middle Eastern region.

The intrusion of the global system into the Middle East acted both as a capability for, and a constraint on, Egypt's foreign policy formulation. In the conflict of values and interests between Egypt and the Western powers following the creation of the Baghdad Pact, the colonial tradition of Britain and France constituted a foremost capability for Egypt in the sense that it rendered the Arab populations more susceptible to Egypt's 'anti-imperialist' and 'neutralist' campaigns. Later the Eisenhower Doctrine enabled Egypt to include the United States in the 'imperialist' category. Consequently, those Arab leaders who rejected Egypt's 'positive neutralism', preferring instead to remain with the Western sphere of influence, were accused by Egypt of being 'tools of imperialism', 'lackeys of colonialism', 'agents of the West' and so on. These accusations affected the perceptions of the indigenous populations within these pro-West Arab states, thus constituting considerable constraints on the policies and actions of their governments.

The development of events in the Arab world during the fifties clearly confirms this point, perhaps nowhere more dramatically than the way in which Jordan was compelled to withdraw from joining the Baghdad Pact in December 1955.[10]

Conversely, as will be illustrated, Egypt's chronic dependence upon the two great powers for military and economic aid constituted a clear constraint on the formulation and implementation of her policies.[11] However, the polarisation of the global system meant that the operational effects of this constraint on Egypt's decision-makers was not crucial. Thus, the refusal of the United States and Britain to meet Egypt's demands for arms was the primary, if not the only reason for the Czech arms deal. Similarly, the competitive nature of the global system enabled the Egyptian leaders to turn to a new patron, in the form of the Soviet Union, when confronted with Dulles's withdrawal of aid for the Aswan Dam. On the other side of the coin, the rupture between Nasser and the Russians over the Iraqi and Syrian Communists in 1959 merely resulted in Egypt's acceptance of American economic aid. Nevertheless, while the constraint was by no means crucial, it certainly was not insignificant. Egypt's gradual dependence on the Soviet Union for her industrial and military expansion, particularly in the post-1967 period, certainly affected her freedom of manoeuvrability in the international arena. Furthermore, Egypt's lack of vital raw materials, especially wheat, meant that at times her very existence was dependent on outside aid.

A further operative constraint, within this context, was the political, economic and military support extended by the United States and NATO to Egypt's adversaries in the region. There can be no doubt, for example, that the American and British military operations in the area in the wake of the Iraqi coup of July 1958 played a significant role in preventing the collapse of the anti-Nasser, Hashemite regime. Likewise the military aid extended by the United States and other NATO countries to Saudi Arabia was a major factor in sustaining the anti-Nasser monarchical faction throughout the long years of the Yemeni civil war. The Eisenhower Doctrine had more or less the same operational effects, since through economic and military aid it tended to maximise the political entrenchment and security of pro-West Arab leaders.[12] It is also alleged that various inducements were offered to King Saud in 1957 by the United States as a part of their efforts to realign Saudi Arabia's hitherto pro-Egyptian orientation.[13] Finally, the United States utilised the threat of military intervention, which was usually manifested either through movements of the Sixth Fleet[14] or by an overt exhibition of US military capabilities,[15] to limit Egyptian 'ambitions' (actual or perceived) in the area.

THE EXTERNAL ENVIRONMENT: THE REGIONAL SYSTEM

In terms of the intensity of interactions, the core of the Middle Eastern regional system, during our period of study, consisted of Egypt, Israel and the countries of the Arab east.[16] The interactions among the members of the core were conducted along two distinct yet interrelated axes. First, there was the conflict between Israel and the Arab states. The extreme enmity existing between the participants in this particular relationship ensured a state of intense and relatively enduring conflict. By 1970, the region had experienced along this axis three major outbreaks of hostilities: the first in 1948 involved Israel and all the Arab states; the second in 1956 was confined to Egypt and Israel; and the third in 1967 again saw Israel confronting the forces of the Arab world.

The second axis of interactions in the core of the Middle Eastern regional system concerned intra-Arab relations. These intensive and multilateral relations reflected both conditions of conflict and efforts at co-operation. In both spheres Egypt was the central and leading actor. While it would be erroneous to suggest that Egypt was a participant in every intra-Arab conflict, nevertheless the regularity of her involvement in inter-Arab rivalry and competition indicates a keen interest in preserving her political and strategic position in the Arab world. It is interesting to note that Egypt's most bitter struggles were conducted against Arab states and leaders perceived by the Egyptians as potential threats to Egypt's leadership.[17] Similarly, in the sphere of inter-Arab co-operation, Egyptian activity reflected and was meant to reinforce Egypt's central position in the Arab world.[18] Thus, while other Arab states can be described as *status quo*-oriented, only Egypt possessed the capability and the will to pursue hegemonial goals in the Arab world. From this point of view, the Egyptian policy of 'positive neutralism' and the principles of 'anti-imperialism' and 'Arabism' can be viewed as serving the function of resisting the penetration of external powers into an area perceived by Egypt's leadership to constitute its own sphere of influence.[19]

The preceding discussion indicates that regional influences on Egyptian policy formulation emanated from two major sources: Israel and the Arab states. While it is true that Egypt's leaders effectively utilised Western support for Israel as a capability in their struggles with other pro-West Arab leaderships, nevertheless Israel has proved to be a major constraint on Egypt's foreign policy. In the first place, Israel constituted a land barrier, hitherto non-existent, between Egypt and the Arab east. Secondly, Israel's military power had to be matched by Egypt, which meant diverting precious resources from other sectors of the economy. Finally, while the other Arab leaders acknowledged that the anti-Israel crusade was dependent on Egypt's active participation for its success, the deterrent power of Israel adversely affected the credibility of this belief, thus turning it into a constraint on Egyptian policy-making. Within this context, Egypt's unwillingness to counter-act the Israeli incursion into Jordan in November 1966 facilitated con-certed attacks by the latter's leaders on the credibility of Egypt's genuine anti-Israel sentiments. The Egyptian leaders, in this case, were derided for their ability to conduct a ferocious verbal war against Israel while conveniently hiding behind the security of UNEF in Sinai.[20] Similarly, Saudi Arabia could argue at the height of the Yemeni war, that rather than fighting Israel, the perceived enemy of all Arab states, the Egyptians indulged in fighting their own 'Arab brethren'.

In the 'Arab circle', however, Egypt was usually accorded a position of leadership and centrality which enhanced its capabilities. Thus, Fahad al-Shair, a member of the Syrian delegation to the 1963 tripar-tite talks on unity, insisted that the Arabs have 'always considered Egypt as the headquarters of Arab nationalism due to its geographic, social and cultural position. [Egypt] was indeed the centre from which the other branches were formed.'[21] This perception was elaborated more fully by the head of the Iraqi delegation, Ali Saleh al-Saadi, when he said:

> The UAR is a strong foundation and a vital and sure base for the Arab nation. That means I cannot say that the Iraqi revolution will act as the base for the liberation of the Arab people, because Iraq does not possess the capability to assume this position. However, it is within the capabilities of the UAR. Consequently, the interests of the Arab world . . . necessitate the existence of the UAR as a base for us.[22]

This image facilitated an attitude among the Arab elite which con-sidered any Arab project not catering for Egypt's active participation, or at least receiving its blessing, to be doomed to failure. For example, Michel Aflaq insisted that there could be no Arab unity without Egypt because 'she could and would successfully oppose any movement to-wards Arab unity which excluded her.'[23] In the same vein, Egypt's threat to withdraw from the Arab League in August 1962 following the 'Shtourah' incident, prompted President Shihab of Lebanon to appeal to Nasser not to withdraw on the grounds that 'the League will have no value if the UAR withdrew from it as the UAR [is] its biggest and strongest member state.'[24] Finally, Heikal relates a con-versation between King Faisal and Nasser in which the King said that his father had given his children one piece of advice: 'He told us to pay attention to Egypt's role, for without Egypt the Arabs throughout history would have been without value.'[25]

The preceding analysis highlights a dichotomous situation in the position of Egypt in the Arab world. While usually constituting a fore-most capability, this perception of Egypt's leading role in the Arab world tended in certain cases to limit the alternatives available to the Egyptian decision-makers. This clear constraint was operative particularly where value-oriented aspirations were involved, such as Arab unity. For example, against his better judgement, Nasser was compelled to agree to an immediate unity with Syria because the Syrians successfully limited his options by reminding him that Egypt was the foremost advocate of the principle of Arab unity, and that it was inevitable that unity should be affected with Egypt under Nasser's leadership. Generally, however, this high regard for Egypt's status in the Arab world constituted a foremost capability for the Egyptian decision-makers in their interaction with the other Arab leaders.

However, while accepting her central and leading position, the perennial inter-Arab conflict indicates that the Arab elites were not prepared to acquiesce unquestioningly to Egypt's 'political domination' of the Arab world. Much of the inter-Arab rivalry was due to the conflicting elite interests of the various Arab countries. Consequently, any Egyptian objective which conflicted with the interests of a particular Arab elite was inevitably met by negative responses which constrained the achievement of these objectives. As such, a major constraint on the formulation and implementation of Egypt's foreign policy lay in the capabilities of Nasser's political rivals in the Arab world. For example, the primary limitation on Egypt's efforts to secure the permanence of the republican regime in the Yemen emanated from Saudi Arabia's uncompromising military and financial support to the Yemeni Imam and his royalist supporters. Similarly, it was the alliance of Syria, Jordan, Saudi Arabia and Tunisia which resulted in Egypt's ignominious withdrawal from the Arab League in August 1962.

THE DOMESTIC ENVIRONMENT

Geography[26]

The geography of a state has been consistently treated by scholars of international relations as a major determinant of foreign policy. One leading textbook of foreign policy analysis views geography as the most permanent element of a state's foreign policy. It places geography at the centre of a number of 'concentric circles' deemed to represent the totality of foreign policy elements.[27] Such interpretation reflects a school of thought which treats geography as an independent variable. In other words, it is argued that the objective reality of a state's geography in itself constitutes a major determinant of foreign policy.

Within the parameters of such an interpretation, it is easy to discern why the objective elements of Egypt's geography actually enhance her capabilities. Egypt lies between the eastern and western parts of the Arab world, and for centuries has constituted the bridge between the two sectors. Egypt has, in Cairo and Alexandria, the largest city and the largest seaport in the Arab world; and because of its strategic location, it has developed extensive contacts with the three continents of Africa, Asia and Europe. Moreover, unlike other Arab states whose legal status rested on artificial boundaries drawn up by the old colonial powers, Egypt has been a distinct geographical unit for over 4000 years.

Such treatment, however, is analytically limited. A systematic analysis of the influence of geography on a state's foreign policy cannot rest exclusively on the objective characteristics of that state's geography, but must be examined through the perceptions of the decision-making elite. Within this context, geography is seen as a dependent variable whose significance for foreign policy is primarily a function of the perceptions of the decision-makers in a specific situation. Thus, in analysing the relation between geography and politics, 'it is essential to keep consistently in mind the distinction between image and reality . . . What matters in making and explaining policies is how the policy-maker imagines his environment to be, not how it actually is.'[28]

In the case of Egypt, the adoption of different and sometimes contrasting policies reflected the diverse perceptions of different Egyptian decision-makers. Some perceived the relative physical isolation of the Nile delta as the most significant factor in Egypt's geographic situation. They thus concluded that nature had set Egypt apart from her neighbours. Such perceptions gave rise to isolationist tendencies which focused entirely on Egypt without reference to the rest of the Arab world. For example, the great Egyptian nationalist leader of the twenties, Saad Zaghloul Pasha, perceived Egypt as a distinct entity divorced from her immediate environment; and he consequently resisted efforts to integrate Egypt's fight against British occupation into the general Arab struggle against colonialism.

Other leaders, however, perceived Egypt's geographic position differently. They saw in her objective position a situation which imposed on the country a dynamic foreign policy not only within the immediate confines of the Arab world, but also in the wider domain of Africa, Asia and the rest of the international system. This view was clearly expounded by Heikal when he wrote:

> Because of its location . . . Egypt has a special position. This position constantly links it with the surrounding region, and brings it, whether it likes it or not, into the arena of world conflict. Thus Egypt cannot, even if it wants to, isolate itself.[29]

Nasser was indeed a disciple of this view. He saw Egypt's geographic situation as affording a clear capability for the pursuit of an activist foreign policy in the Arab world. As early as 1954, he had written that 'we cannot look stupidly at a map of the world not realizing our place therein and the role determined to us by that place.'[30] Thus, when the

Baghdad Pact was perceived in Cairo as an instrument designed to isolate Egypt from the rest of the region, the geographic factor was an important determinant of the Egyptian decision to embark upon an activist regional policy which radically altered the existent relationship of forces in the area. This perception of Egypt's geographic and strategic centrality in the Middle East was also a contributing factor to other Egyptian policies which tended to emphasise the country's activism in the area. These policies included the union with Syria; the projected unions with the other Arab states of Iraq, Yemen, Sudan and Libya; the political and military support to the Algerian, Adenese and Palestinian nationalists; and the intervention in the Yemen.

Demographic Factor

International relations scholars contend that decision-makers formulate and implement policy objectives according to certain perceptions they hold of the relative power of their state compared to the power of those states whose behaviour they seek to influence. One essential element of a state's power is its own population. The influence of demographic factors on the formulation and the implementation of policies depends on a number of objective and subjective factors inherent in the composition and characteristics of a population. One such factor is the size of the population. A large population can be a source of strength, since it can be used as a reservoir for industrial expansion and military might. Yet it can prove a distinct disadvantage through its possible adverse effects on the economic development of the country. Another factor is the quality of the people in terms of their education, health and technical skills. Their level of politicisation is a further variable to be considered, particularly whether they share a common value system or whether they hold diverse attitudes and opinions. Similarly, ethnic heterogeneity can become a liability whereas ethnic homogeneity can prove a distinct source of strength. Finally, population factors must be related to the resources of the country, since an adverse relationship (large population but few resources) will inevitably constitute a major source of weakness.

The population of Egypt is the highest in the Arab world. This fact alone gives her a central position in the Arab world and elevates her to the forefront of military potential in the area. Table 1 illustrates the enormous disparity between the size of Egypt's population and those of other Arab countries. One important feature of the Egyptian population is its high concentration. Ninety-five per cent of the land is barren desert which leaves a narrow strip of land, the Nile delta, to absorb 99 per cent of the population. As such, the density of the population in Egypt is one of the highest in the world. The Nile delta accommodates 900 persons per square kilometre as compared, for example, with Britain's 214 per square kilometre. This immense concentration in villages close to each other creates a state of 'semi-urbanisation', which facilitates easy control by the government,[31] thus strengthening the capability of any established government (its economic repercussions will be discussed later).

TABLE 1

Populations of Egypt and the Other Arab States, 1955–70
(millions)

	Asian Arab states	African Arab states excluding Egypt	Egypt	Total Arab	% of Egypt to total
1955	17.2	25.4	23.0	65.6	35
1958	18.2	27.5	24.7	70.4	35
1961	19.3	29.9	26.6	75.8	35
1964	23.0	49.9[a]	28.9	95.8	30
1967	26.0	48.3	30.9	105.2	29
1970	29.5	52.6	33.3	115.4	29

[a] The sudden increase relates to the attainment of independence by Algeria.

Source: United Nations, *Demographic Yearbook, 1965*, New York, 1966, pp. 128–39; ibid., *1971*, New York, 1972, pp. 132–8.

An important characteristic of Egypt is its unbroken unity over its six or seven millennia of history, which resulted in the remarkable homogeneity of the population. Egyptians are ethnically homogeneous and almost 85 per cent of them follow the Sunni sect of Islam. Egypt suffers, therefore, very little from sectional or racial strife. Moreover, although Egypt's continued existence under foreign rule since the Persian conquest in 528 BC resulted in alienating the mass of Egyptian peasantry from the government, Nasser effectively utilised his pure Egyptian *fellah* [peasant] origins to enhance his capability.

As has been indicated, the size of a population constitutes a capability only if it does not adversely affect the economic capacity of the country. As Table 2 shows, the annual increase in Egypt's population has been around 2.4 per cent, and the increase in population during our period of study amounts to a staggering 55 per cent. The burden of this increase on Egypt becomes clearer when contrasted with the limited increase in agricultural land (see Table 3).

Although the 1952 Agrarian Reform Law has generally tended to increase and improve production,[32] the worsening man–land ratio has contributed to a decrease in the agricultural production per person of population, which in turn has resulted in conspicuous shortages in food materials. In fact, although it has become a net importer on a large scale of food grains, meat, animals and fruit, Egypt still suffers from

TABLE 2
The Increase in Egypt's Population, 1952–70
(millions)

	Population	Increase	Average annual increase	% of average annual increase
1952	21.44			
1955	22.99	1.55	0.52	2.27
1958	24.66	1.67	0.56	2.27
1961	26.58	1.92	0.64	2.40
1964	28.66	2.08	0.69	2.40
1967	30.91	2.25	0.75	2.41
1970	33.33	2.42	0.80	2.40

Source: Arab Republic of Egypt, *Statistical Handbook, 1952–1972*, Cairo: Central Agency for Public Mobilisation and Statistics, 1973, p. 7.

TABLE 3
Population, Cropped and Cultivated Area, 1897–1970

	1897	1917	1937	1957	1960	1963	1970
Population (millions)	9.7	12.7	15.9	24.2	26.0	28.0	33.3
Cropped area (million feddans)	6.5	7.8	8.5	10.1	10.3	10.4	10.8
Land–person (feddans)[a]	0.7	0.61	0.53	0.42	0.39	0.37	0.32
Cultivated area (million feddans)	5.0	5.3	5.3	5.8	5.8	6.1	n.d.
Land–person (feddans)	0.52	0.41	0.33	0.24	0.22	0.22	n.d.

[a] 1 feddan = 1.038 acre.
Source: Kamil Bakri, *Al-Sukan wal Numui al-Iqtisadifi Misr* [Population and Economic Growth in Egypt], Alexandria: Nabi'al-Fikr, 1969, p. 16; National Bank of Egypt, *Economic Bulletin*, vol. 23, no. 1, 1970; ibid., vol. 27, no. 1, 1974.

food shortages.[33] The resultant undernourishment in rural areas has contributed to a steady migration to the urban areas. From 1947 to 1963 for example, the percentage of the rural population dropped from 75 to 62. It is, moreover, estimated that between 1897 and 1960, the urban population grew almost 2.5 times more rapidly than the growth of the whole population.[34] These problems have inevitably demanded much attention from the government which has been compelled to divert precious resources for the purpose of tackling health hazards, unemployment, education and housing. This in itself has constituted an obvious constraint on the formulation and implementation of foreign policy.

Similarly, the huge increase in population tended to affect its quality despite official efforts to expand education and technical skills. Table 4 illustrates the immense effort undertaken by the government to spread education into all sectors of society. At one time it opened new schools at the rate of two every week. Yet as the table clearly shows, due to the population increase relatively little advancement in the educational level of the people was achieved. The drive for family planning was therefore officially endorsed by the National Charter, which referred to the rise in population as 'the most dangerous obstacle that faces the Egyptian people in their drive towards raising the standard of production in their country in an effective and efficient way.'[35]

TABLE 4

The Expansion of Education in Egypt, 1953–70

	1953	1958	1963	1967	1970
Higher education teachers	n.a.	1,789	6,310	9,497[a]	12,641
Higher education students	49,100	83,251	145,651	179,100	218,278
Total number of teachers	63,877	100,400	129,932	159,347	168,330
Total number of students	1,962,388	2,938,716	4,006,282	4,940,302	5,405,747
Percentage of total students to population	9	12	14	13	15

[a] No data available. Figure shown is estimated by averaging the 1963 and 1970 figures.

Source: United Nations, *Statistical Yearbook, 1954*, p. 525; *1955*, p. 570; *1960*, p. 578; *1965*, p. 713; *1969*, p. 737; *1973*, p. 764.

On the whole, therefore, the objective elements of the demographic factor seem to have acted as a constraint on the realisation of foreign policy goals. The huge increases in the size of the population necessitated the concentration of precious resources (materials, money, time, energy) on the domestic environment. Thus, as late as 1967, President Nasser would classify his most pressing problem as 'the fact that another 175,000 people will be born in this country and have to be fed'.[36] Were it not for Egypt's massive population problem, therefore, these resources could have been diverted towards increasing the capabilities of Egypt in her foreign relations with the Arab states.

Perceptually, too, the demographic factor acted as a constraint on the formulation of Egyptian policies towards the Arab world. This is manifested in the ambivalence of the Egyptians towards their Arab neighbours generally, and more specifically toward 'Arab nationalism'. We have already seen that Egypt's past leaders saw themselves primarily as Egyptian nationalists, a perception that led them to divorce Egypt's fight for independence from the general Arab anti-colonial struggle. As late as the mid-fifties, Egyptian intellectuals were advocating isolationist policies and emphasising the merits of an 'Egypt first' attitude.[37] Such attitudes seem to have been shared by most educated Egyptians and, as such, can be considered as merely the reflection of the prevailing system of values.

Reorienting Egyptian attitudes towards their Arab neighbours entailed a massive 'educational' programme – almost an indoctrination campaign. That these efforts were foremost in the minds of the Egyptian leadership, particularly during the period 1955–9, is revealed when one examines the speeches of President Nasser, the broadcasts of Egyptian radios, and the newspaper editorials in this period.[38] Nevertheless, these efforts do not seem to have been completely successful. As late as 1961, Heikal would attribute the failure of the Union between Egypt and Syria partly to the fact that

> in Egypt, the Arab people had not reached the stage of complete mental readiness for Arab unity. The centuries of Ottoman tyranny had isolated the Arab-people to the west of Sinai from the remaining Arab people to the east of Sinai. After the awakening that occurred during Napoleon's rule, Egypt, overwhelmed by this awakening, was unable to shift its attention from its own soil so that it can look across Sinai and discover its Arab position.[39]

In 1963, after nearly ten years of concerted 'Arab oriented' propaganda, Nasser also reiterated his misgivings about the depth of the Arab orientations of the Egyptians.[40]

Economic Factor
The economic element of national power influences the process of policy-making in a number of ways. An economy which is vulnerable to externally generated forces can severely limit the decision-makers' freedom of manoeuvrability. Thus, heavy dependence on imported raw materials, external trade and foreign aid will adversely affect the conduct of foreign policy. For example, it has been argued that the post-1973 pro-Arab postures of Japan and some EEC countries in relation to the Arab–Israeli conflict can be attributed, if not wholly then partially, to these countries' dependence on Arab oil.

In terms of resources and raw materials, Egypt is a poor country. Apart from the canal's income, which totalled $219 million in 1966,[41] Egypt's economy, during our period of study, remained basically dependent on a single commodity, cotton. In 1969, Egypt's export of cotton totalled $276 million[42] which, when added to cotton-based finished products, amounted to nearly 60 per cent of Egypt's total exports. The lack of basic raw materials and currency-earning commodities was bound to retard the Egyptian efforts at industrialisation. Thus, for example, the performance of the steel plant at Helwan suffered considerably as a result of the lack of readily accessible supplies of iron ore and coal. In fact, the coal needed by the Helwan plant was mined in the Ukraine and sent by rail to Odessa. From there it was shipped by sea to Alexandria, where it was dispatched by road to Helwan.[43] These arrangements inevitably resulted in a costly steel product which probably could have been bought at a cheaper price from abroad.

In newly-independent, developing countries such as Egypt, however, the quest for industrialisation carries political implications which overshadow its economic rationale. A major constraint on the decision-makers of these countries has inevitably been the inadequate industrialisation of their countries and their subsequent dependence on foreign capital. Realising the importance of these constraints on their policies, the leaders of most emergent states have usually laid much stress on the goal of 'industrialisation' to the extent that sometimes it tended to acquire greater significance than its economic implications would warrant. In some cases it has become an end in itself, meant to symbolise the nation's ultimate independence from a colonial past. Indeed, in Egypt, industrialisation, as a vital element of the 'modernisation process', became synonymous with the regime's prestige as it was perceived to enhance the country's status in the international system. Moreover, it was obvious to the leaders of Egypt that only through industrialisation could the country's military capability be freed from dependence on outside donors and consequently external control.

The quest for rapid industrialisation was one of the reasons which compelled the regime, between 1958 and 1961, to nationalise all financial institutions and heavy industry and to assume part ownership and direct control over external trade and large scale corporate industry. These sweeping nationalisation measures resulted in increasing the public sector's share of the Gross Domestic Product (GDP) from 15 per cent in 1953 to 34 per cent in 1962.[44] However, the real significance of these measures can be seen by examining their effect on the three sections of the GDP which have a crucial bearing on increasing government's capabilities, namely industry, finance, and transport and communication. Here, the public sector's share of total output increased from 11 per cent in 1953 to 55 per cent in 1962.[45] The emphasis on rapid industrialisation is evident when the provisions of the five-year plan spanning 1959-60 to 1964-5 are examined. The percentage of investment allocated to industry and its infrastructure amounted to half the total investment of the plan.[46] Indeed, while agricultural income grew by only 17.8 per cent during the plan years, industrial income increased by 50.2 per cent.[47] It is clear that the regime's objectives here, and indeed in the entire nationalisation programme, were to increase its capabilities through achieving self-sufficiency, on the one hand, and increasing employment and affecting a more equitable distribution of wealth, on the other.

The results of the nationalisation and the industrialisation measures have been mixed. They have certainly achieved a more equitable distribution of wealth among the population. Employment increased by 22.2 per cent during the plan years, real per capita income rose from $128 in 1956 to $171 in 1965, and there has occurred a discernable improvement in free public service particularly in the areas of health and education.[48] Consequently, these measures contributed to the regime's capabilities by increasing its support among the mass public. However, in terms of economic growth and rapid industrialisation, the results have not been so spectacular. Although an observable improvement in industrial output and an increase in industrial diversity were achieved, the Egyptian economy and its industry remained vulnerable to external forces. This seeming failure of planning was probably the result of two main reasons. In the first place, the rapid increase in population tended to offset the benefits of economic growth. Secondly, the emphasis on rapid industrialisation and Egypt's lack of basic raw materials inevitably led to a steep rise in imports, particularly of capital goods. This resulted in worsening the balance of payments situation, which had been already running at a deficit (notice the steep worsening of the balance of payments over the plan years 1961–4 in Table 5). In fact, in 1964, many factories were compelled to operate below full capacity because of the scarcity of foreign exchange which led to the unavailability of essential raw materials and vital machine spare parts.[49] Nevertheless, the industrialisation process began to pay dividends in the post-1967 period when the export of semi-finished and finished industrial products contributed to a gradual increase in the value of the UAR's overall exports. This, plus a conscious effort to control imports, resulted in ameliorating the trade deficit which, by 1970, had been nearly eliminated.

TABLE 5
Egypt's Trade Balance, 1952–70
($ million)

	Exports	Imports	Balance
1952	431.1	653.5	−222.4
1955	419.0	537.6	−118.6
1958	477.9	689.4	−211.5
1961	484.7	699.7	−215.0
1964	539.1	953.1	−414.0
1967	566.3	792.1	−225.8
1970	761.8	784.3	− 22.5

Source: UAR, *Statistical Handbook, 1952–1964*, Cairo: Central Agency for Public Mobilisation and Statistics, 1965, p. 186; *1952–1971*, 1972, p. 244.

The trade deficit of the sixties, however, constituted an objective constraint on Egypt's foreign policy, since it tended to limit expenditure on sections of the economy vital to the formulation and implementation of foreign policy, such as the armed forces, propaganda organs, etc. Moreover, the deficit contained even more serious overtones. Until 1958, these deficits were financed largely through a fall in the reserves of gold and foreign exchange. From 1946 to 1962, the total amounted to $1082 million, which brought the net reserves of gold and foreign currency from $1062 in 1946 to $−20 at the end of 1962.[50] The crucial factor here is that the annual deficit after 1962 had to be made up by a mounting foreign indebtedness, which in 1969 was estimated at the staggering figure of $3600 million.[51] Between 1958 and 1970, the Soviet Union extended to Egypt economic credits and grants (excluding military aid) amounting to $1023 million of economic aid.[52]

There is no doubt that heavy dependence on foreign aid constitutes a clear constraint on the recipient party's foreign policy. Indeed, it is a double-edged limitation. On the one hand, it is always a variable to be considered by the recipient decision-makers when formulating their policies, and on the other hand, it is a possible weapon for the donor state if it wishes to affect a specific reorientation in the domestic or foreign policy of the recipient country. For example, Heikal contends that during the rupture between Egypt and the Soviet Union over the Iraqi Communists in 1959, Khrushchev wrote a letter to Nasser intimating that 'the present situation [may] give rise to complications for discharging our obligations under the agreement for the construction of the Aswan Dam.'[53] Moreover, it was a conscious policy on the part of the Kennedy administration to extend generous aid facilities, particularly in much needed counterpart funds (i.e. surplus wheat, meat, etc.), to Egypt in the wake of the ensuing recriminations between Nasser and Khrushchev. More specifically, and for the opposite reason, there is some evidence which suggests that American aid was used by the Johnson administration to discourage Nasser from continuing his involvement in the Yemeni war. In May 1966, in response to increased Egyptian militancy, the United States deferred negotiation on an Egyptian request for $150 million worth of surplus food.[50] At the same time, the International Monetary Fund refused to grant an Egyptian request for a loan of $195 million because of alleged dissatisfaction with the economic performance of Egypt through its costly commitments in the Yemen. Given the already mentioned Egyptian dependence on foreign aid for the success of its five-year plan, it is interesting to note that the reopening of the negotiations with the IMF in August 1966 was accompanied in the same month by a peace agreement (though short-lived) over the Yemen signed between Egyptian and Saudi representatives in Kuwait.

Military Capability

A good indicator of a country's ranking in terms of military power in relation to other states in the international system can be discerned from analysing the country's defence expenditure.[55] Apart from facilitating objective comparisons with other states, defence expenditure also provides an insight into crucial elite images such as their need for personal and national prestige, and their quest for leadership.

The pride in Egypt's military leadership was apparent in Heikal's reminder to King Hussein of Jordan that 'the budget of the Egyptian Air Force alone is more than the entire budget of Jordan, including all the foreign aid it gets.'[56] The perceptions of other states are, of course, similarly affected by the objectively observable elements of a state's military strength. It is for this reason that pre-1967 Israel perceived Egypt as the primary threat to her security. Even after the 1967 war, the Israelis continued to consider Egypt as the leading military power in the Arab world.

The defence expenditures of various Arab states is shown in Table 6, which clearly illustrates that in military terms Egypt commanded a central position in the Arab world. The interesting aspect here is that Egypt's defence expenditure frequently exceeded that of the combined expenditure of Iraq, Syria and Jordan, the next three Arab states in military ranking.[57]

TABLE 6
Defence Expenditure of Selected Arab Countries, 1958–70
($ million)

	1958	*1960*	*1962*	*1964*	*1966*	*1968*	*1970*
Iraq	83.5	103.5	125.0	170.3	237.9	253.9	399.4
Syria	65.0[a]	66.5	73.0	91.1	82.6	101.3	161.4
Jordan	38.0	60.0	53.0	59.8	60.5	106.9	104.8
Total	186.5	230.0	251.0	321.2	381.0	462.1	665.6
Egypt	211.0	280.0	314.0	267.1	425.5	506.9	568.3

[a] Estimated by author.

Source: United Nations, Statistical Yearbook, *1961*, pp. 537–93; *1963*, pp. 565–625; *1965*, pp. 597–664; *1967*, pp. 612–86; *1969*, pp. 593–664; *1973*, pp. 629–708.

The much higher expenditure of Egypt on her defence was bound to affect the perceptions of other Arab states who generally accepted Egypt's military leadership in the Arab world. It must be remembered here that until the disastrous defeat of June 1967, the Egyptian army was not perceived to have suffered any serious defeat. The 1956 encounter with the Israelis had been skillfully presented by the Egyptian propagandists as a triumph for Nasser's strategic thinking. They insistently argued that Israel would not have scored her successes had President Nasser not ordered his troops to withdraw from Sinai in order to defend the mainland against the Anglo-French attack. It was generally accepted in the Arab Middle East that the 1956 'setback' was merely a tactical move to achieve the overall strategic objective of 'complete victory' over the tripartite attack. Later on, faced with a hostile enrivonment and a mountainous terrain not conducive to conventional military warfare, the performance of the Egyptian army in the Yemen was more than credible. Consequently, it was agreed that any engagement with the Israeli armed forces would be practically suicidal if undertaken without Egypt's active participation. This high evaluation of the Egyptian armed forces acted as a positive reinforcement for the Egyptian decision-makers who made every effort to maintain the primacy of Egypt's military position in the area. For example in 1961, President Nasser proudly reminded King Hussein that

> The power of the UAR army has reached a stage which will satisfy the hopes of every Arab. If your majesty remembers that the UAR's defence budget at present amounts to $299 million you will understand the sacrifices of the people of this republic. This fact underlines the determination of this people to undertake their responsibility towards the common enemy of the Arab nation.[58]

Naturally, the collapse of the Egyptian army in June 1967 brought into question the high esteem accorded to Egypt's armed forces by the Egyptians and other Arabs. As a result, the pre-June 1967 Egyptian tendency to boast about the power and effectiveness of their military capability gave way to a more cautious and guarded orientation in the post-war period. In a speech on July 22, 1968, Nasser reminded his listeners that it was essential to understand 'that the officers and soldiers are doing a very difficult job . . . Our armed forces must bide their time and be ready to take the opportunity to achieve what they are duty bound to achieve.'[59] Nevertheless, it was still obvious that the success of any future confrontation with Israel would continue to depend upon the participation of Egypt's armed forces. After all, none of the other Arab armies had fared any better against Israel in June 1967, and as such their dependence on Egypt remained very high. Thus, even after the 'setback' of 1967, Egypt continued to be perceived as the leading military power in the Arab world.

This interaction of mutual perceptions in relation to Egypt's military primacy in the Arab world made the military component a vital capability in Egypt's quest for Arab leadership. Very rarely used as a threat (except against Saudi Arabia in the Yemen), the value of the military capability in Egypt's pursuit of her policy objectives in the Arab world lay primarily in the way it affected the psychological environment of the Arab leaders specifically and of the Arab populations generally.

Religious factor

Islam is a primary force in the Arab world. It is the religion of the overwhelming majority of the Arab populations, much of whose values and norms emanate from the inspiration and moral teachings of Islam. Indeed, its relevance to policy-making extends beyond the Arab world to Africa and Asia. President Nasser referred to Islam as 'the circle of our brethren in faith who turn with us, whatever part of the world they are in, towards the same Kibla in Mecca and whose pious lips whisper reverently the same prayers.'[60]

Domestically, the military junta, from the very beginning, appreciated the effectiveness of Islam as an instrument for deriving public support from a traditionally devout and conservative Moslem population. During the tripartite attack on Egypt, Nasser addressed the Egyptian people from the pulpit of the famous al-Azhar mosque in the tradition of the old Caliphs who combined both religious and political authority. However, this particular utilisation of religion as a capability in its role as a support-winning instrument, must be considered as an extreme case. The domestic utility of religion to the Egyptian decision-makers was eloquently described by Ihsan Abd al-Qaddous, one of Egypt's foremost political commentators:

> The regime accepts the cultural value of religion and its significance as the moral basis of society. The regime, however, is definitely committed to a secular concept of national identity, loyalty and legitimacy. It must, nevertheless, use religion (refer to it) in order to retain contact with the masses, until the desired standards of education and economic improvement are attained.[61]

In the Arab world, the utilisation of Islam was unavoidable since it constituted a vital element of 'Arab nationalism'. Moreover, it remains a fact that the richest heritage of Arab history is usually traced to the 'glorious years' of the vast Arab Islamic empire. As such, in the Egyptian leaderships' persistent emphasis on the unified and glorious Arab past, Islam was utilised for the purpose of political assimilation. The leadership correctly perceived the effectiveness of Islam to overcome xenophobic and fissiparous orientations, and consequently they were quite aware of its utility as a capability. For example, Kamal al-Din Hussein, a member of the core decision-making group, asserted in 1963:

> The Arab people . . . believe in the mission of religion and consider the spiritual forces of religion as impetus for the people's strength to achieve their entity and attain their aim. We should also bear in

mind that religion is a basic component on which Arab society establishes its life and future.[62]

Egypt lacks an Islamic 'status'. Unlike other Arab countries such as Saudi Arabia, Jordan and Iraq, Egypt does not possess important 'holy shrines'. However, Egypt's Islamic pretentions lay in the fact that the al-Azhar, the oldest and the most respected Islamic institution in the Arab Middle East and the centre of Islamic intellectualism for over 1000 years, is situated in Cairo. To maximise the effectiveness of al-Azhar as a political instrument and to bring it under close supervision, the Egyptian leadership completely reorganised this valuable institution. Law 103/1961 divided the al-Azhar into five administrations: (1) the supreme council of al-Azhar, (2) the Islamic research council, (3) the cultural administration and Islamic mission, (4) al-Azhar University, and (5) al-Azhar institutions. The law also placed the al-Azhar directly under the jurisdiction of the President.

The stricter control of al-Azhar brought the Egyptian leadership obvious benefits as a result of al-Azhar's immense influence with both the Egyptian public and the Moslems throughout the Arab world. For example, there was undoubted benefit for the Egyptian leadership when no less a figure than the Sheikh of al-Azhar took it upon himself to sanction socialism as an intrinsic component of Islam.[63] This statement was particularly important, as it was made during a period of extreme ideological conflict with Saudi Arabia, whose leaders equated Nasser's socialism with atheism. Moreover, not only was the regime's socialism approved by the Al-Azhar sheikhs but, more importantly, they presented it as a crucial element in the system of values which characterised a new and vigorous Arab and Islamic revival under the leadership of President Nasser. Thus, the al-Azhar Sheikh declared in another instance:

> God has willed that the Arabs should have a fourth golden age to surpass the brilliance of the three previous ones. This has appeared in your age, Mr. President, in which neglected Moslem principles have been reasserted so that government is by consultation, wealth is shared, the masses are equal, justice is universal, and the people rule.[64]

This glorification of Nasser and the attacks directed at his enemies by the al-Azhar establishment continued throughout the President's rule. In April 1967, for instance, the al-Azhar magazine described the Arab kings as those 'reactionaries who have contaminated [Islam] with American gold in order to preserve their crowns and indulge their whims. They have, thus, followed the devil and forgotten God.'[65]

Given the sectionalism within Islam, however, the Egyptian leadership was aware that an over-emphasis on religion could ultimately prove counter-productive. Although the majority of Egyptians adhered to the Sunni sect of Islam, an undue emphasis on religion could have alienated the other sects, such as the ruling Wahabis in Saudi Arabia and Zaidis in pre-1961 Yemen or the influential Shiis of Iraq and the Allawis of Syria. Moreover, an extreme utilisation of Islam would have certainly alienated the economically influential (politically also in the case of Lebanon) Christian minorities of the Arab world. In this case, therefore, emphasis on religion might have become a fissiparous force rather than a cohesive influence.

Consequently, the Egyptian leadership endeavoured to guard against excessive reliance on the religious capability for fear of turning it into a constraint. Islam was utilised only when benefits seemed to outweigh the disadvantages, and at all times the Egyptian regime proclaimed its adherence to secularism in its political and economic activities.[66] Yet even here, a situation of possible conflict existed. Islam, unlike Christianity, is a social, political, legal and cultural system. In the Sharia, the Moslems have a law that deals with all constitutional and legal matters, and as such is treated in orthodox Islamic theory as the only legally acceptable code. Consequently, to the devout Moslem, there can be only one legitimate rule and that is through Islam. This dichotomy between religion and secularism has manifested itself in Egypt through the recurring conflict between the regime and the Moslem Brotherhood organisation. After what was thought to be the regime's mortal blow to the organisation in 1954, the discovery of the Brotherhood's 1965 plot exhibited the extent of the organisation's power and influence not only among the poorer classes but also with the educated sections of the society.[67]

The utility of Islam to the Egyptian decision-makers seemed to depend primarily on the issue involved. It is evident that the Egyptian leadership used religion to attain maximum return without running the risk of having it transformed into a constraint on their policies. After a period of trial and error, the Nasser regime settled on a formula which divorced Islam from political organisations and economic activity yet utilised it with varying levels of intensity if and when it proved helpful for the purpose of elite perpetuation and entrenchment.

Pressure Groups and Public Opinion
Pressure groups are defined as sectional groups, clusters or organisations bound by vocational and/or associational interests who seek to influence policies. Groups who participate in the decision-making process (e.g. political parties, and in this particular case the defence establishment) do not fall within this specific conceptualisation, which is concerned primarily with influence emanating from outside the formal decision-making structure. This influence would usually vary according to the nature of the political system and the group's accessi-

bility to the leadership. Important in this relationship is the power of deprivation a group is capable and/or willing to exercise, or threaten to exercise, on the leadership while making its demands. It is evident that in the Egyptian case, the authoritarian characteristics of the political system and the fundamental mechanics of the charismatic relationship renders such power fairly minimal. The one exception here is when the leader himself perceives a specific group as particularly significant for the preservation of his regime.

As has already been discussed, the regime's successive blows against its perceived political rivals effectively diminished the power of pressure groups to an extent as to make it almost non-existent. By 1956, the junta had eliminated almost all of its political rivals. The political parties were dissolved and declared illegal and their leaders were either imprisoned or deprived of all political rights. The Agrarian Reform Law had dealt a severe blow to the traditional power of the landowning classes. The Moslem Brothers were effectively repressed.[68] The educational institutions were purged and the intellectuals and artists placed under the supervision of a governmental council headed by the Minister of Education. The hold of the regime was further consolidated when a number of laws were passed during the years 1960–5 which crippled the economic power of the industrial, financial and commercial classes of Egypt. The feudalists, too, suffered further blows which completely destroyed their remaining power. Moreover, seeking closer control of the news media, Nasser and the regime nationalised the press in May 1961 by vesting the ownership of newspapers and publishing houses in the National Union. Consequently, after 1961 the press ceased to execute its traditional role of probing and criticising; rather its functions became to mirror and explain the regime's attitudes and policies. Thus, for example, in the wake of President Nasser's abrupt adoption of a conciliatory posture towards the Arab heads of state in December 1963, the editors of the Egyptian press met and decided to immediately cease all the bitter press campaigns which they had been conducting against other Arab states for over two years.[69] During the relative relaxation of censorship which accompanied the public debate occurring on the wake of the Six-Day War, Heikal candidly admitted that the press could not reveal pre-1967 errors because of political pressure.[70] During this period, some of the more powerful editors and newspapermen even began to question the advisability of nationalising the press, as illustrated in the following comment by Heikal:

> The future of the Egyptian press depends upon a frank definition of the concept of ASU ownership of the press. Is it political ownership or material ownership? ... Does the ASU want the press to serve its readers, the working masses, or does it want the press to serve the

cause of petty and futile squabbles? Does it want the press to be a means of freedom in an open society or a means of authoritarianism in a closed society?[71]

However, while such views were tolerated, and in some instances, encouraged, they did not substantially change the relationship between the press and the regime. Freedom of the press was not, nor could it be, a cherished value in Nasserite Egypt; rather it was entirely dependent on the consent of the leadership.

Political considerations relating to the process of elite entrenchment seem to have been a major determinant of the regime's policies. Even the sweeping socialist measures of 1960-1 appear to have had a political as well as an economic rationale, because they tended to be directed more at minorities perceived to be antipathetic to the regime. For example, out of the 850 people whose property was sequestered after the Syrian secession, the Jews, followed by the Syrians and Lebanese, seemed to be the hardest hit whereas the Egyptian Moslems by comparison came out rather lightly, although they constituted the largest group of identifiable company directors, as illustrated in Table 7.

TABLE 7
Composition of Groups Affected by 1961 Sequestration Measures

	% of 1391 identifiable company directors[b]	% of 641 persons sequestered[a]
Egyptian Moslems	66	25
Syrian and Lebanese	13	18
Egyptian Copts	4	3
Jews	3	50
Others	14	5

[a] Those whose names could be identified.
[b] Listed in *Egyptian Stock Exchange Year Book, 1960.*
Source: Issawi, op. cit., p. 62.

While heavily restricting the powers of the bourgeoisie and landowning classes, the leadership courted the working classes who were expected to form the regime's basic support base. In July 1961, the government reduced industrial working hours to 42 hours per week and declared that 25 per cent of the net profits of any factory should be distributed to employees and workers. In February 1962, the minimum wage was almost doubled to 25 piasters a day while prices were kept under strict control. The 1961 laws, furthermore, decreed that two out of seven members of a company's board should be elected representatives of the workers and salaried employees. This was raised in 1963 to four out of nine and the distinction between workers and salaried employees was abolished. The workers were encouraged to organise but strikes were made illegal. The same procedure was followed in the agricultural sector. While the redistribution of land earned the regime the support of the peasants, the government through the co-operatives kept a close supervision over land and farmers.[72] It is thus obvious that while the regime courted and benefited both the industrial and agricultural workers as a group, it kept them under strict control. Moreover, the more workers were made to identify their interests with the regime's, the less their effectiveness as a pressure group became.

It is, therefore, clear that President Nasser operated in comparative freedom from the constraints of pressure groups which would be the envy of many other leaders and regimes. The comparative lack of effective pressure on the Egyptian leadership had a mixed effect. It was disadvantageous in the sense that it deprived Nasser and the leadership from the benefits of debate and dissent. However, this shortcoming was more than offset by the leadership's capability, through centralisation, to take decisions relatively quickly and implement them effectively without the actual or perceived hinderance of argument (e.g. the nationalisation of the Suez Canal Company, the socialist measures of 1961–2, the union with Syria, etc.).

Finally, we come to the influence of 'public opinion' on the decision-makers of Egypt. First of all, however, we should examine the analytical clarity of the term. Professor Philip Reynolds argues that due to the multiplicity of opinions operating in a political community, the monolithic assumption inherent in the term 'public opinion' can be misleading. In fact, Reynolds asserts that politicians sometimes use the term deliberately as a justification for policies adopted for other reasons. Accordingly, he classifies public opinion into political opinion (parliament, political parties), informed opinion (journalists, commentators), pressure group opinion (industry, financial institution, etc.) and mass opinion, which is our concern here. Reynolds sees mass opinion as generally ill-informed, inarticulate and with little influence particularly in foreign policy. He, nevertheless, admits that mass public opinion may have some bearing on foreign policy 'in the sense of setting broad limits to the behaviour of policy-makers'.[73]

While this study has adopted a different conceptualisation to the one elaborated above, it agrees with Reynolds' isolation of 'mass opinion' from the rest of 'public opinion'. In this study, it is posited that whereas pressure groups can influence decision-makers on both the tactical and strategic levels in the sense that the opinions of such groups are taken into consideration by the decision-makers while formulating major policies and day-to-day tactical and 'implementing' decisions, mass opinion affects decision-making only on the strategic level, i.e. in major policies and objectives. In other words, mass opinion tends to constitute a broad parameter for what is possible in the formulation of policies.

In the case of Egypt, it is difficult to ascertain the influence of mass public opinion on the Egyptian leadership because of the charismatic relationship existing between the President and his people. Basically a dichotomous situation arises here. On the one hand, it is assumed that such a relationship would minimise the effect of mass public opinion on the leader, yet on the other hand, the 'special bond' existing between the charismatic leader and the people necessitates an 'intense receptivity' to mass demands on the part of the leader. This account-ability to the people was bound to increase as their level of political awareness increased.

The regime's conscious effort to politicise Egyptian society in foreign affairs, in addition to the dynamic nature of Egypt's involvement in international relations, contributed to a dramatic upsurge in the 'political awareness' of the mass public which had become evident even as early as 1956.[74] In this, the newly acquired values, images and expectations became perceptual limits beyond which a policy could have probably run the risk of causing cognitive dissonance,[75] and subsequently, alienation and rejection. Within this context, it is possible to attach some credibility to statements such as the one made by Nasser in 1957 in which he rejected any suggestions for international super-vision of the canal on the basis that public opinion would simply not allow it.[76] It is almost certain that Nasser was not telling the whole truth. Nevertheless, the attitudes of hostility engendered in Egypt in the wake of the tripartite attack would have acted as a clear constraint on Nasser were he to consider compromising on the issues of inter-national supervision.

Capabilities and constraints were defined at the beginning of the chapter as positive or negative contributions to the achievement of the totality of a state's foreign policy. The preceding analysis has viewed this contribution as actual or perceived influences on the formulation and conduct of foreign policy. As such, capabilities and constraints have been conceptualised here primarily as a 'stock of factors' or a 'reservoir of resources' that exert either a positive impetus for, or a negative limitation on, the pursuit of a dynamic foreign policy. Con-sequently, the preceding analysis has been 'general' rather than 'specific' in nature. In other words, the main emphasis has been on analysing the features of the various 'factors' or 'resources' in order to explain their influences on foreign policy in general, and by implication on the specific period under study. Where it was deemed necessary to elaborate further in order to highlight the significance of a particular 'factor' to our specific topic, relevant examples were utilised to explain the relationship. Thus, while the analysis is meant to illustrate the various influences on the formulation and conduct of Egypt's foreign policy towards the Arab world, it certainly need not be confined to this narrow segment of Egypt's international relations, but can be utilised for the understanding of Egypt's behaviour in the international system as a whole.

8   Institutions and Processes

The term political elite has been the subject of much controversy and numerous definitions. At its most basic, it is defined as groups of people who either exercise directly or are in a position to influence very strongly, the exercise of political power.[1] However, other theorists prefer to limit this definition by arguing that in every political elite there exists an identifiable smaller 'ruling' elite whose preferences regularly prevail in cases of differences on key issues. This group has a greater share of power than any other group, is more highly organised and more coherent structurally and motivationally than any other group.[2]

Using this categorisation, the Egyptian decision-making elite can be divided into three categories classified in a scale of descending importance in terms of the power and influence they possessed and the frequency with which they exercised this influence:

(1) *The principal decision-maker.* This category refers to President Nasser's central and dominant position in the Egyptian decision-making process. Throughout the period, he was the virtual decision-maker, having been personally responsible for the foreign policy sector.

(2) *The ruling elite (inner circle).* Those who were regularly consulted by Nasser and could influence his decisions on various issues. They were also occasionally allocated powers to make formal decisions in certain areas. This group comprised the cabinet, the defence establishment, and the foreign ministry. Perhaps one should also include the influential editor of *al-Ahram*, Muhammed Hasneen Heikal, within the inner circle.

(3) *The political elite (peripheral circle).* Those who participated in the decision-making process without having been allocated any powers to make formal decisions. They exercised intermittent and diffuse influence mainly through their role as a gauge of public opinion. This group included the National Assembly, the National Union and the Arab Socialist Union.

THE PRINCIPAL DECISION-MAKER

Professor Joseph Frankel divides group decision-making into three distinct patterns. The first two are characterised by the agreement of all, or a majority of, the members of the group in reaching a particular decision or pursuing a defined policy. The third pattern is dominated by one member of the group who leads it 'by virtue of his position, his special knowledge or his personality. [Accordingly], he becomes the virtual decision-maker, and the other members of the group can be accommodated within the [decision-making] model as environmental influences.'[3]

A principle decision-maker, Frankel's third category, is more likely to emerge in the sector of foreign policy rather than domestic policy since, unlike the domestic environment, governments tend to have an almost total monopoly on foreign affairs. This is due to their command of the best available sources of information and their possession of the foremost capabilities for formulating and implementing policies. It follows that a strong and dominant leader, particularly in an authoritarian system (that which lacks any institutional opposition), can transfer this governmental near-monopoly on foreign affairs to his own person. As such, the participation of the subordinate authorities (i.e. state organs) in the decision-making process takes the form of information and advice in the pre-decisional stage and implementation in the post-decisional stage. Yet at all times the final and ultimate authority remains with the central and dominant figure. Professor Boutrous Boutrous-Ghalli, in analysing the working of Egyptian foreign policy states that 'the formulation of foreign policy . . . is strictly the prerogative and sole responsibility of the Chief Executive. The extent to which the Executive is guided by the council of his principle associates, including the Minister of Foreign Affairs, is a matter of personal choice.[4]

Accordingly, the role of the subordinate authorities in the decision-making process of Nasser's Egypt was confined purely to the function of influencing policies, where influence is defined as the 'participation in the decision-making process without the power to make a formal decision'.[5] This power lay with the Chief Executive, President Gamal Abd al-Nasser – the principal decision-maker.

However the preponderance of President Nasser in the decision-making process did not fully emerge until 1955. Nasser's power and authority gradually increased throughout this year and the next, reaching its zenith by the end of 1956 when the last British soldier had withdrawn from Egypt after the failure of the Suez expedition. By contrast, between 1952 and 1955 all decisions were taken by the Revolutionary Command Council, consisting mainly of the core Free-Officer group which planned and executed the July 1952 coup. As such, the decision-making process in that period followed the first two patterns of Frankel's group decision-making model. Charles Cremeans confirms this when he writes that:

in the early days of the regime, . . . all basic policy decisions, including formulation of aims and planning of tactics, were made within the Revolutionary Command Council . . . There was lively interchange of ideas, with all members of the group presenting their opinions and insisting on being convinced of the wisdom of the majority decision. Often there were violent disagreements and emotional scenes. Nasser's personality was dominant but, . . . policy as well as tactics were the product of group decision.[6]

Indeed, in one instance, Nasser is said to have been outvoted by seven to one on an important policy decision. As a result, he resigned from the Revolutionary Command Council; but two days later, his colleagues relented and invited him back to the council, allowing him to have his own way.[7]

1952–5: GROUP DECISION-MAKING

When power is 'transferred' in a traditional–legal context, authority (i.e. legitimate control) is automatically bestowed on the recipient party, since in this case authority is embodied in, and becomes a manifestation of, the legitimacy of the political system. However, the act of 'power usurpation' occurs outside the traditional–legal framework and is, by definition, diametrically opposed to it. Consequently, authority does not follow automatically but has to be acquired for the purpose of permanent political entrenchment. The acquisition process consists of two distinct yet interrelated and complementary factors: the consolidation of power and its legitimisation.

The consolidation process relates to the gradual accumulation of power. Intrinsic in this definition is the inevitable deprivation of power from other competing groups. In the case of Egypt, the junta was faced with an initially lukewarm response from the Egyptian people and consequently had to embark on the consolidation process almost immediately after usurping power. Its first act was a clear exhibition to one and all of the strength of its resolution and intent. On August 12, 1952, less than a month after gaining control, the junta ruthlessly suppressed a minor revolt by workers at the textile factory of Kafr al-Dawar and mercilessly hanged two of the ring-leaders.

After this 'exhibition of strength', a series of acts followed designed to break the power of potential adversaries. In September 1952, the régime enacted its Agrarian Reform Law, which dealt a severe blow to the landowning classes depriving them of much of their traditional economic and financial power. In January 1953, all political parties were dissolved, and fifteen months later, leaders of these parties (Wafdists, Sa'adists, Liberal Constitutionalists, and others) were deprived of all political rights for ten years. This was followed by the wide-scale arrests of Communists, and a purge inside the army of 'counter-revolutionary' elements. The mass media was the next object of attack. After several allegations by the junta pertaining to the corruption of the press and its opposition to measures taken by the regime, strict supervision over the press was established. Thus, with the radio already under their control, the regime achieved almost complete control over the media. An 'educational purge' was next in line when Kamal al-Din Hussein, Minister of Education and a member of the Revolutionary Command Council, expelled many student activists and dismissed forty university professors.

Perhaps the most dangerous adversary of the junta was the organisation of the Moslem Brotherhood, a revivalist mass movement[8] which boasted some 2 million members in 1949.[9] In 1952 its leadership proposed that the Revolutionary Command Council should accept their supervision for a period of ten years until '. . . a Moslem state fulfilling all precepts of Moslem law and run by the new generation they were preparing'[10] could be achieved. Although the Revolutionary Command Council did not acquiesce to this demand, they did tacitly acknowledge the strength of the Brotherhood when the abolition of political parties in January 1953 excluded the Brotherhood on the pretext that it was not a party but an organisation.

The junta's first move in its efforts to contain the Brotherhood's power was to establish the Liberation Rally, a government-controlled mass organisation based on an infrastructure composed mainly of students and unionised workers. One of the main functions of the Rally was to counteract the Brotherhood's power, particularly in street demonstrations. However, the junta seemed reluctant to use its coercive capabilities against the Brotherhood except in a limited form (such as in February 1954), preferring to wait for the Brotherhood to overplay their hand. This the Brotherhood did when a poorly organised attempt on Nasser's life ignominiously failed. The regime swiftly retaliated by arresting some 18,000 members.[11] Six of its leaders were executed and the 'supreme guide', al-Hudaibi, was sentenced to life imprisonment.

During this period, a power struggle arose within the Revolutionary Command Council between its two dominant personalities, Colonel Nasser and General Nagib. Nagib's strength lay in his popularity with the people, the Brotherhood, the Communists, and the old political parties, all of whom applauded his zealous adherence to parliamentary rule. Real power, however, namely the loyalty of the junta and the army (except of Khalid Mohyiddin and a section of the cavalry) remained with Nasser. During February and March of 1954, Nagib was first outvoted in the Revolutionary Command Council and then completely outmanoeuvred by Nasser and the junta in the struggle for popular support. During the Brotherhood Trials that followed the attempt on Nasser's life, Nagib was implicated and subsequently placed under house arrest in November, never to be politically active again.

Hence, by the end of 1954, the junta had successfully eliminated almost all of the potential threats to its survival.

The second factor which contributes to the political permanency of any new ruling elite is its legitimisation (i.e. its quest for mass acceptability). Furthermore, in the case of the military elite in developing countries, the basic structural characteristics of the military are in themselves a legitimising device, since 'by its definition and nature, the army is a national body representing the people as a whole without factional considerations.'[12] Moreover, 'its hierarchical nature [renders] it the darling of the right and its democratic mass basis the favourite of the left.'[13] These favourable characteristics are compounded in the Middle East by the traditional culture of the region which 'rests upon a religion that accords great prestige and legitimacy to the military'.[14] Hence, in their subsequent efforts to gain mass acceptability, the junta could operate from a fundamentally secure base.

It is, of course, easy to identify in retrospect certain policies such as agrarian reform, anti-colonialism, the promise of and striving towards a welfare state, the fight against corruption, and the like as support-winning measures that helped to win the regime mass acceptability. However, it is difficult to assess empirically the extent to which these policies were the result of premeditated planning by the regime to acquire legitimacy, since the writings of some of the Free Officers suggest that the primary motivation behind the 'reforming' policies were on the whole ideologically oriented.[15] They are unanimous in identifying their coup as a mission to eliminate imperialism, social oppression and corruption, which were all denounced as morally inequitious and identified as having divided and weakened the nation.

Yet it is also valid to suggest that part of the motivation behind these reforming acts and policies lay in the junta's awareness of the needs and aspirations of the people. A main feature of the input–output interaction between the social system and its political sub-system is the regime's sensitivity to the demands being made upon the political system. Accordingly, the junta in Egypt could have hardly been unaware of the political payoffs these reforming policies would yield, and as such, in this respect at least part of the motivation that lay behind their enactment was the obvious effort to gain mass acceptability.

The Agrarian Reform Law was one such act. It limited maximum holdings to 200 feddans,[16] hence releasing half a million feddans for distribution among landless peasants. It also decreed the establishment of agricultural co-operatives and workers' unions and formalised landowner–tenant relations designed to minimise the preceding exploitative relationship.[17]

The dissolution of the 'corrupt' political parties and the formation of the 'Liberation Rally' also served as support-winning measures, particularly with the more sophisticated urban Egyptians sickened by the corruption and scandals that had pervaded the earlier order. The Liberation Rally was especially popular, as one of its declared functions was the creation of a welfare state.

At the same time, the junta laid much emphasis on the traditional values and norms of Egyptian society which centred on the ideals of Islamic orthodoxy. In the context of the legitimisation process, the emphasis on Islam could be interpreted as a device employed by the regime to reduce the abrupt impact of the junta's 'revolutionary' measures on a basically traditional and conservative society. Thus in August 1954, Nasser, accompanied by other high-ranking ministers and government officials, made a highly-publicised pilgrimage to Mecca;[18] and in September, a draft charter for an Islamic Congress was issued. Its Secretary-General was to be Anwar al-Sadat, a member of the Revolutionary Command Council, and its aims were to spread Islamic culture and promote active co-operation among Islamic countries. Additionally, the regime emphasised the role of the Liberation Rally as a vehicle for the teaching of Islam to the Egyptian youth.

Thus, in the early period, much of the junta's energies were directed towards cementing their authority. As has been shown, the methods they employed and the policies they pursued served to consolidate their position and contributed toward its legitimisation. Yet by 1955, having more or less achieved the consolidation of its power, the military elite began to discover a new legitimising device – the emergence of Nasser's charismatic leadership.

POST-1955: NASSER AS THE PRINCIPLE DECISION-MAKER

Max Weber, the originator of the concept, defines charisma as
>a certain quality of an individual personality by virtue of which he is set apart from ordinary men and treated as though endowed with supernatural, superhuman or, at least, specifically exceptional qualities . . . These are not accessible to the ordinary person, but are regarded as divine in origin, or as exemplary, and on the basis of them the individual concerned is treated as a leader.[19]

Thus, the basic definition concerns a relationship – the charismatic relationship in which the people perceive qualities in an individual which compel them to follow him, and as such '. . . it is the duty of those to whom he addresses his mission to recognise him as their charismatically qualified leader.'[20]

The emergence of Nasser as a charismatic leader began in 1955 with the activation of his 'anti-imperialist' policies. These policies were partly Egypt's response to forces operating in the external environment. Primary among these forces was the Western powers' perception (particularly the United States) of a bi-polarised international system in which there was little room for a neutralist orientation among any of the system's units.[21] Consequently, pursuing a policy of containment of the Soviet Union and its allies, and endeavouring to safeguard their interests in the area, Britain, France, the United States and Turkey fostered the idea of a Middle-East regional defence organisation which later gave birth to the Baghdad Pact. To Nasser and the junta any Western-conceived plans in the region were merely an extension of the West's 'imperialist' policies, and hence, were utterly unacceptable.

This 'show of independence' ran contrary to the prevailing psychological environment of the decision-makers in the West, who perceived such actions within the boundaries of their rigidly conceptualised bipolar system. As a result, they showed increasing reluctance to offer economic or military aid to Egypt and proceeded to shift their focus of activity to Iraq as the potential centre of their proposed alliance. In Egypt, Nasser and the junta interpreted these policies as an effort on behalf of the Western powers to weaken Egypt internally and to isolate her strategically from the rest of the region. Consequently, as decision-makers arrive at their decisions by confronting their values with their image of the environment,[22] the Egyptian response, that of virulent and uncompromising defiance, seems, in retrospect, to have been inevitable.

Since Nasser was the dominant personality inside the Revolutionary Command Council, this policy of defiance was increasingly identified with him. As such, the decision-making process was becoming event more personalised until all government policies were thought to emanate from Nasser. In other words, demands made on the political system were being directed more at Nasser and less toward the regime as a whole.

Part of the explanation for this emerging phenomenon can be traced to the cultural traditions and social experiences of the Egyptians themselves, for throughout recorded history the main feature of the political structure in Egypt has been its authoritarian character, centred primarily on highly centralised government with a powerful Chief Executive.[23] The acceptance by the people of this type of government was probably facilitated by the fact that in the villages, which had always been Egypt's core societal unit, authority had, for centuries, been bestowed on one person (al-Rais: the leader). Hence, a powerful charismatic leadership was, in all probability, more relevant to the prevailing Egyptian situation than other types of institutions.[24]

However, the major catalyst in the emergence of Nasser's charismatic leadership was undoubtedly the overwhelming enthusiasm with which his anti-Western policies were greeted inside Egypt and within the Arab world as a whole. The main reason behind this enthusiasm was the almost total alienation of many Arabs from the West[25] to which Nasser's policies gave expression. Thus, Nasser's 'defiance of the West' in a series of dramatic and highly publicised acts such as his virulent attacks on the Baghdad Pact, his Czech arms deal, and the momentous nationalisation of the Suez Canal Company coincided with the prevailing political orientations of the Arabs. Moreover, these were the first acts for almost a century and one-half to counteract the sense of social and political inferiority Egyptians had acquired throughout their long history of subservience to the West.[26] These support-winning measures were reinforced by the glory Nasser had attained in Bandung in April 1955, as one of the leaders of the non-aligned world. His image was even further enhanced when the Anglo-French withdrawal from Egypt after Suez was perceived by many Arabs as a resounding defeat of 'imperialist' forces by Nasser.

This perceived victory of Nasser over the combined military might of Britain and France bestowed upon him almost superhuman qualities. Professor John Badeau states that 'with the Suez Canal crisis, Nasser suddenly filled the Middle-Eastern horizon, becoming . . . a regional hero. To restless and frustrated Arab nationalists he indeed seemed a second Saladin, turning the table on Western imperialism.'[27] From now on the Egyptians would look upon Nasser 'no longer as the mere leader of a military junta but as a god and a saviour of his people'.[28] In other words, referring back to Weber's conceptualisation, the charismatic relationship between Nasser and the Egyptian people had finally and clearly emerged.

The process of acquiring personal charisma stimulates and contributes to the process of attaining the status and power of the principle decision-maker. This analysis is true for three interrelated reasons. First, the sheer force of mass adulation in a charismatic relationship elevates the leader to a position far above that of his colleagues in the decision-making process, thus forcing upon him a new 'role behaviour'. Second, the leader's need for his colleagues, in view of his mass support, is considerably diminished. Third, his colleagues, being a part of the general environment, must be affected by the dynamics of the charismatic relationship. However, it must be emphasised here that the two concepts are not coterminous. In other words, while the acquisition of charisma is a contributing factor toward the attainment of centrality in the decision-making process, achieving a position of dominance in the decision-making structure does not necessarily bequeath charisma upon the occupant.

As stated above, the Suez crisis and Nasser's central role in this crisis was the final culmination, indeed the crowning, of the charismatic process. Suez was the most important catalyst in establishing Nasser's power over the Egyptian people as a whole and within the decision-making structure. Anthony Nutting attributes Nasser's eventual dominance to positive acts by Nasser during the crisis: '. . . whereas formerly he had always consulted his colleagues before taking any important decision, he now told them what he wanted done and brooked no argument with his judgement.'[29] Charles Cremeans also analyses the role relationship amongst the group of officers who had constituted the actual decision-making structure in Egypt. However, he posits that only part of the reason behind this change in perception and role-playing could be attributed to a change in Nasser. Cremeans thus argues that

> an even greater change took place in the attitudes of the people around him. Men closely associated with him for years who had argued with him through interminable strategy sessions, giving as good as they got, began referring to him as el-Rais (the leader, or the president) and quoting his opinions as the final word on every subject.[30]

An interesting observation derived from the foregoing discussion relates to the obvious linkages between the national and the international environments.[31] It has by now become evident that Nasser's primacy in Egypt did not follow any startling achievements in his domestic policies but was a direct consequence of his perceived 'successes' in the foreign policy sector. The attacks on the Baghdad Pact, the Czech arms deal, the nationalisation of the canal, and, probably the most vital of all his measures, the decision not to 'surrender' but to confront the 'imperialists' over the canal – these were all policies that were directed at, and were responsive to, the external environment.

As Nasser's political dominance and hegemony in Egypt emerged after Suez, he endeavoured to legalise his position constitutionally. The Egyptian constitutions of 1956, 1958 and 1964 gave the President of the Republic sweeping powers, making the cabinet and the legislature wholly subordinate to him. The President's constitutional functions included the appointment and dismissal of vice-presidents, prime ministers and cabinet ministers, and the power to dissolve parliament (the National Assembly). He was accorded the authority to conclude treaties, declare war (after the approval of the National Assembly) and proclaim a state of emergency. Moreover, the appointment of ambassadors and army officers also fell within his jurisdiction. In law, therefore, as the highly centralised and intensely personalised form of decision-making emerged, 'the President [was] not constitutionally responsible to any institutional checks upon his authority.'[32] And although the Constitutional Bill of September 27, 1962, set up a twelve-member Presidential Council with the theoretical function of bearing most of the presidential powers, in reality its only purpose was to relieve the President from secondary and time-consuming tasks. In any case, the life span of the Presidential Council did not exceed eighteen months, and it was finally abolished under the Constitutional Bill of March 23, 1964.

Apart from the constitutional endorsement of Nasser's authority, his institutional entrenchment was further cemented by political measures. The formation of the United Arab Republic in February, 1958, installed him as the leader of the first unionised Arab state and brought back to Egyptians, Syrians and the rest of the Arabs the memory of the earlier union between the two regions under the great Saladin. Domestically, the nationalisation of the press in 1960 afforded him complete control over the mass media and the publishing industry. The confiscation of the property and fortunes of all the remaining Egyptian capitalists and feudalists immediately following the Syrian secession from the UAR, ensured the final obliteration of a class which could have emulated in Egypt the role its Syrian counterpart had played in the secession. In the realm of development, the construction of the Aswan High Dam served as a symbol of 'forward-moving' Egypt and emphasised Nasser's ability to implement his declaratory policies no matter how difficult and monumental the task may have seemed to the average citizen.

By the early sixties, therefore, Nasser's hegemony over the decision-making structure and among the Egyptian people was such that setbacks in foreign and domestic policies did not seem to affect his position as a charismatic leader or as the principle decision-maker. The dissolution of the United Arab Republic and the disastrous involvement in the Yemen war, for example, were instances of the failure of policies personally identified with Nasser's vision for the future of Egypt and the Arab nation, yet no infringement on Nasser's actual or constitutional powers occurred. Indeed, when he himself offered his resignation after Egypt's humiliating defeat in the June war of 1967, the enormous and spontaneous reaction of the Egyptian masses coupled with the unanimous reluctance of any of his colleagues to assume Nasser's responsibilities swept him back to power within only one day of his resignation;[33] this act vindicated and emphasised his charismatic hold on the Egyptian people as a whole and on his colleagues within the decision-making process.

Therefore, beginning with the period spanning the years 1955–6 and continuing thereafter, President Nasser was the principle figure in the decision-making process in Egypt. Until his death in 1970, he was personally responsible for Egyptian policy generally and for the foreign sector specifically. The individuals participating in the decision-making process lacked the authority to make formal decisions unless it was personally delegated by the Chief Executive himself. Thus in an analysis of the decision-making process in Egypt, these individuals can only be treated as environmental influences. In this case, any study of Egyptian foreign policy, whether theoretical (i.e. concerned with formulating generalised hypotheses) or historically period-oriented, must start from the premise of Nasser's central and dominant posture in the process of foreign policy-making. Unlike the pluralistic models of political behaviour in which the Chief Executive derives his authority from the perceived legitimacy of the political system, the charismatic relationship between the people and their leader in Egypt elevated President Nasser to a position of dominance over the legal–institutional structure, thus making the perceived legitimacy of the political system wholly dependent on Nasser's authority alone.

PERSONALITY FACTOR

There is no doubt that the personality factor is an important determinant in the shaping of perceptions which, themselves, account for much of the political system's reaction to external stimuli. It is also obvious that 'personality analysis' is much more relevant in the study of authoritarian political systems where the leader is the dominant sub-system, than in states of more complex institutional structure, i.e. those possessing more major sub-systems. Moreover, when the dominant sub-system is also a charismatic leader, personality factors assume a distinctly vital and central role due to the leader's assumption that he is the sole representative of his people. As such, a study of the leader's personality, its uniqueness and its idiosyncracies, is essential to a more complete understanding of the foreign policy of an authoritarian state.

In a seminal study of the Protestant reformer, Martin Luther, Erik Erikson argues that the earlier experiences encountered in the pre-adulthood phase are particularly important to the development of the 'reformer's personality'.[34] Erikson concentrates on the relationship between the ideology of the reformer and the 'identity crisis' which he defines as 'the major crisis of adolescence [which] occurs in that period of life cycle when each youth must forge for himself some central perspective and direction, some working unity, out of the effective remnants of his childhood and the hopes of his anticipated adulthood.'[35] It is thus essential, for the purpose of this study, to examine Nasser's childhood and his adolescence in order to attain a clearer insight into his later values and ideological orientations.[36]

Nasser was born in Alexandria in a poor neighbourhood and grew up in a relatively deprived environment. These humble origins affected him deeply. They tend to explain his later sympathies with, and his efforts to eradicate the plight of, the poor. They also explain his own unpretentious life style. He once said, 'I am always proud of having originated from a humble family, . . . and I promise to remain poor all my life.'[37] Probably even more significant than their own economic deprivation was the feeling of social inferiority Nasser's family experienced on account of their being native Egyptians who lacked the sophistication of the predominantly non-Egyptian and Coptic urban upper class. Wilton Wynn asserts that it was during his childhood that Nasser suffered the humiliation that brought home to him a maddening fact – his family was looked down on as inferior simply because they were Egyptians, because they spoke Arabic instead of French, because they were baladi (native Egyptians). It was then that the emotional groundwork was laid for that tremendous psychological drive in Nasser – the drive to make himself and his people proud, and not ashamed to be Egyptian.[38]

A further factor which contributed to Nasser's 'identity crisis' was his own unstable family life due mainly to his father's frequent transfers, which deprived the young boy of a settled life both inside and outside his home. Between the ages of three and seventeen, Nasser changed homes nine times.[39] Moreover, his relationship with his father, in contrast to that with his mother, whom he dearly loved, was frequently strained. When his mother died and his father remarried, Nasser's alienation became so acute that he had to leave his father's home and live with relatives.

These domestic crises were reinforced by a general political crisis that plagued Egypt throughout the twenties and thirties, and together they contributed to a sense of alienation from the existing social and political system. Nasser himself asserted that his personality was 'conditioned by my family background and upbringing, allied to a general feeling of dissatisfaction and defiance that spread throughout the whole of my generation in schools, universities and subsequently in the armed forces'.[40] This dissatisfaction felt by Nasser's generation was primarily directed at their existing leaders, whom they perceived to be impotent in the face of the humiliating British domination of Egypt. This was certainly compounded by a feeling of frustration at their own inability to change the *status quo* which alone would have eradicated their sense of humiliation.

This general alienation from the existing social and political system compounded by his own unsettled home life made the young Nasser a rebel, an avowed nationalist, and partly contributed to his total of nine school transfers between the ages of five and seventeen.[41] He began to devote himself to political demonstrations and anti-British activities at the expense of his formal education. In 1935, he organised and led a demonstration near the British army barracks in which two students were killed and he himself received a head wound. Much of Nasser's later values and attitudes, such as his preoccupation with 'anti-imperialism', Egypt's 'prestige' and 'leadership', can be traced to the perceptions he had of the existing Egyptian political and social order of the mid-thirties. These perceptions can be discerned from a revealing letter he wrote to a friend in 1935 concerning the existing situation in Egypt:

Today the situation is critical and Egypt has reached an impasse. It seems to me that the country is in a state of despair . . . Who can stop the imperialist? There are men in this country with dignity who do not desire to die like dogs. Yet where is the burning nationalism of 1919? Where are the men who are willing to sacrifice themselves for the independence of our homeland? Where is the man who can recreate the country so that the feeble humiliated Egyptians can live again, free and independent? Where is dignity? . . . It is said that the Egyptian is so cowardly that he fears the slightest sound. We must, then, have a leader who will take him into battle for his country, transforming him into a thunder that will shake persecution to its very foundation.[42]

One salient aspect of the letter is Nasser's almost fatalistic belief, at this stage, in the central role of the leader who will 'transform the feeble Egyptian into a thunder'. This clearly shows that he was a believer in the 'great man theory'; the individualist who leads men into deeds that rewrite history. Indeed his heroes, then, were all individualist Egyptian nationalist leaders such as Mustafa Kamil and Saad Zaghloul. It is also known that his leisure time was spent reading the biographies of great historical leaders like Alexander the Great, Julius Caeser, Napoleon, Mahatma Ghandi, etc. This orientation must, to a great degree, explain the later ultra-centralisation of Nasser's political structure and his seeming unwillingness, even inability, to delegate power or transfer authority to a grass-root political organisation.

The second important aspect of the latter is its heavy emphasis on the term 'dignity'. From an early age, Nasser sought to counteract the humiliations he encountered on the personal level as a poor native Egyptian, and on the national level as a member of a 'colonised' community, by an almost obsessional emphasis on personal dignity. A later 'humiliating' incident, which affected Nasser deeply, occurred in February 1941 when the British ambassador surrounded the royal palace with British forces and forced King Farouk to appoint a pro-British Prime Minister. Nasser later recalled that the incident 'completed Egypt's shame and yet put new spirits into us. It shook many people out of their apathy and taught them that there is a dignity which deserves to be defended at any price.'[43] The term 'dignity' was widely used in Nasser's speeches and interviews. In fact the main recurring theme of Nasser's speeches during the period of our study such as 'the fight against colonialism', 'the quest for regaining Egypt's prestige', and so forth, were all, at least substantially if not fully, motivated by a desire to give his country and his humiliated countrymen a feeling of pride and a sense of dignity. Asked once what he thought was the greatest achievement of the Egyptian Revolution, President Nasser immediately answered, 'the restoration of our self-confidence and sense of dignity as a people'.[44]

STYLE FACTOR

Nasser's personality development undoubtedly contributed to a unique style in the formulation and conduct of foreign policy. Nasser's courage, coupled with an almost uncanny confidence in his own tactical skill, made him take decisions and formulate policies that were both unorthodox and unexpected. Many of these decisions were rapid responses to international stimuli. The usual speed that accompanied the formulation of these decisions was facilitated by the highly centralised character of government. Many of these responses were naturally risky, yet cannot be considered as reckless. The most illuminating case here was undoubtedly Nasser's momentous decision to nationalise the Suez Canal Company barely ten days after the American announcement to withdraw their aid to the Aswan Dam project. The charge of 'recklessness' in the decision to nationalise the canal company was based upon Egypt's perceived isolation in a region dominated by hostile powers, and on the huge military disparity between these powers and Egypt. Yet, according to Nasser, this decision was arrived at coolly and rationally. It was taken, Nasser alleges, after a careful consideration of various alternatives and an effort to 'measure the situation by putting himself in the place of Eden'.[45] Nasser, later on, recounted the process with which the decision was taken in the aftermath of the American announcement:

> Basically, [the problem] became a simple one. There could be no question of shelving the plans; the money had to be found; and the only means I had of increasing the national revenue by any marked degree, was by nationalizing the Suez Canal . . . I knew that I was taking a calculated risk. I knew of my personal experience of Anthony Eden that he would feel bound to take action to protect British interests; but I was almost certain, too, that Britain did not have enough troops in Kenya, Cyprus or Aden, their nearest bases to carry out an immediate attack. I believed that, in the time needed for him to mobilize sufficient forces, it would be possible for us to reach a peaceful solution.[46]

Even the series of decisions taken by Nasser in May 1967, could not be termed reckless. While the end result was catastrophic, the decisions themselves could be described as risky yet quite rational, given the perceived capabilities of the conflicting parties at that time and Nasser's hitherto frequently successful utilisation of foreign policy as a legitimising device for his regime. Throughout the winter of 1966–7, Nasser had been virulently attacked by the Arab kings for allegedly harbouring less than hostile intentions towards Israel and for 'hiding behind the security of UNEF'. Consequently, apart from using them as a 'signal' to Israel not to take military action against Syria, Nasser's decisions to request the withdrawal of UNEF from Sinai, to assert Egyptian sovereignty over Sharm al-Sheikh, and to close the Straits of Tiran to Israeli shipping, were taken in order to cement the domestic and regional positions of his regime. Once the implementation of these decisions achieved his political objective, Nasser immediately proceeded to de-escalate the crisis by offering to send his Vice-President, Zakariya Mohyddin, to Washington. Nasser obviously, and quite reasonably, calculated that rather than be drawn into the conflict themselves, the superpowers would compel Israel to accept the newly created situation, thus leaving Nasser with a great political victory which would silence his critics and restore his credibility and prestige. However, neither Nasser, nor the rest of the world it seems, had calculated for the presence in Israel of leaders who were just as adept as Nasser at risk-taking.

The nationalisation of the canal company and the decisions of May 1967 epitomise another aspect of Nasser's style. Nasser asserted more than once: 'I do not act, I react.' As such, he was a pragmatist who was willing to experiment and who, in the implementation of policy decisions, was prepared to utilise improvised means if necessary. In this, Nasser did not allow his ideological convictions to severely restrict his manouevrability. Within the broad parameters of a general principle, he would pursue various and sometimes even contradictory objectives. For instance, his interpretation of the principle of 'anti-imperialism' allowed him to direct vicious attacks on the United States and its perceived 'friends' in the Arab world, while not letting it restrict him from accepting American economic aid. Also, there was much pragmatic rationality behind the enunciation, on the wake of the Syrian secession, of the seemingly confused thesis of 'Egypt as a state and a revolution', since it allowed the Egyptian decision-makers to conduct diplomatic transactions with other Arab leaders while simultaneously inciting their respective populations against them. Professor Majid Khadduri writes on this subject that although Nasser was 'ideologically committed to certain overriding objectives, he was not a utopian reformer for whom one simple solution would make everything come out right.'[47]

In handling people, Nasser possessed and exhibited great skill. Those who met him were usually surprised by the calm and personal dignity that he displayed. He was widely read and well informed, which made him excel in arguments and discussions. This debating ability is evident when one consults the minutes of the tripartite talks on the subject of unity between the UAR, Syria and Iraq in March and April of 1963. Suspicious of unity with the Baath, and using the talks as a debating forum, he completely dominated every session, controlling the tempo and tone of the arguments almost at will. He consistently succeeded in getting the Iraqi and Syrian Baathists to quarrel with, and even contradict, each other. Seasoned politicians and articulate intellectuals such as Bitar, Aflaq and Abd al-Karim Zuhur were lectured to by Nasser as though they were raw school-children.

His frequent speeches to the Egyptian public were brilliant rhetorically. These speeches sometimes lasted for several hours and were usually interjected with colloquial passages and filled with witty remarks (sometimes abusive) directed at his contemporary enemies. By manipulating the Arabic language, he coined many slogans which became widely used throughout the Arab world, such as his references to the leader of Iraq in 1959 as the 'Kassem of Iraq' which in Arabic means 'the divider of Iraq'. In another instance he replaced 'Shaab' with 'Saab' thus referring to 'Mahkamat al-Shaab', the Iraqi Peoples' Court, as 'Mahkamat al-Saab', the Court of Abuse. However, although his speeches were mainly directed at the emotions of his people, who usually reacted immediately and enthusiastically, many of these speeches were also educational, containing much information about Egypt's economic, social and foreign policies.

A particularly noticeable trait in his style of public speaking was the feeling of intimacy which he exuded, thus letting the 'masses' feel that they shared with him the most closely-guarded secrets of state. He filled his speeches with phrases such as 'between you and me', 'brothers let me tell you frankly', 'I shall read you a letter from Khrushchev', 'today we are being frank with each other', and so on. This technique gave the masses an impression of accessibility to the decision-making process, while at the same time educating them on matters of domestic and foreign policy. Throughout, he persisted in assuring his public that his information to them was always correct. Thus, his speeches would frequently contain phrases such as: 'We speak the same language in secret documents. We speak the same language in the speeches and public announcements.'[48]

Finally, his rhetorical ability coupled with his espousal of the Pan-Arab cause contributed towards an innovative and substantive change in the style of conducting foreign relations among Arab states. Prior to 1955, foreign relations were the domain of statesmen who utilised secret diplomacy as the primary instrument of foreign policy. Egypt, using its leader's rhetorical ability and his increasing popularity among the Arab people, was the first country to use propaganda as a major instrument for achieving Egyptian objectives. With the advent of the transistor radio in the Middle East, Egypt increased the power and transmission time of her radio service and used it to appeal directly to the peoples of other Arab states over the heads of the indigenous leadership. Realising the obvious effectiveness of this new method, other states soon emulated the Egyptians in concentrating on propaganda techniques to the detriment of other foreign policy instruments.

THE SUBORDINATE INSTITUTIONAL STRUCTURE

Due to the nature of the power relationship within the Egyptian decision-making process, a study of the various institutions will naturally highlight both their subordinate role and the hegemony of the presidency. Thus, such an analysis will mainly be an extension of the preceding discussion of Nasser's central position in the decision-making process. While these institutions participated fully in the process of policy formulation and execution, their significance lay primarily in their ability to modify decisional outcomes either through their control of information channels, their accessibility to the presidency in an advisory capacity, or through a position which afforded them influence in the choice of a particular method of implementation. Thus, an analysis of these institutions will elaborate the role (however small) they played in the foreign policy decision-making process. Moreover this shift of emphasis in the analysis (i.e. on the institutions themselves rather than on Nasser), while producing similar conclusions as above, should further help us understand Nasser's predominance by highlighting the structural weaknesses of these institutions which contributed to the hegemony of the presidency.

The ruling elite – the cabinet

The most striking feature of the Egyptian cabinet throughout Nasser's rule was its relative structural uniformity. Thus, of the cabinets that spanned the period between Nasser's assumption of power in April 1954 and his death in September 1970, the membership of officers or ex-officers in the cabinet averaged over 40 per cent.[49] The majority of these officers were the original Free Officers who had participated in some form or other in the execution of the July 1952 coup.

This structural uniformity contributed to the eventual subservience of the cabinet to the presidency in two ways. In the first place, the cabinet, particularly in the crucial period between 1954 and 1961 which saw the final emergence of Nasser's charismatic authority, was filled with Nasser's trusted friends. These were either his old army friends who were the original members of the Free Officer's inner circle, and who had come under his influence as long ago as the late thirties and the early forties, or they were civilian technocrats who had supported the revolution at its inception. These were men like Mahmoud Fawzi and Abd al-Muneim Qaissouni, who sympathised with Nasser's policies and who shared his vision for the future of Egypt. Consequently, situations of potential conflict arising from disagreements on broad outlines became minimal and afforded Nasser the opportunity for independent action.

Secondly, an examination of Table 8 illustrates the heavy emphasis on specialisation within the Egyptian cabinet. Thus, while individually cabinet ministers could exert more influence on the president in matters

TABLE 8

Occupants of Selected Key Ministries of Egypt, 1954–61

	Defence	Interior	Foreign Affairs	Economy & Treasury	National Guidance Affairs	Social Affairs	Education	Planning	Health	Public Works	Industry	Agriculture
1 Sept 54	Abd al-Hakim Amer	Zakariya Mohyddin	Mahmoud Fawzi	Abd al-Muneim Qaissouni	Salah Salim	Hussein Shafei	Kamal al-Din Hussein	Abd al-Latif Baghdadi	Nur al-Din Tarraf	Ahmad Abd al Sharabasi	Hassan Marei	Abd al-Razzak Sidqi
30 June 56	,,	,,	,,	,,	Fathi Radwan	,,	,,	,,	,,	,,	Azziz Sidqi	Said Marei
5 Mar 58	,,	,,	,,	,,	,,	,,	,,	Muhammed Abd al-Nusseir	,,	,,	,,	,,
7 Oct 58	,,	,,	,,	,,	Salah Bitar	,,	,,	Abd al-Latif Baghdadi	,,	,,	,,	,,
17 Aug 61	,,	Abd al-Hamid Saraj	,,	,,	Sarwat Okasha	,,	Amjad al-Tarabulsi	,,	,,	,,	,,	,,
18 Oct 61	,,	Zakariya Mohyddin	,,	,,	,,	,,	Said Muhammed Yousif	,,	,,	,,	,,	Muhammed Najib Hashaad

relating to their own specific departments, collectively they became less effective in influencing broad policy matters, particularly in the foreign affairs sector. Thus, the cabinet as an independent decision-making institution was weakened to the extent that Nasser himself began to exhibit extreme annoyance and displeasure if his ministers participated in discussions not strictly related to their own departments.[50] The President encouraged this trend by creating parallel institutions to the cabinet which were allowed to share executive power with the president. Such a body was created in September 1962 and was called the Presidential Council, whose duties were to relieve the President from administrative burdens. It was made the supreme executive authority but was desolved in March 1964.

The cabinet, therefore, was merely a collection of the heads of specialised departments which influenced policy decisions only in so far as these decisions related to the departments themselves. Indeed, there were very rare collective discussions of international issues. Nutting relates that at the height of the 1967 crisis, the cabinet had collectively discussed the explosive situation only once in the middle of May after the return of Sidqi Suleiman, the Prime Minister, from the Golan Heights.[51] Probably the most illuminating comment on the relationship of the cabinet to the presidency was made by Salah Bitar, a member of the Unionist Cabinet during 1958 and 1959:

> There was no really free discussion on any debate of broad ideas among the Ministers. Nasser was the first in everything – in foreign and home policy and in economic and social policies. I did not at all contest his capacities or his leading place – he deserved that place, but I contested the idea that others had no place.[52]

The ruling elite – the defence establishment

Of all the cabinet departments, only the Defence Ministry succeeded in attaining a measure of independence from the immediate control of the presidency. Its influence on foreign policy became far greater than that of the cabinet as a whole or of the Foreign Ministry. The reasons for this seeming anomaly can be traced to Nasser's own perceptions of the position of the military in Egypt. Even at the height of his charismatic authority, he persisted in regarding the armed forces as the backbone of his regime. This was probably due to his own conspiratorial experiences as a young army officer which nourished his image of the army as a crucial variable in the domestic balance of power. As such he became very sensitive to the demands of the military. He once remarked: 'The army is my parliament. The army has [not] carried out the Revolution simply to make me a ruler and then to leave me and go. I have to satisfy the army that the demands for which the Revolution was carried out are being realized.'[53] This respect for the armed forces allowed it a measure of political autonomy in Egypt which was denied to other groups. It led, later on, to a conflict beween the presidency and the defence establishment under Marshal Abd al-Hakim Amer, which only came to public notice during the debates that followed the 1967 war.[54] Heikal goes as far as saying that a 'peaceful coup' had in fact occurred in 1962 which resulted in something like a 'duality of authority' between Nasser and the defence chiefs. According to Heikal, this led Nasser to seriously contemplate not seeking the nomination for the March 1965 presidential elections.[55] Nasser himself admitted that prior to 1967 the military had succeeded in establishing a measure of independence from his political control.[56]

This independence became an obvious constraint on the conduct of foreign policy. One of its clearest manifestations was the military's continuous intrusion into spheres of duty accepted generally to be within the domain of foreign policy. Thus, not only were they accorded complete freedom in appointing military attachés in embassies abroad but it appears that sometimes they were also able to appoint ambassadors. Nasser's role in the inevitable and consequent conflict which arose between the Foreign Ministry officials and the defence establishment, indicated a propensity towards placating the military, since the protestations of the Foreign Minister and his deputies were frequently overruled by Nasser.[57] Nasser's seeming reluctance to curb or limit the military's power contributed to an increasing polarisation between the political and military factions of the leadership. It, indeed, became a constraint on Nasser's freedom to conduct foreign affairs. This was clearly illustrated by an instance relating to the Yemeni war, where Nasser is believed to have favoured gradual disengagement through political conciliation, while the defence chiefs sought an escalation of the war effort until a prestigeous military victory could be achieved. Robert Stephens authoritatively related that after nearly three and one-half years of an inconclusive and costly campaign, Nasser appointed the flexible Ahmad Muhammed Numaan to the Yemeni premiership in place of the dogmatic General Sallal, and encouraged him to seek a settlement with the Saudis. Accordingly, Numaan carried out his own unilateral negotiations with the Saudis and presented a peace plan which was apparently accepted by Nasser. However, the military leaders, incensed at not having been consulted, rejected the plan. Nasser, to Numaan's surprise duly reversed his earlier endorsement and appointed the hawkish General Hassan al-Amri as Prime Minister.[58]

The appointment in 1966 of General Shams al-Din Badran, a close friend of Marshal Amer, as the Minister of Defence reinforced the political influence of the defence establishment and contributed to the military's increased insularity from presidential control. Consequently, when Nasser dismissed Amer and fifty other top military commanders on the wake of the June War debacle, the defence establishment, which had grown accustomed to its independence, clearly resented Nasser's interference. This led to the abortive coup of August 1967 which resulted in the arrest of Marshal Amer (and his subsequent suicide) and General Badran, together with 149 other army and security chiefs.[59] The failure of the coup and the consequent demise of Amer and Badran, brought the defence establishment under closer super-vision by the political leadership, and as a result, the post-1967 period saw the influence of the defence establishment over the formulation of Egypt's foreign policy become substantially diluted.

The ruling elite – the foreign ministry
The Foreign Ministry was involved primarily in diplomatic transac-tions and the day-to-day implementation of decisions reached by the presidency. This is not to suggest that a Foreign Minister of Mahmoud Fawzi's stature failed to exert influence on Nasser. On the contrary, the president valued the opinions of his Foreign Minister considerably and always took heed of his advice, especially on matters relating to United Nations and extra-regional affairs. In inter-Arab affairs, how-ever, the ministry was relegated to a secondary role. For example, during his years of office, Hussein Zulficar Sabry, the Deputy Foreign Minister, visited only one Arab capital, Damascus.

One important point which contributed to the structural weakness of the Foreign Ministry was Nasser's preference for gathering informa-tion about the Arab world from sources outside the ministry. This in itself seriously undermined a fundamental rationale for the existence of the ministry, namely its function as an organ of study and research for disseminating and analysing incoming information. Nasser, how-ever, preferred to gather his information on the Arab world from the international press, particularly the Lebanese newspapers, and he relied on advice from a loosely knitted 'task force' consisting primarily of some of the original Free Officers. Thus, Anwar al-Sadat was apparently in charge of the Arabian Peninsula and Kamal Rifaat in charge of Syria and Lebanon. Moreover, as has already been discussed, Marshal Amer frequently interfered in the appointments not only of military attachés but also of ambassadors, overriding in the process the frequent objections of the Foreign Minister.

The major structural weakness of the Foreign Ministry, therefore, relates to the multiplicity of organs and institutions that dealt with matters relating to the external environment – matters that should have been the sole responsibility of the Foreign Ministry. These organs competed with the Foreign Ministry in executing its functions, and as a result, the ministry's power, prestige and influence were severely restricted.[60]

The political elite – the national assembly
The influence of parliament on foreign affairs is usually minimal unless

it is independent of the government, since its 'concurrence is necessary to pass implementing legislation and to appropriate the required means'.[61] Even in this sense, it merely operates as a platform for discussions of important issues. It presents its opinions as representing the general mood of the people and the country, thereby hoping to exercise influence on the leadership.

In Egypt, however, the National Assembly was created by the leadership itself and consequently became entirely dependent on the executive. An independent legislature on the Western model was rejected by the junta, partly to eliminate the possibility of competition for power, but also because they could see 'no advantage for Egypt in the establishment of a parliament in which men serving the interests of big landlords, or of Iraq, or of London, Washington or Moscow, would sit masquerading as Egyptians'.[62] Thus, according to Article 192 of the Republican Constitution promulgated in January 1956, all members of the National Assembly were to be nominated by the National Union, which itself was to be organised by the presidency. The electoral law which followed in March 1957 provided for a National Assembly of 350 seats, and the elections were held in July of the same year. The National Union executive committee, comprising three leading members of the junta – Baghdadi, Amer and Mohyddin, and working in close liaison with President Nasser, screened all 2528 applicants, rejecting 1210 and leaving 1318 actual contestants. In five constituencies all the original candidates were eliminated and replaced by regime-picked choices; and all cabinet members and some former army and police officers were elected unopposed.[63]

As a result, the National Assembly was completely dominated by the executive branch of government. The first Egyptian assembly had Baghdadi as its President and the first UAR assembly was presided over by Sadat, the latter being the only nominee for the post, thus getting elected by 568 votes – all those present in the assembly.[64] Not even the much heralded worker-dominated third assembly, elected in March 1964, could escape the straight-jacket imposed upon it by a dominating executive;[65] and as such, like its predecessors, its influence on foreign affairs remained minimal. Consequently, rather than executing its real functions of questioning and probing governmental policies, the assembly acted merely as a rubber-stamp for executive decisions. It met only to listen to the President and members of the leadership elaborating on their government programmes and explaining policy decisions already taken.[66] In this context, the assembly acted simply as a support for a commanding executive, providing it with a semblance of constitutional legitimacy. Its effectiveness in influencing policies was generally minimal, and in the foreign sector was particularly negligible.

The political elite – the political party

The influence of Western-type political parties occurs outside the formal decision-making structure through their members, who formally participate in the decision-making process either in the executive or in the legislative branch. The allegiance of individual members to their respective parties are partly a result of their adherence to the party's ideology or 'programme' and partly because they usually owe their political positions to the party. Thus, in a developed and mature democracy, parties of various ideological orientations compete with each other for support from the electorate for the purpose of gaining access to, and acquiring influence on, the formal decision-making process.

After a short period of experimentation, the junta in January 1953 decided against the adoption of Western-type political parties which had operated in pre-1952 Egypt, on the grounds that these parties were not prepared to subordinate their own interests to the general good of the people and the country.[67] It was argued that, in contrast to the mature democracies of the developed world, Western-type political parties would prove counter-productive in underdeveloped countries still suffering from corruption, social and economic injustices and foreign domination.[68] Within this context, Nasser observed that if parties were allowed in the UAR, there would be a party acting as an agent to the American CIA, another upholding British interests, and a third working for the Soviets.[69] Moreover, as was the case with the National Assembly, the military junta was averse to allowing any other institution a measure of independence from the executive. In their 'fight' against 'reaction' and its 'external mentors', the leadership could not allow any real measure of power-sharing with what they perceived as corrupt political parties.

The junta, therefore, in Article 192 of the 1956 constitution, created the National Union, a mass organisation which, according to Heikal, 'organizes and controls political activities in the country for the people's interests'.[70] Nasser went further, by insisting that general policies relating to planning, economic development and *external relations* would be submitted to the union and that 'its decisions would be the foundation upon which the government will formulate and implement its decisions.'[71] However, in reality the National Union's real functions were much more modest and were elaborated by Nasser, himself, on another occasion, namely: 'to know the problems of the masses, . . . and to get in touch with the government and ask for solutions to those problems'.[72] In other words, through its organisational structure, the National Union was supposed to act as a channel of communication between the public and the leadership. Yet, even here, the directional flow of communication was, in most cases, downward. In fact, by 1961, the union had proved to be a dismal failure on the organisational, ideological, and even mobilisational levels.

In accordance with the radicalisation of Egyptian politics after the Syrian secession, the National Union was abandoned by Nasser because 'reactionary elements [had] managed to paralyse its revolutionary effectiveness.'[73] Instead, a new political organisation whose membership was dominated by workers and peasants was created and christened the Arab Socialist Union (ASU). According to the official explanation, the aim of the new organisation would be to educate and organise the masses, and to safeguard the republic from capitalist, feudalist and foreign elements.[74] Its relations with the regime were defined by Heikal as 'seeking, through democracy, to keep state authorities under its supervision in order to protect the economic and social achievements of the Revolution'.[75] Yet here, as in the case of the National Union, the promise was greater than the ensuing reality, because contrary to Heikal's hopeful comment, control continued to flow in the opposite direction – from the state authorities to the ASU. In this, the new organisation fared little better than its disgraced predecessor. It is thus difficult to disagree with Leonard Binder's assertion that in Egypt political parties are created to serve as 'means of mobilizing sentiment for the regime and . . . rendering the masses unattainable to alternative leaders'.[76]

The inability of the two organisations to influence policies, therefore, was the result of a fundamental weakness in their organisational structure which concentrated power in the hands of the Executive Committee at the top of the organisational pyramid. This committee was mainly made up of members of the executive branch. For example, the presidential decree of June 11, 1960 filled the committee entirely with cabinet members of old trusted ex-officers – men such as Baghdadi, Mohyddin, Sadat, Shafei, Hussein, Amer, Rifaat, etc. Moreover, the controllers of the Egyptian and Syrian National Union committees were Kamal al-Din Hussein and Abd al-Hamid Saraj respectively.[77] Similarly, as Table 9 shows, the Supreme Executive Committee of the newly created ASU was dominated by the executive branch of government. Moreover, in a subsequent shake-up of the organisation in 1966, the number of the membership of the Executive Committee was reduced to seven. These were Nasser, Amer, Mohyddin, Shafei, Sadat, Ali Sabri and Sidqi Suleiman, the new Prime Minister.[78] Thus, both parties, like their sister organisation the National Assembly, were accorded subservient status and functions and were made wholly dependent upon the executive. One perceptive commentator insisted that these organisations failed to execute their theoretical functions because 'the leadership wanted to lead the masses from the top . . . leaving them only the right to applaud and approve.'[79] By 1968, even Heikal had become so exasperated with the ASU that he advocated its complete overhaul.[80]

TABLE 9
ASU Supreme Executive, 1962–4

Background	Members
Officer	Gamal Abd al-Nasser
Officer	Abd al-Latif al-Baghdadi
Officer	Abd al-Haikim Amer
Officer	Zakariya Mohyddin
Officer	Anwar al-Sadat
Officer	Hussein al-Shafei
Officer	Kamal al-Din Hussein
Officer	Ali Sabri
Officer	Hassan Ibrahim
Civilian	Nur al-Din Tarraf (Dr)
Civilian	Ahmad Abd al-Sharabasi
Officer	Kamal al-Din Rifaat
Civilian	Mahmoud Fawzi
Civilian	Abd al-Muneim Qaissouni (Dr)
Civilian	Aziz Sidqi (Dr)
Civilian	Mustafa Khalil
Officer	Abbas Radwan
Officer	Abd al-Qadir Hatem

Source: H. Hrair Dekmejian, *Egypt under Nasser: A Study in Political Dynamics*, London: University of London Press, 1971, p. 148.

Thus, the influence of the political party on policy as a whole, and foreign policy in particular, was almost non-existent. Unlike the mass-mobilising, single-party systems of the Communist world, the two unions lacked the prestige, legitimacy and stability of their Communist counterparts. While the CPSU, for example, as the guardian of Communist ideology, has conferred legitimacy on successive Soviet leaderships, in Egypt after 1958, the regime did not owe its legitimacy to any institution but to the charismatic leadership of Nasser. As an Egyptian journalist observed: 'It was not the popular organizations that organized the ideological orientations of the masses, . . . rather it was the bond between the masses and the revolutionary leadership.'[81]

THE PROCESS OF POLICY FORMULATION

It is evident that the process of policy formulation in Egypt was dominated by President Nasser. As has been explained, he became the virtual decision-maker; and the participation of others in the decision-making process (be they individuals, agencies, or institutions) was, in the final analysis, almost wholly dependent on their own accessibility to Nasser himself.[82] In this case, the ratio of their influence on policy was directly proportional to their accessibility to the President. For example, there is reason to believe that by virtue of his intimate friendship with Nasser, the influence of Muhammed Hasneen Heikal, the editor of the newspaper *al-Ahram*, on policy generally and foreign affairs particularly, exceeded the influence of major formal institutions such as the National Assembly, the National Union and even in some cases the Foreign Ministry.

The charismatic relationship between the people and their President initiated a direct linkage between the two which circumvented important institutions, thus weakening them considerably as independent, power-yielding, decision-making organs. Moreover, these institutions, being a part of the general environment, were themselves affected by the dynamics of the charismatic relationship. Consequently, the power to question, probe, disagree and modify or change, was replaced by the function of applauding and endorsing. This subordinate role robbed the Egyptian decision-making process of the dynamism its Western counterparts possessed through the vigorous participation of the various institutions and agencies in the decision-making process, either in the pre-decisional or in the post-decisional stages. Instead, the decision-making process in Egypt centred around the person of the President, and as such, can hardly be referred to as a process. Thus, the concept of flow in the interaction between the various decision-making organs was almost non-existent in Egypt. At most, it was so minimal as to render it insignificant.

This is, of course, not to suggest that the President operated in isolation from other organs of the decision-making process; such a situation is simply impossible. What is relevant here is that it was he who dictated the frequency and the intensity of this interaction with the other organs. As such, no formal or identifiable decision-making procedures seem to have existed; instead, the decision-making process, in form and content, seems to have depended almost entirely on the President's own discretion.

9 Values and Images

It is clear from the analysis of the preceding chapter that the decision-making process in Nasser's Egypt was dominated by a very small core-group composed mainly, but not exclusively, of ex-officers who exhibited remarkable cohesiveness over time as a result of their long and intimate association, their shared experiences and expectations, their common institutional interests, and probably most importantly their recognition of the central role and the charismatic authority and leadership of President Nasser. Consequently, the foreign policy decision-making process in Egypt lacked the institutional complexity of its counterparts in the liberal democracies of Western Europe and North America, and as such, foreign policy decisions in Egypt emanated almost exclusively from the above mentioned core decision-making group. Moreover, the cohesiveness of the group contributed to a high degree of perceptual uniformity and congruence of values among the members of the group. It is this perceptual consistency and the relative freedom from institutional constraints which facilitated the adoption of the simplified framework expounded in Chapter 6 of this study, which viewed decisions as the end results of interactions, occurring in the psychological environment of the decision-makers, between their values and their image of the operational environment. In other words, a cognitive interaction between the decision-makers' perception of reality and the various values they hold produces a response in which a specific change in the operational environment is sought. Thus, while the latter is important in its capacity to influence decision-making through objective change, nevertheless at any given moment values and images (psychological environment) are the determinants of the decisions and policies arrived at by the decision-makers.

The first component of the psychological environment is the 'image'. As a concept, the image refers to a set of closely related perceptions of the environment. Its relevance to the study of foreign policy was first advocated by Kenneth Boulding in 1956[1] when he argued that decision-makers do not respond to the objective facts of the situation but to their image of the situation. In other words, it is what they think the world is like, not what it really is, which determines the behaviour of decision-makers. Within this context, the decision-makers' evaluation of reality would generally depend on the type of information available to them, their idiosyncratic personality traits, and their conception of the

'National Role'.[2] The importance of the concept of image to the study of foreign policy decision-making has already been indicated in Chapters 7 and 8, where it was shown that in some instances differing perceptions of one objective fact had led to different, even contradictory, courses of action. In this chapter, however, the analysis of perceptions will concentrate on the way they interacted with the various values held by the decision-making elite.

'Values', as the second component of the psychological environment, constitute an important segment of the perceptual patterns of the decision-makers, in so far as 'the accumulation of knowledge is . . . not merely the mechanical sum of messages received and stored, but includes their organization according to certain principles and values, to meet . . . needs and desires.'[3] There is, however, little agreement among the analysts who have utilised the concept as to its precise meaning. This study will adhere to the general definition formulated by George J. Graham, which viewed values as abstract concepts 'whose contents are believed, by actors in a social or political context, to be something of special worth'.[4] The conscious adoption of values at the declaratory level by the decision-makers conceptualises them as the 'principles' of foreign policy. Values and principles are usually conditioned by the political culture and the historical legacy of the community.[5] However, they are neither static nor permanent. Their importance and relevance will vary according to the particular environmental situation within which the decision-makers are operating at the time, and their permanency will be affected by changing objective and subjective factors.

In analysing these values, we shall first endeavour to determine the 'operative elite perceptions'[6] which contributed to their espousal as principles of Egyptian foreign policy. It must be admitted, however, that any conclusions arrived at must remain to a certain extent speculative, for it is impossible to ascertain definitively such intangible factors as perceptions, expectations and motivations of individuals. Nevertheless, a perceptual analysis offers a set of probabilistic statements based on recurring cognitive patterns which can be identified and assessed through a careful study of the speeches, statements, interviews and writings of the national 'elite'. The utility of this method, therefore, lies in its ability, through the identification of recurring cognitive patterns, to recreate an approximation of the prevalent perceptual prisms of the decision-making elite and the dominant Egyptian imagery of the period. As such, the utilisation of this method should offer at least partial explanations of elite behaviour.

After outlining the perceived components of Egyptian principles, an assessment of their functional role in the decision-making process will be attempted. This includes the fulfillment of such functions as motivation, transfer of responsibility, justification and legitimisation.[7] Thus, these principles are, on the one hand, independent variables in their capacity to motivate policies yet, on the other hand, they are equally utilised to justify policies of the decision-making elite, based on other considerations such as the need to legitimise their rule, etc.

The following discussion will concentrate on four main principles (declaratory values) which during this period of study can be seen to have influenced Egyptian policies and actions. These principles were: anti-imperialism, Arabism, leadership and prestige.

ANTI-IMPERIALISM

The principle of anti-imperialism, as espoused by the decision-making elite, was a natural corollary to their perception of the objectives of the Western powers in the area. An article written by Heikal at the end of 1958 which closely approximates to the perceptual patterns of the decision-making elite of Egypt, alleged that the Western powers were pursuing three major objectives in the Middle East. Foremost among these objectives was the age-old concept of 'divide and rule'. He argued that the Western powers took the view that if the Arab states were not united within military pacts under Western domination, manipulation and spheres of influence, then they should not be united at all. Secondly, Heikal identified Israel's safety as a major concern of Western policies, and he contended that the realisation of this objective necessitated the fermentation of conflict within the Arab world. Finally, he argued that the 'West' would do all in its power to keep the rich oil resources of some Arab countries as remote as possible from the 'Arab radical movement'.[8]

The concept of 'divide and rule' seems to have been paramount in the perceptions of the Egyptian elites. In Nasser's speeches and interviews, too, it constituted a recurring theme. For example, even in the comparatively less militant atmosphere of 1965, Nasser insisted in a major address that

> throughout the years, imperialism was working for the division of the Arab world. Imperialism wanted to sow the seeds of dissent among the Arab states. Not only was imperialism against the unity of the Arabs, but it was against their unity of purpose, because in spite of artificial boundaries, the unity of purpose had always constituted a powerful force which was able, over the years, to confront imperialism.[9]

As the above quote indicates, much of this perception had its roots in the Egyptians' historical experience with foreign domination. References to Egypt's past experience with British, French and other foreign interests were time and time again resorted to in the writings of the elites generally, and in the interviews and speeches of Nasser particularly. For example, explaining his rejection of a World Bank offer to finance the Aswan Dam in 1956 on condition that the Bank should be allowed some supervisory capacity over the Egyptian economy, Nasser related that his immediate response was: 'how can I hand over my treasury and my accounts to you . . . we had experience of this. It was on this basis that we had been exploited and occupied. The result was that Cromer came and sat here in Egypt.'[10]

Much of the political involvement of the United States, Britain and France in the area during the fifties and sixties, tended to act as positive reinforcement for the above perceptions. These acts included the creation of the Baghdad Pact, the refusal to meet Egypt's demands for arms, the withdrawal of aid from the High Dam project, the Suez crisis, the Eisenhower Doctrine, the military interventions in the Lebanon and Jordan, the Algerian war, the persistence of Britain's colonial status in the Arabian Peninsula, the suspension of US aid to Egypt in 1965, and the general pro-Israeli attitudes of the Western powers.

In such an atmosphere, the occasional 'good will' gesture and 'non-imperialist' policy was usually lost in the overall perception of mistrust and suspicion. In Deutsch's cybernetic language, the perceived accumulation of animostic and subversive 'signals' reached a 'noise' level which tended to overwhelm the occasional 'supportive' signal. A salient example was the failure of the 1954 canal agreement to affect a reorientation in Anglo-Egyptian relations. Within the parameters of the perceptual model, two reasons for this failure could be offered. In the first place, the Egyptian historical experience of British domination gave rise to the perception that the canal agreement was the 'exception' rather than the 'rule'. Secondly, the Egyptian tendency to perceive the 'West' as a unitary entity (derived from the ability of the Western powers in the fifties and sixties to co-ordinate their policies on most issues relating to the area) meant that Britain's reputation in the area was dependent on policies and actions over which she often had little control. The same analysis is true of Egyptian responses to Britain's decision in February 1966 to withdraw from the Arabian Peninsula, and the US efforts in 1962 and 1963 to mediate between Egypt and Saudi Arabia over the Yemen. In the latter case, the examination of Nasser's speeches and Egyptian newspaper editorials, clearly indicates a perceptual inability on the part of the Egyptian elite to separate American support for Saudi Arabia from British activity in the Arabian south. Only in the case of France, can one discern a reorientation in Egyptian attitudes and a consequent improvement in relation as a result of France's disengagement from the Algerian war.

Finally, not only did the Egyptian elite perceive Western motives in the area to be primarily 'imperialist', but they became progressively convinced that these 'imperialist' designs were being increasingly channelled at the Egyptian regime as the leader of the 'anti-imperialist' movement. The basis of this perception could probably be traced to the Suez crisis in which the British and French decision-makers took the view that stability in the area would not be achieved unless Nasser's regime was overthrown. The Egyptian leadership, therefore, began to suspect that the West would utilise almost any method to undermine the Egyptian political system. During the Yemen war, this suspicion grew into an obsessive belief that if the Yemeni revolution were to be liquidated, then 'imperialism' through its 'reactionary' agents in the Arab world would 'transfer the battle against socialism and progress and against the people of Egypt in Cairo'.[11]

Given this perceptual pattern, it is clear that 'anti-imperialism' constituted a major motivation for Egyptian policies. There is, indeed, a general consensus among Middle Eastern analysts that Egypt's virulent anti-West policies in the fifties and sixties were motivated, if not wholly then predominantly, by the psychological factors discussed above.[12] This view is, of course, further supported by the analysis in Chapter 8 relating to the early development of Nasser's personality during the twenties and thirties, which was a period of protracted conflict and turmoil characterised by extreme anti-British sentiment and activity. It is also worth noting that the entire membership of the military junta (with the exception of General Nagib) and many of Nasser's future friends, advisers and confidants were of the same age group as that of Nasser, and as such, they too were subjected to the same psychological and political influences of the era.

Apart from its motivating (and in a sense, constraining) role as an independent variable, anti-imperialism served other functions which were primarily designed to maintain the political order and to strengthen the authority of the decision-making elite. Thus, the regime used this principle to communicate screened and distorted events in order to transfer responsibility for its own failures. Thus, the withdrawal in 1967 of Egyptian troops from the Yemen after five years of inconclusive fighting was justified on the basis that 'the dispute over Yemen ended when Britain decided to evacuate South Arabia. The forced evacuation of British colonialism from South Arabia meant that the Egyptian army had no choice but to withdraw from Yemen.'[13] Moreover, the failure of Egypt's efforts to achieve either an organic or a functional unity of the Arab states, which to some extent could be attributed to the hegemonic orientations of the Egyptian elite,[14] was transferred by the Egyptian regime to the anti-unity efforts of the 'Western powers and their Arab lackeys'.[15] In this sense, therefore, 'anti-imperialism' was used as a reservoir of continuing anti-West sentiment on which the regime could draw to minimise its own failures. A salient example here can be seen in the response of the regime to the Arab–Israeli conflict. In their efforts to explain to the Arab public their inability to defeat Israel, the Egyptian leaders repeatedly endeavoured to make amends for their own deficiencies by attributing Israel's obstinate persistence on 'imperialist' activity in the region. Thus, in the post-1967 period,

Nasser would remind his listeners that 'liberating the homeland from Israel was no easy matter, because Israel did not stand alone. It opera- ted as a stooge of world imperialism and colonialism.'[16] Indeed, Israel 'was merely a manifestation of the system of imperialist world domina- tion'.[17] By the same token, in the delicate period immediately following the June 1967 war, the regime deliberately blamed its own disastrous failures on the fictitious participation of the United States and Britain in the war.[18] While later admitting their 'error', this transfer of respon- sibility served as a stabilising factor in an uncertain and potentially explosive situation.

Anti-imperialism as a principle was also used in its functional role as a justification for Egyptian policies. For example, the Egyptian regime rationalised its paradoxical participation in the Arab Security Force in September 1961 with 'reactionary' Jordan and Saudi Arabia to defend 'feudalist' Kuwait against 'progressive' Iraq on the basis of anti-imperialism. The Egyptian leaders argued that in this case, the most immediate and pressing objective was the replacement of the 'imperialist' British forces who had answered an appeal from the ruler of Kuwait.[19] A similar argument was utilised to explain Egypt's abrupt change towards an anti-Soviet orientation in 1959 after more than four years of close co-operation with the Soviet Union. Nasser, disregarding other possible factors, explained that 'the consciousness of our people has become strong enough to know that our campaign against the communist agents aims at protecting our homeland from a new imperialism.'[10] Moreover, Egypt's perennial conflict with the other Arab states was also rationalised, and its almost vicious intensity justified, in terms of Egypt's anti-imperialist crusade.[21] The verbal war against the Shah of Iran, according to the Egyptians, was also con- ducted on the basis of his close ties with the United States and Israel.[22]

The question that arises here is whether anti-imperialism was the sole motive behind these policies, or indeed whether it played a sub- stantive part in the formulation of these decisions. It is obvious that many factors can be identified as constituting the probable motive for any particular policy. Thus, while the Egyptian leadership's decision to participate in the Arab Security Force may have been motivated by anti-imperialism, it could have also been motivated by personal ani- mosity towards the Iraqi leaders, or by an effort to emphasise Egyptian centrality in the Arab world, or by the hope of future Kuwaiti aid, or other such considerations. Similar arguments can be applied to Egyptian–Soviet relations in 1959, for while the suspicion of a 'new imperialism' on the part of the Egyptian leaders may have been genuine enough, their anti-Soviet orientation could also have been motivated by their fear of the Communist party as an alternative leader, or by their anger at Khrushchev's personal attacks on Nasser, or it could be explained as an effort to normalise relations with the United States. In short, in any decisional situation there are many interacting factors present, and consequently it is both simplistic and inaccurate to pursue a single-factor analysis, since decisions constitute the end results of multiple interactions and processes. Nevertheless, while anti-imperialism may not have been the sole determinant of these decisions, it is also erroneous to argue that it played no significant part in their cognitive formulation. However, what is important here is that in these cases, 'anti-imperialism' provided the Egyptian leaders with an easily comprehensible explanation which, apart from its mobilisational functions, directed attention away from motives relating to personal ambitions and power politics.

The final function of 'anti-imperialism' as a principle, relates to its role as a legitimising factor. Legitimacy, in this case, refers to the acceptance by the society of their decision-making elite as the authoritative allocators of values.[23] The legitimacy of the Egyptian decision-making elite was enhanced and reinforced by the pursuit of anti-imperialist policies that reflected the dominant value-system of the period. Most Middle Eastern analysts[24] agree that the authority and prestige of Nasser's regime throughout the fifties and sixties was enhanced by its anti-imperialist policies which first emerged as a response to the creation of the Baghdad Pact.

ARABISM

Arabism is an amorphous concept based primarily on emotional and sentimental attachments to a perceived entity called 'the Arab nation'. It presupposes a high level of homogeneity among the inhabitants of the Arab states based on mutual perceptions of a common cultural, linguistic and religious heritage. It emphasises the achievement of the 'Arab nation' under Islamic rule and prescribes a unified future.[25] It is used interchangeably by analysts as well as political leaders with 'Arab nationalism'.

Arabism as a value of Egypt's foreign policy-making was gradually evolved between the years 1952 and 1958, reaching its zenith in the latter part of 1958 in the period following the establishment of the United Arab Republic and the collapse of the pro-West Iraqi monarchy. It has been already illustrated that in the early years of the revolution, there was minimal identification by the military leadership, and indeed by the Egyptian people as a whole, with 'Arab nationalism'. There was merely an awareness by the young leaders that Egypt had obvious ties with the Arab, African and Moslem worlds, and of those the 'Arab circle' was the most closely connected with Egypt.[26] However, as Egypt's involvement in regional Arab politics, particularly after the Baghdad Pact, grew in intensity, Egyptian identification with 'Arabism' became more pronounced, more forthright and less self-conscious. Thus by 1958, Nasser could declare that 'Arab nationalism is not a word or a motto; it is a great and a high principle.'[27]

R. Hrair Dekmejian, in his book *Egypt Under Nasir*, used the technique of 'content analysis' of Egyptian radio broadcasts between January 1952 and December 1959 to ascertain the movement of nationalist ideology. In a graphic illustration which is reproduced here (Fig. 4), he shows that while Arab nationalism achieved ascendancy

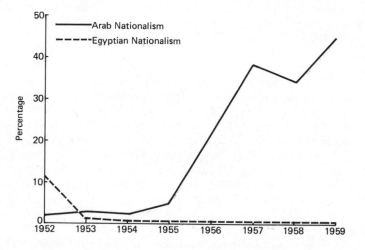

Fig. 4 The Movement of Nationalist Ideology

Source: H. Hrair Dekmejian, *Egypt under Nasir: A Study in Political Dynamics*, London: University of London Press, 1971, p. 94.

over Egyptian nationalism at the end of 1952, the complete orientation towards the former did not emerge until February 1955. The creation of the Baghdad Pact was the major catalyst in this shift. The leadership's assessment of the Pact's effect on Egypt's political and strategic interests, which was reinforced by their residual anti-imperialist orientations, resulted in their decision to reject the pact and to fight its mentors. An evaluation of the best means to undermine the pact produced the second stage. It was soon realised that the most effective method was to appeal directly to the fermenting nationalist and anti-West sentiment by using Nasser's personality and his rhetorical ability, and by utilising an innovation rapidly spreading through the Middle East – the transistor radio. The activation of these policies produced the third and final stage – the dynamic involvement of Egypt in Arab politics and affairs, which itself became the vehicle for inculcating the Egyptians with this value.

Within the above context, we can see that unlike anti-imperialism the principle of Arabism was espoused by the decision-making elite primarily as a response to political and strategic factors which operated beyond the parameters of the elite's psychological and historical experiences. In other words, whereas 'anti-imperialism' constituted a major variable in the early stages of the development of the elite's personalities, thus influencing their later attitudinal and intellectual orientations, 'Arab nationalism' as a value was far removed from the crisis condition of the twenties and thirties and consequently played no significant part in shaping the perceptual patterns of the future elite. The Egyptian leadership was not averse to admitting this fact. During the unity talks of March–April 1963, Nasser told the Syrian delegation with surprising frankness: 'the national feeling in Syria has been clear for a long time. In Syria when an infant is born, he utters the words, Arab nationalism and Arab unity . . . Here in Egypt, this feeling emerged only in 1955 or 1956.'[28] Thus, while admitting the tenuous historical basis of Arabism in his own country, Nasser perceived Arabism to be a major ideological factor outside Egypt and particularly in the Arab east. However, as has been argued, he spared no effort to inculcate this value in the Egyptian people.

Within this context, three major functional roles of 'Arabism' can be discerned. In the first place, it constituted a motivating force for Egyptian policies. There can be no doubt that Arabism was an important factor (yet only one among many) in Egypt's nationalist drive in 1958, the so-called 'year of victory'. Moreover, in more specific terms, it can offer probable, yet necessarily partial, explanations for Egypt's involvement in the fiascos of Gaylani's unsuccessful uprising and Shawaf's abortive coup in Iraq. Whatever the motives for Egypt's involvement in these two attempts to topple Kassem, the important variable here is the elite's belief in the residual nationalism of the people of Iraq.[29] This perception may indeed have led to a fatal overestimation of the realistic chances of success these attempts actually had.

The second functional role of 'Arabism' was that of a limitation. The espousal of Arab nationalism by the Egyptian elite acted as a constraint on their freedom of manoeuvrability in choosing different policy alternatives and pursuing various courses of action. On the one hand, Egypt's pursuit of an Arab policy could have restricted her manoeuvrability in other spheres of possible Egyptian participation. For example, while gaining her undoubted support in the Arab world, the emphasis on Egypt's Arab character might have resulted in some loss of credibility in the African sphere. The Egyptians seem to have been aware of this possibility, since much intellectual and political energy was channelled into emphasising the alleged lack of contradiction between 'Arab nationalism' and 'African unity'.[30]

The second limitation occurred within intra-Arab regional politics and was, in a sense, system-generated as a result of Egypt's nationalist activities in the area. While her espousal of a nationalist posture and her leading role in Arab politics contributed to Egypt's strength and centrality in the regional system, they paradoxically also constituted clear systemic constraints on her freedom of manoeuvrability in intra-Arab politics. A major manifestation of this argument can be discerned from the political moves (confirmed by Syrians and Egyptians) which led to the formation of the United Arab Republic. While the Syrian delegation pressed for immediate union, Nasser expressed strong reservations and advocated a long period of transition. The Syrians, therefore, proceeded to limit Nasser's options by reminding him that many weeks had elapsed since the Syrian Chamber of Deputies passed a resolution demanding union with Egypt without any response from the Egyptian National Assembly. This, according to the Syrians, had affected the feelings of their people regarding Egypt's nationalist pretentions. Moreover, they insisted that as a result of the increasing 'Communist infiltration' and 'reactionary intrigues', it was incumbent upon Egypt as the leading nationalist force in the Arab world to 'save' Syria from disintegration and collapse.[31] Nasser, in a speech made after the secession, clearly illustrated the Syrian utilisation of this systemic constraint. He explained,

> I told them: Let us pave the way for unity because unity needs preparation, because unity is tantamount to troubles and problems, and because it is an inter-mixture. I said this but they told me: where are the aims you have advocated? where are the aims you have proclaimed? will you go back on those aims? ... will you leave Syria to be torn by strife? will you let Syria be lost? I said: Never, to me ... it is a sector of the Arab homeland in which I have laid my faith. I said: I agree to the unity ...[32]

Egypt's involvement in the Yemen could also be partially attributed to this systemic constraint. Nasser explained that Egypt intervened in the Yemen because 'we felt that we were doing a duty imposed upon us by the principles which we have upheld for the sake of the unity of the Arab struggle.'[33]

'Arabism' was also used to justify, and mobilise support for, Egyptian policies. Utilising the inherent attraction of 'Arab nationalism' and 'Arab unity' to the educated and modernising sectors of Arab societies, the Egyptian leaders consistently denigrated other Arab leaders, who, for various reasons, did not share Egyptian views and aspirations, as 'traitors who had turned against their Arabism and their homeland'.[34] As was the case with anti-imperialism, the utility of 'Arabism' as a tool for justification and mobilisation lay in its simplicity, directness and emotional appeal. It was, thus, an ideal vehicle for reducing complex explanations to one easily comprehensible and readily acceptable interpretation. For example, Nasser could justify his diversely motivated conflict with the Iraqi and Syrian Communists simply on the grounds that they had 'lost their Arabism, [and] cannot be treated as Arabs'.[35]

LEADERSHIP

An often quoted passage from Nasser's book *The Philosophy of the Revolution* closely reflects the Egyptian elite's perception of their leading role in the Arab world. Nasser wrote:

> History is . . . charged with great heroic roles which do not find actors to play them on the stage. I do not know why I always imagine that in this region in which we live, there is a role wandering aimlessly about seeking an actor to play it. I do not know why this role . . . should at last settle down, weary and worn out, on our frontiers beckoning us to move, to dress up for it and to perform it since there is nobody else who could do so . . . We and only we, are impelled by our environment and are capable of performing this role.[36]

As we have seen in the discussion in Chapter 7 relating to Egypt's capabilities, this view was supported not only by objective factors, but also generally by the perceptions of other Arab elites. It is important to make the crucial distinction that while the elites in the other Arab countries may have resented Egypt's 'hegemony', they, nevertheless, tended to perceive correctly the objective elements of her ascendancy in the Arab world.[37]

An interesting, but by no means definitive, method of ascertaining the perceived strength of various Arab states *vis-à-vis* each other, is to measure the number of times each state was approached by another state to affect some form of union between the two. Since these efforts were primarily, yet admittedly not entirely, motivated by domestic or intra-Arab considerations that directly related to the maintenance of the elites in power, the state which received the highest number of 'approaches' can be assumed to have been perceived as the most prestigious. In this method, a score of two will be awarded for every received approach, and in the case of a mutual initiative, each state will get a score of one. The period under consideration is 1955–70. With a score of fourteen going to Egypt as opposed to only three for her nearest rival (Table 10), this method tends to confirm Egypt's perceived centrality in the Arab world. The table includes every effort which was made to create some form of union between two Arab states in the given period. As such, those Arab states not included in the table took no part in any initiative for unity.

Table 10 further shows that all the efforts for unity with Egypt tended to come from the so-called 'progressive' Arab states. This is important, because it re-enforces the assumption that Egypt was perceived not only as the strongest and most populous state in the Arab world, but also, and more importantly perhaps, as the leader of a 'nationalist'

TABLE 10
Measurement of Egyptian Centrality in Arab Unity Efforts

To:	Egypt	Syria	Iraq	Jordan	Yemen
From:					
Egypt	—	—	—	—	—
Syria	4	—	1	—	—
	(58, 63)		(63)		
Iraq	6	1	—	1	—
	(58, 63, 64)	(63)		(58)	
Jordan	—	—	1	—	—
			(58)		
Yemen	4	2	—	—	—
	(58, 63)	(58)			
TOTAL	14	3	2	1	0

and 'revolutionary' struggle. This perception included the view of Nasser as the leader of this nationalist struggle and the person most able to articulate the aspirations of the majority of the educated classes.[38] Within this context, Nasser's own charismatic leadership became interlocked with that of Egypt. Consequently, it is common to find among analysts and commentators interchangeable references to Egypt's centrality in, and Nasser's leadership of, the 'Arab nationalist movement'.

Nasser himself reflected and reinforced this view. He saw no necessary contradiction between Egypt's centrality and his own leadership. On the contrary, in frequent references, he seemed to believe that each was the logical, almost inevitable derivation of the other.[39] Indeed, sometimes this perception led to grandiose statements which over-exaggerated his influence and power in the Arab world. For example, he once intimated that his views expressed 'the opinions of the millions living throughout the Arab nation'.[40] Whatever the real merits of such claims, the important point here is that they represented powerful perceptual currents which made Egypt's leadership of the Arab 'progressive movement' a declared principle of Egypt's foreign policy. The National Charter thus asserted:

> The great part of the responsibility for pioneer revolutionary action devolves upon the popular leadership of the UAR, since natural and historical factors have laid upon the UAR the responsibility of being the nucleus state in this endeavour to secure liberty, socialism and unity for the Arab nation.[41]

Given this elaboration of the perceptual patterns of the Egyptian decision-making elite, it is obvious that Egypt's claim to the leadership of 'pioneer revolutionary action' in the Arab world constituted a motivating force behind some Egyptian policies. For example, this can explain the immediate identification of the Egyptian regime with the Iraqi coup in July 1958, both in political and military terms, in the face of an uncertain and highly volatile international situation.[42] It can also offer a partial explanation for Egypt's seemingly hasty and spontaneous military intervention in the Yemen. However, as has already been pointed out, given the multiplicity of factors operating in one decisional situation, 'revolutionary leadership' cannot be posited as the sole motivation for these policies but merely as one probable explanation. It is worth noting here that Egypt's leadership of the revolutionary 'struggle' was also utilised as an easily identifiable and highly mobilisational justification for Egyptian policies. Heikal, for example, asserted that it was 'the unity of aim which . . . made Abd al-Nasir stand with al-Sallal and his popular revolution on the consideration that it was a free Yemen will'.[43]

A further function which 'leadership' served was in its contribution to the legitimacy of the Egyptian decision-making elite. In the first place, it appealed to people's vanity by positing Nasser's regime (and by association, the Egyptians as a whole) as the 'leaders' of the 'Arab world'. The resultant increase in support, coupled with Nasser's perceived international prestige, elevated his regime to a position of eminence beyond the reach of alternative political leaders. Heikal, as an important communicator of the regime's values, frequently reflected and reinforced the perception of Nasser 'as an answer to Arab aspirations';[44] 'as the personal commander of the Arab revolution';[45] 'as the leader of a struggle for destiny in historical circumstances';[46] and 'as an Arab symbol which transcends local boundaries'.[47] There can be no doubt that such views, which the Egyptian news media nourished and reinforced, contributed to the legitimacy of the regime by increasing its domestic mass support. For example, in attacking the Rogers peace initiative of spring 1970, Heikal explained that the USA considered 'Egyptian independence an obstacle to its objectives in the area in view of the significance of Nasser's leadership'.[48]

Finally, leadership acted as a limiting factor on the ultimate realisation of Egypt's goals and aspirations in the Arab world. The perception of Egypt as the 'nucleus state' indicates that the Egyptian elites considered Egypt to be the foundation upon which Arab unity would evolve. As such, they perceived the interests of the Arab world to be necessarily and by definition, synonymous with those of Egypt. Consequently, they expected Egyptian policies to be supported wholeheartedly by other states since these policies were supposed to advance the ultimate interests of the 'Arab nation'. This attitude, however, only served to alienate many Arabs from Egypt. Heikal candidly admits this. He suggests that in its role as the leading participant in the complex Arab interactions, Egypt contributed as much to the ultimate crisis of the 'Arab revolution' as to its initial strength and momentum. This, according to Heikal was inevitable as Egypt's opinions were bound to be reinforced by its full weight which tended to exert counter-productive pressures on other revolutionary forces.[49] Salah Bitar added credance to this assertion when he alleged that 'the rupture between Nasser and the Baath Ministers in 1959, was caused by a certain Egyptian hegemonic view of the Union.'[50]

Leadership as a principle, constituted a major force in the first half of the period of this study. However, the Syrian secession followed by the Yemeni war and the gradual deterioration of the Egyptian economy, contributed to a progressive decline in the perceived importance of this principle. The new configuration of forces in the Arab world which arose as a consequence of the 1967 Arab–Israeli war saw the final abandonment of this principle by the Egyptian leadership. In 1968, Nasser, almost with relief, confided that 'beforehand every-one was depending on us, as the war in the Yemen showed. Now everyone is depending upon himself and this is much healthier.'[51] One such group was the Palestinians, who were warmly congratulated by Nasser for 'championing their own cause by themselves and defending their rights by themselves'.[52] Accordingly, when in 1970 a foreign journalist tried to contrast Nasser's healthy political position after the June war with Napoleon's situation after Waterloo, Nasser quickly retorted that 'the Arab revolution, the Arab nation, and the Egyptian people are above any individual.'[53] With massive domestic problems, with Israeli troops sitting on the east bank of the canal, and with the economy dependent on foreign aid extended by the 'reactionary' states of Saudi Arabia, Kuwait and Libya ('reactionary' until the Qadhafi coup of September 1969), the cost of leading the 'Arab revolutionary movement', in the post-1967 period, had outstripped the benefits.

PRESTIGE

This is a concept which is difficult to measure or explain objectively. In the case of Egypt, it is certain that the almost fanatical emphasis on the prestige of Egypt as a value of Egyptian policy-making related directly to the obsession of Egypt's decision-makers with 'dignity'. This obviously dated back to their perception of, and sensitivity to, the ignominy of Egypt's long years under foreign domination. In this sense, Egypt's dignity and hence its prestige were both a psychological factor (a state of mind) which influenced the perceptual process of the Egyptian elites, and a declared political value (a principle) which served several functional roles. Nasser's evaluation of the crucial role of dignity in the determination of Egyptian policies is clearly ascertained when his speeches and interviews are analysed. In these, Egypt's dignity and prestige were consistently and repeatedly endorsed and emphasised. A typical example is his assertion that Egypt's 'new society' was built to become 'the stronghold of dignity and prestige for every individual'.[54]

As in the case of 'leadership', President Nasser's own prestige became inseparable from that of Egypt. As the perceived leader and spokesman of Egypt and the Arab world, he grew increasingly sensitive to criticisms levelled at him or at his regime. While he saw fit to indulge in the most bitter personal attacks on other leaders, any reciprocal criticisms usually engendered a wave of indignation on his part.[55] This seeming inability to accept criticism sometimes thrust him into petty and meaningless quarrels. He once bitterly attacked the BBC for showing an allegedly 'insulting' programme about the Yemen war.[56] In 1960, he banned the American magazine *Newsweek* from Egypt simply because 'it contained an article in which it was asserted that Mr. Dag Hammarskjoeld talked harshly to the President of the UAR.'[57]

'Prestige' as a principle of Egyptian foreign policy played an important role in motivating and justifying major policy decisions. It seems that the decision to nationalise the Suez Canal Company, for example, was not merely a response to the withdrawal of American aid, but also a function of the decision-makers' perception of the manner in which it was done, which was deemed 'insulting to the dignity of Egypt'.[58] Zakariya Mohyddin endorsed this view when he told the British ambassador, Humphrey Trevelyan, that 'it is not so much the withdrawal of the money which we mind. We can find other ways of financing the High Dam. It is the way in which it was done.'[59] Similarly, when in December 1964 the US ambassador related his government's 'concern' over Egypt's attitudes to the Yemen and the Congo and hinted that it might affect US food shipments to Egypt, Nasser in a major speech angrily replied:

> I am telling those who do not approve of our behaviour to go and drink the Mediterranean and if this is not enough, then they can try the Red Sea as well. We are not prepared to sell our independence for thirty, forty or fifty million pounds. Furthermore, we shall cut the tongue of anyone who dares to insult us . . . . We do not tolerate pressure and we do not accept humiliation. We are a people whose dignity cannot be sacrificed, not even for a thousand million pounds.[60]

Thus, the prestige of Egypt and the dignity of its people constituted a fundamental principle of Egyptian foreign policy-making. Given the prominence of 'dignity' as a value in Nasser's early psychological development, it is possible to give credance to statements made by him, such as: 'I shall fight for the prestige and dignity of Egypt to the last drop of my blood, because these are the principles with which I have grown.'[61] As such, it could be argued that of all the principles discussed in this section, prestige and dignity constituted the basic infrastructure upon which other values and principles rested.

CONCLUSION

Having outlined the major principles of Egyptian foreign policy and the functions they served, it must be noted that many analysts would argue that these so-called principles are little more than empty slogans that have no intrinsic motivational function. Rather, because of their popular appeal, they are primarily utilised by the leaders for the functions of justification, legitimisation and communication. For example, in this specific study, these analysts would argue that there is no reason to believe that anti-imperialism or Arabism actually motivated Egyptian policies, but that they were merely convenient tools for the regime to justify its policies, or legitimise its rule. From this criticism, two interrelated questions emerge. Firstly, can motivation be isolated from the other functions of principles, and secondly, is there such a thing as a 'principle of foreign policy'?

Regarding the first question, it seems to this writer that isolating the motivational role of a 'principle' ('slogan' in the critics terminology) from other functions carries an inherent contradiction. Thus, for example, the assertion that Nasser and his regime utilised anti-imperialism only to justify their policies or to mobilise support for them, presupposed *a priori* the prevalence of anti-imperialism as a *value* of the society. If this were not the case, then evidently anti-imperialism would not be able to engender the support or the justification desired by the political leaders. Now, since decision-makers are constrained by the need for support from society and since they are an intrinsic part of the environment, then clearly the value held by the society would act as a motivating force for the decision-makers' policies.

If, on the other hand, the critics are arguing that the authoritarian nature of Nasser's regime precluded the need for support from society, thus negating the preceding reasoning, then this would indicate that there was no original requisite for Nasser and his regime to resort to anti-imperialism for the purpose of justification and/or mobilisation. The remaining logical explanation for their utilisation of anti-imperialism, therefore, can only be that it constituted a *personal* principle of Nasser and his regime. Either way, therefore, the illogicality of isolating the motivational role of values and principles from their other functions is indicated.

Having established the motivational role of principles, the second question is easily answered. In an analogy with the study of 'political science', it has been observed that 'there is no more vicious theorist than the man who says, "I have no theory; I just let the facts speak for themselves".' This statement was used to refute the 'traditionalists' claim that theory had no utility for the study of politics. The theorists argue that 'some kind of theory (or conception or viewpoint) inherently determines which facts are selected, how they are ordered, and in what manner they are interpreted.'[63] The same argument can be used for our purposes. Since principles have a distinct motivational role, then they are an important variable of the cognitive process which determines the selection, organisation and interpretation of perceived facts, data and messages. Values and principles are, therefore, important determinants of foreign policy-making and should not be dismissed as mere slogans or empty rhetoric.

10　Political Objectives

Analysts of foreign policy behaviour have not always been rigorous in their usage of the terms 'values', 'goals' and 'objectives' in so far as these terms have tended to be used interchangeably. Needless to say, such failure to delineate the conceptual boundaries of these terms has sometimes proved a source of confusion.[1] In this study, therefore, a distinction between the three terms will be drawn according to a descending order in their level of abstraction. At the highest level, we shall place the 'values' of foreign policy, as these are primarily abstract and general concepts that represent the emotional and/or philosophical dispositions of the decision-makers. However, when these values are applied to a concrete world situation, they are translated into one or more aspirational and ultimate 'goals' of foreign policy. Yet given the existence of various environmental constraints on state action,[2] these goals are usually redefined in terms of lower-level, more realistic and less ambitious 'objectives' of foreign policy. The advantages of utilising this framework can be illustrated by adumbrating United States behaviour in the international system during the fifties and sixties. Not many would argue with the contention that the major value of American foreign policy in the fifties was 'anti-Communism'. When the abstract and philosophical tenets of 'anti-Communism' were applied to the world situation as it existed during that period, they shaped the aspirational goal of eliminating from the international system the forces of 'international Communism', particularly as they were manifested in the regimes of the Soviet Union and the People's Republic of China. However, the obvious environmental constraints on the achievement of such a goal necessitated its redefinition into a number of lower-level objectives (both in terms of abstraction and aspiration), including the minimum objective of 'detente' and the intermediate objective of 'containment'. Within this context, objectives can, therefore, be defined as compromise solutions to tensions existing between aspirations and perceived and actual environmental limitations.

The preceding analysis can be utilised for the understanding of Egypt's objectives in the Arab world. The application of Egypt's values to the Arab world gave rise to Egypt's aspirational goal in the area; namely, the goal of 'Arab unity'. Unity would constitute the means for asserting the strategic implications of anti-imperialism, the ideological manifestations of Arabism, the political orientations of leadership, and the psychological needs of prestige. However, the capacity to achieve this goal was intrinsically dependent upon actual and perceived environmental influences and limitations. This tension between the aspirational manifestations of 'Arab unity' and the constraints on its achievement within specific environmental situations, produced a series of definitions of 'Arab unity' by the Egyptian decision-making elite, each of which reflected a new definition of the situation. Thus, Nasser argued in August 1961 that 'Arab unity' 'extends on an Arab front which begins with Arab solidarity and ends with constitutional unity'.[3] This, to Nasser, did not mean an inevitable or a natural progression. Rather, within the context of environmental limitations, Nasser explained that 'solidarity is a step towards unity. It is the answer if we cannot achieve unity.'[4] Therefore, as far as the Egyptian leadership was concerned, 'unity' was not a static concept; rather it was seen as a continuum along which decision-makers were allowed some freedom of manoeuvrability to determine the most feasible policy alternative within a particular definition of the situation. The following analysis, therefore, will concentrate on the various political objectives which the Egyptian decision-makers pursued within the continuum of Arab unity in different phases of Egyptian policies. Three major objectives were discerned to be operative during Nasser's presidency: a maximum objective of 'comprehensive and constitutional unity', a minimum objective of 'Arab solidarity', and an intermediate objective of 'revolutionary change' (Fig. 5). Moreover, a historical analysis will be employed in order to elaborate the operational changes occurring in each phase which tended to influence the perceptions of the decision-makers and which, as a consequence, produced the various policy alternatives or 'objectives'. The application of such an analysis, however, means an inevitable overlap with sections of Part I of this study. Nevertheless, this has been kept to a minimum and it is considered an unavoidable price to pay if the continuing interaction between the operational and psychological environments is to be highlighted. The analysis will begin with the period that witnessed the utilisation by the Egyptian leadership of the maximum option along the continuum.

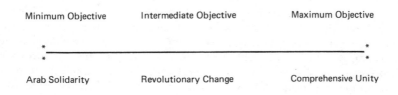

FIG. 5 The Continuum of Arab Unity

THE MAXIMUM OBJECTIVE: COMPREHENSIVE UNITY

The espousal of the maximum objective by the Egyptian leaders occurred in the period immediately preceding the creation of the United Arab Republic[5] and reached its highest intensity with the collapse of the pro-British Iraqi monarchy in July 1958. The enthusiasm with which the union was received in Syria and the neighbouring countries, as witnessed by the highly emotional welcome accorded to Nasser on his first visit to Syria and in the ramifications it had on the populations of Lebanon, Iraq and Jordan, enforced the Egyptian leadership's perception of the 'pro-unionist' sentiment in the countries of the Arab east.[6] Consequently, the Egyptian regime intensified its propaganda campaign against the allegedly 'anti-unionist' rulers of Iraq, Jordan and Lebanon,[7] in which direct emotional appeals were made to the 'Arabism' of the inhabitants of these countries.

The civil war in the Lebanon which led to Chamoun's downfall, followed by the collapse of the virulently anti-UAR Iraqi monarchy and its direct repercussions on the stability of the Jordanian monarchy, acted as positive reinforcements for prevalent Egyptian perceptions. On the one hand, these 'successes' reinforced the aspirations of the decision-making elite, thus making the 'ultimate goal' seem a 'realisable objective'. On the other hand, it minimised the perceived environmental limitations occurring at the operational level. In this, the leaders seemed to believe that the 'nationalist orientations' of the people, when reinforced and encouraged by Egyptian propaganda, would ultimately eliminate their 'anti-unity' rulers, thus opening the way for 'comprehensive Arab unity'.

This orientation appeared to reach its highest intensity during July and August 1958. This can be clearly ascertained from the speeches of the Egyptian leaders, from the news items and editorials of the Egyptian press, and from the radio broadcasts of Cairo and Damascus. Apart from the constant reiteration of the words 'Arab unity' and 'Arab nationalism' in the speeches and writings of the Egyptian elites,[8] an intensive campaign was directed at the countries of the 'Fertile Crescent' deemed susceptible to the cause of 'Arab unity'. In the case of Iraq, Egyptian news media concentrated its efforts on eulogising, and publicising the endeavours of the outspoken leader of the 'unity now' forces, Colonel Abd al-Salam Aref, at the expense of his more reticent superior, Brigadier Abd al-Karim Kassem.[9] As far as Jordan was concerned, the months of August and September witnessed the most persistent and intensive radio campaign against the rule of King Hussein, which was directed at the 'people' and 'soldiers' of Jordan.[10] Moreover, there is evidence to suggest that the Egyptian efforts were not limited to the propaganda instrument alone. Twenty-three Jordanians were arrested on the night of 26–7 July on charges of gun-running from Syria. In the trial that followed, they allegedly admitted that 'they were trained in the use of arms and explosives in Syria in order to carry out an armed insurrection in Jordan.'[11]

It is important, however, to note that the Egyptian decision-makers have never admitted their espousal of this objective. On the contrary, they have persistently and categorically denied any intention on their part to pursue the objective of 'comprehensive unity'.[12] In their defence, it could be argued that Egyptian activities during this period did not radically differ from the general post-1955 Egyptian activist policies in the Arab world. Consequently, in this view, Egypt's propaganda campaign did not necessarily prove Egyptian espousal of the maximum objective; rather it merely reflected a natural Egyptian preference for pro-UAR Arab leaders who would be more sympathetic to Egypt's ideological and political orientations.

This line of argument, however, disregards two essential points. Firstly, the perceptual pattern of the Egyptian decision-making elite in 1958, as ascertained from their speeches, interviews and writings, shows an emphasis on 'Arab unity' which was clearly absent from the earlier phase. Secondly, applying the concepts of 'precedents' and 'learning process'[13] to Nasser's experience in the talks which led to the formation of the UAR, it is clear that the successful Syrian tactics (limiting Nasser's options by appealing to Egypt's, and his, 'leading nationalist role' in the Arab world) could not have left him unaware that the same tactics could be utilised again by other nationalist leaders to 'impose' unity on Egypt. The fact that Nasser not only persisted with, but also increased, his encouragement of nationalist and unionist elements in the post-UAR period suggests that, at the very least, he was not averse to the idea of comprehensive unity.[14] It seems reasonable, therefore, to conclude that the quest for comprehensive unity by the Egyptian decision-makers during the period of February to September 1958 was implicit in their policies and attitudes.

However, by the end of September, a shift in Egyptian policy from comprehensive unity to Arab solidarity occurred. This was basically a response to the rapid deterioration of the earlier held expectations and hopes placed in Iraq's and Jordan's eventual entry into the UAR. In Iraq, a power struggle between the leaders of the coup facilitated the ascendancy of General Kassem, who was backed mainly by 'Iraq first' and Communist elements over Colonel Aref and his unionist groups. In Jordan, the almost incredible powers of survival of the King shattered the earlier hopes for a nationalist and unionist revival. Consequently, as the emphasis on comprehensive unity became more ill-attuned to such developments, the shift from the maximum to the minimum objective occurred. The first indication of this change in Egypt's policy appeared in an interview given to the Indian journalist Karanjia by Nasser at the end of September. In the interview, Nasser insisted that what interested him above everything else was 'Arab solidarity which constituted the firm basis upon which Arab nationalism could be built'.[15] According to Nasser, 'solidarity' would make 'the Arab states stronger through their co-operation in the economic, military and cultural fields, and in the sphere of foreign policy'.[16]

THE MINIMUM OBJECTIVE: ARAB SOLIDARITY (PHASE ONE)

Arab solidarity as an objective of Egyptian foreign policy is located at the minimum end of the continuum of 'Arab unity'. While advocating co-operation and unified action among the various Arab countries, solidarity lacked the most vital aspect of comprehensive unity – it did not insist on the constitutional unification of the Arab states. It was thus primarily based on the mutual and universal respect for the sovereignty of all Arab states. Consequently, other Arab leaders were more receptive to the premises of this objective, as it entailed minimum incursion on their own power. In fact, it tended to reinforce rather than diminish their political positions. A leader's public adherence to the 'nationalist' policy of solidarity with the UAR invariably increased his domestic support while rarely constituting a threat to his own authority.[17] Moreover, as diplomacy was the traditional instrument utilised for the implementation of the minimum objective, it was believed that this would decrease the general tension in the area and consequently the national ferment of the indigenous populations would generally subside.

The operational effects of 'Arab solidarity' resulted in the gradual normalisation of intra-Arab relations. As the propaganda campaigns against Jordan and Saudi Arabia subsided better relations followed. In mid-July 1959, the borders between Syria and Jordan were reopened, and this was followed by the resumption of diplomatic relations, severed since July 1958. Although relations were temporarily strained in the wake of the assassination of Jordan's Prime Minister Huzzah al-Majali, the conciliatory environment engendered by 'Arab solidarity' soon facilitated a rapproachement between the two countries. In an exchange of letters in February 1961, the two leaders, echoing the basic tenets of 'Arab solidarity', agreed to view their differences with 'a spirit of fraternal forgiveness and deep understanding of the motives each of [them held] for his own attitude'.[18] Relations with Saudi Arabia followed a similar pattern. In September 1959, King Saud arrived in Cairo for a state visit during which it was agreed that the two countries should renew 'unrestricted and absolute' co-operation. This was, indeed, followed by two years of tranquil, diplomacy-oriented interaction between the two states. Even in Iraq, as the Communist influence began to decline by mid-1960, the UAR leaders endeavoured to curtail tensions by considerably decreasing the intensity of their propaganda campaigns against, and the level of subversive activity in, Iraq. Thus in January 1961, the UAR Foreign Minister, Mahmoud

Fawzi, attended the Arab foreign ministers conference in Baghdad and held talks with General Kassem. As a result, in April, Iraq reopened her borders with Syria which had been closed since 1959. In fact, the month of April witnessed extensive diplomatic interaction amongst the Arab states. There were meetings of the Arab economic council, the Arab social affairs ministers and the Arab chiefs of staff.

The actual and perceived environmental constraints which contributed to the change from the maximum to the minimum objectives were not exclusively limited to external forces, but were also due to factors emanating purely from the domestic environment and acting independently of the inter-Arab milieu. Nasser's increasing problems in Syria meant an inevitable decrease in resource allocation (in time, energy and materials) to the foreign sector. This necessitated the adoption of a less activist (i.e. more conciliatory) policy in the Arab world which would demand minimal resource allocation, hence the attractions of Arab solidarity. Nevertheless, as we have seen, domestic problems in Syria continued to mount until the Syrian army staged a military coup in September 1961 and unilaterally withdrew Syria from the union.

As has already been discussed,[19] Egypt perceived the secession as a 'reactionary' and an 'imperialist' plot. It precipitated a bitter disillusionment with the maximum objective and probably ushered the final abandonment by the Egyptian decision-makers of comprehensive unity as a viable policy objective. This is evident from Nasser's performance in the unity talks with Syria and Iraq in March and April 1963, in which he seemed to treat these talks more as a forum for scoring debating points and less as a constructive prelude for actual unity. Moreover, when Brigadier Sallal of the Yemen intimated his wish for the re-establishment of the earlier federation between the UAR and the Yemen, Nasser politely yet firmly rejected any idea for a new federation.[20] The nationalist and pro-unionist government of Iraq received the same response from the Egyptian leadership in 1965. Nasser told the Iraqis: 'we need at least five years to study the ways of unity . . . and I am against any sudden unity.'[21]

However, the immediate result of the Syrian secession lay in its effect on the psychological environment of the Egyptian decision-making elite. They became convinced that the secession was the direct result of the new drive by the reactionary elements in the area whose forces had been considerably strengthened during the calm environment of the preceding two years.[22] In other words, 'Arab solidarity', which was instrumental in bringing about this calm environment, was perceived to be partly responsible for the secession. The Egyptian decision-makers, therefore, embarked on redefining their objectives in the Arab world within a significantly more activist and intransigent framework.

THE INTERMEDIATE OBJECTIVE: REVOLUTIONARY CHANGE (PHASE ONE)
The central thesis upon which this post-secession objective rested was
enunciated by Heikal at the end of 1961. Surveying the intra-Arab
situation and inter-Arab relations in the light of the Syrian secession,
Heikal adumbrated the theory of Egypt's duality of roles – that of a
state and of a revolution. He wrote:

> We should distinguish between two things: Egypt as a state and as a
> revolution . . . If as a state, Egypt recognizes boundaries in its
> dealings with governments, Egypt as a revolution should never
> hesitate or halt before these boundaries but should carry its message
> beyond the borders in order to initiate its revolutionary mission for
> a unitary Arab future . . . We should do our best to co-operate with
> governments, but we should refrain from extending such co-opera-
> tion if it were to affect the people's movements. This policy must be
> pursued whatever the consequences or the difficulties may be.[23]

It is obvious that while reflecting a more intransigent orientation on
the part of the Egyptian decision-making elite, the thesis of Egypt's
duality of roles contained a basic conceptual ambiguity. This related
to the inherent paradox of assigning two contradictory functions to
one unit of action. In other words, Government A will find it difficult
to carry proper diplomatic interaction with Government B if it perceives the latter to be supporting dissident elements within its borders.
This basic dichotomy between the two functions characterised many
of the official statements and documents of the period. For example,
the contradiction is evident in the UAR Charter. On the one hand, it
declared that 'unity cannot be nor should it be imposed . . . [since]
coercion of any kind is contrary to unity.'[24] Later on, however, it
asserted:

> The United Arab Republic, firmly convinced that she is an integral
> part of the Arab Nation, must propagate her call for unity and the
> principles it embodies, so that it would be at the disposal of every
> Arab citizen, without hesitating for one minute before the outworn
> argument that this would be considered an interference in the affairs
> of others.[25]

In their efforts to overcome this basic conceptual ambiguity, the
Egyptian elite insisted that in cases of incompatability, the primacy of
revolutionary activity over traditional state relations must be clearly
and unequivocally asserted.[26] As such, the objective of 'revolutionary
change' can be placed in the continuum of 'Arab unity' somewhere
between the minimum end of 'Arab solidarity' and the maximum
extreme of 'comprehensive unity'. While falling short of calling for
actual constitutional and organic unity, nevertheless, unlike the static
posture necessitated by 'Arab solidarity', it advocated a 'revolutionary'

activist policy in order to achieve a 'unitary Arab future'. Thus, by positing themselves as the guardians of the 'revolutionary struggle' in the area, the Egyptian leaders bestowed upon themselves the right to try and induce structural changes in the 'reactionary' countries. This could be achieved either through direct (though not necessarily physical) intervention or by the support accorded to indigenous revolutionary forces. Consequently, the thesis of the duality of roles, which emerged as a response to an alleged reactionary threat, provided the Egyptian elite with the intellectual justification for a policy of 'revolutionary' intervention which overrode conventional diplomatic regard for state sovereignty.

Inter-Arab relations during the period which followed the secession clearly illustrate Egypt's operationalisation of its objective. Diplomatic relations with Jordan were severed immediately after Jordan's recognition of the new Syrian regime, and after King Saud was accused of complicity in the secession, Egypt directed a concerted and vicious propaganda campaign against Jordan and Saudi Arabia. The same treatment was extended to the new 'reactionary' Syrian government and to the 'medieval' Imam of the Yemen. In fact, in its efforts to induce the desired structural changes in these countries, Egypt was directing its propaganda campaigns against almost every state in the Arab world. Furthermore, Egypt's efforts were not confined to the propaganda instrument alone. In August 1962, the Egyptian military attaché in Lebanon defected to Syria and supplied the authorities with a long list of Egyptian agents operating there. Moreover, Egypt's massive military intervention in the Yemen was, at the very least, a partial manifestation of the objective of 'revolutionary change'.[27]

It is important to note here that within the context of 'Arab unity' as a continuum, the espousal of the intermediate objective offered the Egyptian elites several inherent advantages. Foremost among these was its implication that future unity was primarily dependent on the compatability of the social systems of the states involved. By making the evaluation of this compatability a function of Egyptian perceptions, it made 'unity' wholly reliant on Egypt's own needs and aspirations. Unlike the circumstances which led to the formation of the UAR, the Egyptian leadership would no longer have its options on unity so limited as to be almost entirely dependent on external forces. Moreover, the ambiguity of Egypt's duality of roles was itself effectively utilised in explaining some paradoxical and sometimes diplomatically embarrassing policy decisions. A clear example of this occurred when Egypt unilaterally decided to publish the minutes of the secret talks on unity in March–April 1963. The Egyptian leaders admitted that the publication amounted to a breach of diplomatic practice, but excused it on the grounds that the unity talks 'were not talks among governments but among Arab revolutionary forces representing popular leaderships . . . Therefore, the principle of diplomatic secrecy was inoperative in this case.'[28] It is interesting to note that as late as 1966, the 'duality of roles' was being used to explain general Egyptian policy inconsistencies.[29]

'Revolutionary change' constituted the main policy objective of the Egyptian decision-making elite in the Arab world during this period, which spanned over two years. In this, the protracted inter-Arab conflict, labelled by some 'the Arab cold war', probably reached its most intensive and acrimonious level. Yet by the end of 1963, two new environmental limitations had to be considered by the Egyptian decision-makers: the Yemen war, which was proving to be an almost ruinous burden on Egypt's weak economy, and Israel's diversion of the head-waters of the river Jordan.[30] The evaluation of the new 'situation' necessitated a redefinition of 'Arab unity' which compelled the Egyptian decision-makers to revert again to 'Arab solidarity' as the primary objective of Egyptian foreign policy.

THE MINIMUM OBJECTIVE: ARAB SOLIDARITY (PHASE TWO)
Ironically, the intellectual tenets of the new phase of 'Arab solidarity' had its roots in the militant period which immediately preceded it. During the phase of 'revolutionary change', Egyptian decision-makers had repeatedly rejected the allegation that Egypt's revolutionary activism had divided and weakened the Arab ranks, by insisting that the unity of 'aim' was more important than, and had to precede, the unity of 'ranks'.[31] They argued that subordinating the ideological imperative (i.e. socialist revolutionary change in the 'reactionary' Arab states) to political considerations would, in the long run, be essentially counter-productive, as it would compromise the revolutionary forces in these states and lead to the strengthening of the 'forces of reaction' as evident in the earlier phase of 'Arab solidarity'.

Drawing from this intellectual base, the Egyptian leaders explained Egypt's deradicalisation of her Arab policy after 1963 by arguing that Israel's diversion of the river Jordan constituted a new environmental factor which had radically changed the regional situation and which consequently had to be considered in the assessment of the intra-Arab balance of forces. It thus transpired that in response to the newly created environmental constraints, the unity of 'effort' among the Arab governments was allowed to take precedence over the unity of 'aim'. Within this context, Nasser, in February 1965, explained the new phase in these terms: 'Everything depends on the unity of the Arabs, and I don't mean the constitutional unity whose realization is difficult at the present time. I am referring to the unity of effort which precedes the unity of purpose.'[32] It is obvious that while not overtly inclined to advertise the fact, the Egyptian decision-makers did take into consideration the intrusion of a further environmental constraint which contributed to the deradicalisation of Egypt's regional policy, namely the ruinous cost of the Yemeni war.

During this phase, the Arab governments exhibited far greater determination, and showed much more genuine concern, to pursue the tenets of 'Arab solidarity' than the earlier pre-secession period. Indeed, 1964 and 1965 were probably the most harmonious years in the post-Baghdad Pact period of Arab inter-state relations. The first Arab summit of January 1964 led to the establishment of the 'Arab Military Unified Command', and the second summit held in Alexandria in September 1964 resulted in the creation of the PLO. In the interim period, the relations between Egypt and Jordan improved to such an extent that King Hussein was persuaded to recognise the republican regime in the Yemen at the expense of the royalists. Moreover, Nasser signed with President Aref of Iraq an accord creating a joint presidential council and a unified military command. More importantly, diplomatic relations with Saudi Arabia were resumed in March 1964, and an agreement over the Yemen reached in September.[33] When this accord was sabotaged by the two Yemeni factions, Nasser and Faisal tried again in August 1965 to create the conditions necessary for a lasting peace in the Yemen. However, the conflicting Yemeni parties succeeded yet again in stifling these efforts, and no substantive agreement was reached.

The breakdown of the peace talks in the Yemen was almost immediately followed by Faisal's advocacy of an Islamic summit, a proposal which was treated with the utmost suspicion by the Egyptian decision-makers, who perceived it within the confines of their anti-imperialist learning experiences. Responding to Faisal, therefore, Nasser declared that the Egyptians were against the 'Islamic Pact' just as they were against 'The Baghdad Pact and the Eisenhower Doctrine'.[34] Consequently, as the Egyptian leaders became progressively alienated from the conservative Arab governments, they found themselves moving closer to the new, neo-Marxist and virulently 'anti-reactionary' Syrian regime. Thus by mid 1966, the Arab world had become yet again ideologically polarised between the 'progressives' and the 'reactionaries', and consequently, Arab solidarity had to give way for a new phase of 'revolutionary change'.

THE INTERMEDIATE OBJECTIVE: REVOLUTIONARY CHANGE (PHASE TWO)
This revision to militancy occurred as a result of a perceptual process not very different from that which had caused the earlier period of revolutionary change. Faisal's advocacy of an Islamic conference, followed by his tour of the conservative Middle Eastern states of Iran, Jordan, Morocco and Turkey, were equated in Egyptian minds with the previous activities of Jordan and Saudi Arabia during and after the Syrian secession. In this, Faisal's calls for Islamic unity were interpreted

by the Egyptian leaders as a renewed offensive by the reactionary
forces, whose strength had increased as a result of the tranquility of the
preceding two years.[35] This perception acquired positive reinforcement
when President Nkrumah of Ghana and President Sukarno of Indonesia, two important leaders of the non-aligned movement, were deposed and replaced with pro-Western, right-wing regimes. Thus, the
perceived anti-progressive (and consequently, anti-Egyptian) activities
in the Middle East were placed within the wider international context
of 'an imperialist and reactionary onslaught against the national
revolutions in Asia, Africa and Latin America'.[36] Therefore, rather
than allow the 'reactionary' forces to repeat their Syrian success of
September 1961, the Egyptian decision-makers decided to pre-empt
this perceived possibility by themselves going on the offensive against
the conservative regimes. As such, the effort to induce structural
changes in the 'reactionary' states became, once again, the primary
objective of the Egyptian leadership, and as far as the summit conferences were concerned, these had 'been proved false and void, and
[had to] be replaced by the unity of the Arab revolutionary forces'.[37]
Egypt had again moved up the continuum of Arab unity from the
minimum to the intermediate objective.

During the period of Egypt's adherence to the objective of revolutionary change, the political interactions in the Arab world mirrored
the ideological polarity between the 'radical' camp spearheaded by
Egypt and Syria, and the '*status quo*' camp led by Saudi Arabia and
Jordan. Consequently, diplomatic interactions between the two
opposing camps came to a halt and propaganda warfare was intensified.
As a result, the hitherto tranquil and co-operative intra-Arab environment was suddenly pervaded by intense and acrimonious inter-state
hostility that was to characterise the Arab political situation until the
Arab–Israeli war of June 1967.

THE MINIMUM OBJECTIVE: ARAB SOLIDARITY (PHASE THREE)
Within the context of the intra-Arab political situation, the June war
had a profound impact not only on the actual configuration of forces
in the Arab world, but also on the theoretical assumptions which under-
lay previous inter-Arab behaviour. One such assumption was Egypt's
leadership of the Arab 'progressive' forces which required intensive
Egyptian revolutionary activism. The changing circumstances of the
post-1967 period necessitated a critical evaluation by the decision-
makers of Egypt's role in the Arab world. Three factors were immediately discernable. In the first place, because of the presence of
Israeli soldiers on Egyptian soil, Egypt's primary foreign policy preoccupation centred on the 'eradication of Israeli aggression'. Secondly,
the war-induced economic problems severely limited Egypt's capabilities and imposed on Nasser a primarily Egyptian rather than an Arab

orientation. Finally, Egypt's ensuing economic dependence on the 'reactionary' states[38] naturally vitiated the possibility of Nasser or Egypt leading the 'anti-reactionary' crusade. These factors meant that Egypt was obliged to adopt a friendly orientation towards the other Arab states regardless of ideological considerations. Accordingly, in a tone which was in stark contrast to the militancy of the earlier period, Nasser contended that the mobilisation of 'the Arab forces [required] massive efforts at the level of Arab governments as well as the level of the masses.'[39] Thus, a combination of external and domestic constraints compelled Egypt to discard the intermediate objective and to pursue the objective of 'Arab solidarity'.

Unlike the other periods, the post-1967 phase of Arab solidarity proved to be less fragile and more enduring. Egypt's relations with the Arab states including its traditional 'reactionary' enemies were normalised to such an extent, that Heikal, moved by the irony of the situation, reminded his readers that Saudi Arabia, which had assiduously tried to exhaust Egypt's resources during the Yemeni war, was contributing five years later to Egypt's economic solvency.[40] Indeed, Egypt's conciliatory orientation became such that it was repeatedly called upon to intervene diplomatically between conflicting parties in the Arab world. Thus, for example, it was Egypt who mediated between the Lebanese government and the Palestinian guerrillas in the spring of 1969. A more crucial role was the one played by President Nasser in bringing together the two opposing parties in the Jordanian civil war of September 1970. While this act was probably the crowning achievement of Nasser's pursuit of the objective of 'Arab solidarity', it also proved to be the last one before his death. However, President Nasser's demise from the Arab political scene did not affect the relatively enduring nature of Arab solidarity in the post-1967 period. Indeed, the Arab policy of President Sadat clearly indicates the present primacy of the minimum objective.

A CONCEPTUAL OVERVIEW

A feature of the preceding analysis has been the vital yet implicit role of 'feedback' in the formulation of Egypt's various objectives towards the Arab world. The analysis has shown that these objectives were primarily a perceptual response by the Egyptian decision-makers to specific changes in the operational environment. It was these changes that provided the 'feedback' effects which, along with other independent environmental stimuli, constituted the inputs into the foreign policy system discussed in Chapter 6.

This process of interaction between the operational and psychological environments can be illustrated by analysing the changes in the various policy objectives adopted by Egypt towards the Arab world. Thus, for example, the decision in late 1958 to adopt the objective of Arab solidarity at the expense of comprehensive unity was a perceptual response on the part of the Egyptian decision-makers to specific feed-back effects and environmental inputs in the form of the ascendency in Iraq of the Communist forces over the 'Arab nationalists', Hussein's unexpected survival in Jordan, and the numerous domestic difficulties encountered in Syria. Intrinsic in this response were certain values held by the Egyptian elites, such as their zeal to preserve Egyptian prestige, and their adherence, whenever possible, to the principle of 'non-inter-ference'. The resulting response embodied in the adoption of Arab solidarity contributed to the advent of relatively calm inter-Arab relations. A theoretical schema can thus be constructed: a perceptual interaction between values and images occurs when a decision-maker perceives an objective change in the operational environment. This produces certain responses from the decision-maker which affects a further change in the operational environment (see Fig. 6).

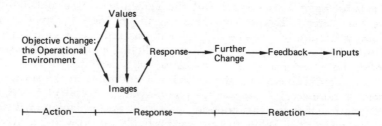

FIG. 6 The Process of Interaction between the Operational and Psychological Environments

The schema can be similarly utilised to explain the adoption of the objective of revolutionary change which occurred primarily as a response to the Syrian secession (change in the operational environ-ment). The secession was perceived by Nasser as a plot by his 'reac-tionary' adversaries in the area whose forces had been consolidated through Egypt's lack of activism during the phase of Arab solidarity (image). This was reinforced by Nasser's innate suspicion of, and his ideological antipathy to, 'reaction' and 'imperialism' (value). The per-ceptual interaction of these two variables produced the activist phase of the objective of revolutionary change (response), which in turn contributed to a period of intense ideological and political enmity in the Arab world, with the Yemeni war as its central manifestation (further change in the operational environment): This analytical process could be similarly applied to the other phases of Egypt's Arab policy.

While this ability to highlight the adaptive capacity of the foreign policy system is a feature of the model used in this study, it must, nevertheless, be pointed out that such a treatment by no means provides the definitive answer to the 'feedback' problem in foreign policy analysis. Two major shortcomings remain. In the first place, the development treatment of a state's foreign policy realignments over time confines the applicability of the model to specific cases of interaction where a target state or a group of states can be identified. In other words, when the object of the study is an analysis of a state's behaviour in the international system as a whole, the applicability of the formula 'action–response–reaction' is impaired due to the absence of a central focus. Secondly, there can be no doubt that the introduction of the dynamic element to the model, while contributing to a fuller explanation of a state's foreign policy, requires further analytical development. A more rigorous application of the formula 'action–response–reaction' would need to isolate the impact of each feedback upon the various components of the decision-making process, and the corresponding responses of these components. The analyst would then be able to determine the way in which these 'micro-responses' are aggregated to produce a 'macro-response' from the foreign policy system as a whole. Yet this problem at present seems insurmountable; for while it has been successfully solved in analysing one foreign policy decision at a time,[41] it will almost certainly prove a great obstacle to a general analysis of a state's foreign policy. At this stage in the intellectual development of foreign policy analysis as a rigorous sub-discipline of the social sciences, scholars in the field possess neither the methodological dexterity, nor the sophisticated tools of analysis, necessary to overcome the present impasse. It is perhaps in the direction of the two problems cited above that future research should be channelled if a comprehensive and coherent theory of foreign policy behaviour is to be successfully developed.

11 Economic Objectives

Some analysts contend that in conjunction with Egypt's political objectives for Arab unity ran mainly covert, but sometimes explicit, economic objectives. These analysts argue that the economic objectives were motivated by Egypt's need to create new markets for her semi-finished and finished industrial goods, and to obtain fresh sources of raw materials for her industry.[1] This interpretation rests on what is held to be an Egyptian quest for Arab economic unity on a model similar to the European Common Market, from which Egypt, as the leading industrial power in the area, would derive immense benefits.[2] Professor Charles Issawi, a leading expert on Middle East economics, endorses this view by arguing that in return for selling her goods Egypt could draw on 'oil and foreign exchange from the Persian Gulf and Libya, grains and livestock from Iraq, Syria and Sudan, and various kinds of fruits and vegetables from Lebanon and Jordan'.[3]

How much of the impetus for Arab unity was engendered by Egypt's desire to maximise her economic wealth is difficult to ascertain precisely or objectively. There does, indeed, seem to have been a tendency on behalf of the Egyptian policy-making elite to regard the non-industrial countries of the Middle East and Africa as convenient potential outlets for Egyptian manufactured goods. It was officially stated in the early sixties that it was 'only through export that the UAR industrialization drive could achieve its objectives once a state of self-sufficiency has been attained'.[4] Professor Majid Khadduri relates an interesting instance which seems to endorse this view. In the wake of the 1958 Iraqi coup, Egyptian economic experts suggested to their Iraqi counterparts that in any future union with the UAR, the Iraqis should concentrate on agricultural development, since Egypt's industrial capacity was sufficient for both countries. However, when the Iraqi experts intimated that their planning placed a high priority on industrialisation, the Egyptians allegedly retorted that 'the adoption of an agricultural policy by Iraq would be the price for Arab unity'.[5]

Such attitude on the part of some of the Egyptian elites, even though they could be held to represent a rational assessment of the economic situation of the two countries, could only contribute to Arab suspicions of Egyptian hegemonic aspirations. Thus, primarily as a result of such Arab perceptions, all Egyptian efforts during the fifties to create an Arab Common Market which, according to the Egyptians, would

154

resist Western 'exploitation' by keeping 'Arab wealth' in 'Arab hands',[6] consistently failed. Not until June 6, 1962 was Egypt able to persuade other Arab countries, namely Morocco, Kuwait, Syria and Jordan, to enter into an economic unity agreement.[7] A year later, Iraq and Yemen added their signatures to the agreement but, because of ideological and political differences, Lebanon and Saudi Arabia did not participate in the agreement.[8] The agreement stipulated that the contracting parties should make their countries a single customs entity; that they should unify their tariff laws and import and export policies and legislation; and that they should regulate their economic policies and tax and social security systems. To implement these proposed measures, the member countries provided for the establishment of an Arab Economic Unity Council (AEUC) in Cairo, whose membership was to be composed of delegates from all member countries.

Theoretically, the provisions of the agreement certainly favoured a country like Egypt whose industrial base was much broader than the other Arab states. The advantages to Egypt were further enhanced in August 1964 when the AEUC adopted a resolution providing for the removal by the end of 1973 of all customs duties and other trade restrictions among member countries. However, the actual operational results of these hopeful prospects proved to be much less spectacular. Thus, for example, not only did the volume of Egypt's exports to Jordan and Syria during 1965 and 1966 prove to be extremely discouraging, but the nature of these exports tended to be mainly non-industrial, agricultural products such as rice, salt and potatoes. Only Egyptian–Iraqi trade showed any signs of improvement during this period. Yet this was due to the cordial political relations between the two countries, rather than to their adherence to the provisions of the agreement.[9] Indeed, by 1967, it had become apparent that, given the political realities, the Egyptian propagated idea of an Arab Common Market was going to be very difficult to achieve. Like the search for political unity, the quest for some form of economic union was, in the final analysis, dependent on the perceived environmental limitations. In this case, the suspicion of Egyptian domination was one such constraint.

Oil is a clear example of mutual suspicions existent amongst the Arab countries. The Egyptian elite have always been aware of oil as a valuable commodity and as an effective economic weapon. One newspaper article bluntly stated that a primary advantage of Arab unity was that the benefits of 'Arab oil' would no longer be monopolised by a handful of states but would be shared by 'all Arabs'.[10] It must, therefore, have been welcoming to Egyptian ears to hear leaders such as Abd al-Salam Aref of Iraq make the occasional promise to share his country's oil wealth with other Arab countries.[11] However, all efforts to plan and rationalise oil consumption and production within a general framework of economic development for all the Arab countries failed.

The most important of these efforts was the first Arab Oil Conference held in Cairo in 1959, which called on every Arab oil-producing government and oil company to contribute 5 per cent of its annual profits to a central financial organisation which would divert the money into development projects in various Arab countries. However, because of suspicions relating to Egypt's motives,[12] this proposal was never implemented. This failure constituted a constraint on further attempts to utilise oil for general economic development or as a weapon against the perceived 'imperialists' and the 'supporters of Israel'.[13]

Although the Egyptian decision-makers have, on occasions, indignantly denied coveting Arab oil or considering the Arab states as mere markets for Egypt's industrial output,[14] it is, nevertheless, doubtful that they were unaware of the benefits Egypt could have derived from some form of economic as well as political union. Indeed, the preceding discussion shows a clear Egyptian perception of these benefits. However, such a conclusion must remain in the realm of conjecture, since an analysis of the objective data affords little support for the above assumption. Tables 11 and 12 do not indicate the existence of a substantial trade movement between Egypt and the Arab countries between 1958 and 1970.[15] While as a result of two decades of rapid industrialisation, the figure for Egypt's exports to the Arab world in 1970 shows a considerable increase over the 1958 level,[16] nevertheless this figure represented less than one-third of Egypt's exports to the Eastern bloc in 1970.[17] It seems, therefore, that although the Egyptian decision-making elite may have had a defined economic objective in the Arab Middle East, there is no evidence that such an objective was actively pursued or put into operation. It seems that apart from the efforts to establish an Arab Common Market, the Egyptian leaders confined their interest in achieving their objective to spasmodic newspaper editorials, press interviews and speeches. For example, the period between 1958 and 1967 witnessed very little aid from the rich oil countries deemed vulnerable to 'Nasserism'. Professor Malcom Kerr, in an article, devotes much space to emphasise Egyptian desire and ability to exercise political leverage on the Arab oil countries in order to induce these states to contribute part of their vast wealth to Egypt. Yet Kerr admits that by the end of 1965, the total Kuwaiti (probably the most 'vulnerable' state to 'Nasserism') financial assistance to Egypt amounted to a 'very modest $80.5 million'.[18] It is probably indicative of the Arab political situation that the $230 million aid extended to Egypt after the June war by the oil countries occurred at a time when Egypt no longer possessed the capability or motivation to pursue an activist policy in the Arab world.

Probably the best operational test of Egypt's economic objectives in the Arab world can be found in Egypt's involvement in Syria during the union. The consensus of opinion prevalent after the secession held

TABLE 11
Total Egyptian Trade with the Arab League Countries
(in $ million)

	1958 Imports	1958 Exports	1963 Imports	1963 Exports	1967 Imports	1967 Exports	1970 Imports	1970 Exports
Arab east[a]	20.7	15.5	58.3	25.9	68.5	50.0	76.4	96.5
Maghreb[b]	3.0	2.5	1.8	6.7	3.5	6.5	3.9	10.3
Sudan	2.7	5.5	6.2	2.8	6.6	3.5	17.2	16.8
Total Arab trade	26.4	23.5	66.3	35.4	78.6	60.0	97.5	123.6
Total of all Egyptian trade	684.6	459.9	1143.3	650.8	988.3	606.4	786.6	761.7
% of Arab trade	3.8	5.1	5.8	5.4	7.9	9.9	12.4	16.2

[a] Iraq, Jordan, Kuwait, Lebanon, Saudi Arabia, Syria, Yemen.
[b] Algeria, Libya, Morocco, Tunisia.
Source: Figures compiled from various editions of United Nations, *Yearbook of International Trade Statistics, 19* , New York: Department of Economics and Social Affairs, 19 ; and al-Jumhuriya al-Arabiya al-Muttahida, *al-Nashra al-Tijariya al-Sanawiya* [Annual Trade Bulletin], *19* , Cairo: Central Agency for Public Mobilisation and Statistics, 19

TABLE 12
Egyptian Exports of Selected Industrial Products to the Arab League Countries
(in $'000)

	1958	1963	1967	1970
Air conditioning & Refrigeration	23.0	141.1	327.8	770.6
Medicine & pharm.	152.1	132.6	329.6	878.4
Iron & steel structures	230.2	246.8	143.5	843.7
Electrical appliances	—	8.8	78.3	605.3
Indust. & agri. mach.	—	6.4	57.3	54.4
Clothing	417.9	852.4	944.5	1,453.3
Cars, buses & spare parts	168.5	230.7	443.2	1,325.4

Source: Various additions of al-Jumhuriya al-Arabiya al-Muttahida, *al-Nashra al-Tijariya al-Sanawiya*, Cairo: Central Agency for Public Mobilisation and Statistics, 19

that Egypt's alleged effort to 'colonise' Syria was a crucial variable in the latter's desire to secede from the union. Many commentators, in this case, pointed to Syria's lack of industrialisation after four years of union as proof of Egypt's motives. This point is indeed confirmed by Professor Issawi's analysis of the first five-year plan in Syria. Issawi found that 40 per cent of the total investment was allocated to agriculture and irrigation against 18.7 per cent for industry. These figures compared with 23.5 per cent and 33.7 per cent, respectively, in Egypt. However, he asserted that such a policy was justifiable in terms of Syria's limited industrial capacity and her traditional dependence on agriculture. He only criticised the political wisdom of the plan, which would only induce the Syrians to perceive their country becoming an 'agricultural dependage of Egypt'.[19]

With regards to the claims that Egypt had made Syria a colony of hers, this rested on the argument that the Syrian markets were flooded with the cheaper Egyptian commodities and industrial products. Consequently, it was argued that Egypt's benefits from the union far exceeded those of Syria. However, an examination of the composition of trade between the two countries does not support this contention.[20] Moreover, the balance of trade between the two countries during the Union years (see Table 13) seems to indicate that whatever the intentions of the Egyptian leaders, no actual exploitation of Syria occurred.

TABLE 13
Syrian Trade with Egypt
($ million)

	Imports	Exports	Balance of trade Surplus	Deficit
1958	7.1	4.6		2.5
1959	11.7	19.1	7.4	
1960	14.7	17.0	2.3	
1961	18.4	11.4		7.0

Source: United Nations, *Review of Economic Conditions in the Middle East, 1959–1961*, New York: Department of Economic and Social Affairs, 1962, p. 160.

In conclusion, it can be surmised that during our period of study, any economic objective the Egyptian decision-making elite might have formulated with regards to the Arab world was either not operationalised or only half-heartedly tackled, as in the case of the proposed Arab Common Market. Nevertheless, the Egyptian elites could not have been unaware of the benefits Egypt could derive from an economic union. As such, these objectives seem to have existed primarily in the form of elite expectations and aspirations which were not allowed by the Egyptian decision-makers to be translated into clear-cut, vigorously pursued policy objectives. Like the quest for comprehensive unity, the Egyptian decision-makers soon realised the environmental limitations, inherent in the perceptions of the other Arab elites, that would constrain the achievement of their economic objectives. As such, Egypt seems to have adopted a reactive rather than an initiatory attitude towards its economic objectives in the area.

12 Instruments

As has been argued, the formulation of foreign policy objectives is primarily a cognitive process. However, these objectives have to be implemented in the operational (external) environment. The implementation process requires the utilisation of one or more methods, called the policy instruments. These can range from diplomatic bargaining at one end to the use of physical coercion at the other extreme. The preference for one instrument over another depends on a number of objective and perceived environmental influences which can be either externally or domestically generated. Thus, for example, the superior military power of state A would normally tend to eliminate the possibility of military force being used by state B as a means of achieving its foreign policy objectives towards state A. Furthermore, a cohesive society whose members share a common set of norms and values is usually less susceptible to the instruments of propaganda and subversion than a society in which no universal agreement on a common value-system exists. Moreover, a country which is blessed with immense indigenous wealth will tend to resort to foreign aid as a primary instrument for achieving its foreign policy objectives.

In their efforts to achieve their own foreign policy objectives in the Arab world the Egyptian decision-makers utilised a number of instruments. These were diplomatic bargaining, propaganda, cultural activities, clandestine methods and the use of physical coercion.

DIPLOMACY
Diplomacy is the traditional instrument of foreign policy. It is characterised by the interaction of official representatives of two or more states with the purpose of maintaining, modifying or changing their international relations. In the past, diplomatic activity was usually conducted on a bilateral basis through ambassadors. These days, however, there is an increasing tendency towards personal diplomacy involving the direct participation of the foreign ministers, prime ministers and heads of states. Personal diplomacy can take the form of direct, bilateral interactions, multilateral conference negotiations and parliamentary diplomacy in such bodies as the United Nations or the Arab League. In the Arab world the emphasis on the diplomatic instrument has usually occurred in phases of general deradicalisation of inter-Arab politics. Thus, in Egypt the implementation of the mini-

mum objective of Arab solidarity has been generally sought through diplomatic activity, whereas in periods characterised by the primacy of the intermediate objective of revolutionary change, a shift of emphasis towards the instrument of propaganda, subversion or force was clearly discernible.

The highly centralised nature of the Egyptian government, coupled with Nasser's undoubted flair in conducting foreign affairs, made personal diplomacy the main feature of Egypt's diplomatic activity. Indeed, direct diplomatic negotiations were an extremely suitable vehicle for Nasser's extraordinary verbal ability. In the tripartite unity talks, for example, he completely dominated the proceedings of the discussions. On frequent occasions, he succeeded in getting the Syrians and the Iraqis to contradict each other and whenever a particular discussion came to an end (usually with Nasser having had the upper hand), it was always the Egyptian President who would take the initiative in directing the following discussion to an area in which he was specifically interested.

However, due to the highly volatile nature of inter-Arab politics, President Nasser found very few opportunities to exhibit his diplomatic skills. The main phases of diplomatic activity in the Arab world occurred during the phases of 'Arab peaceful coexistence' between 1964 and 1966. This period was characterised by a general mood of moderation which was epitomised by the three summit conferences. One clear example of Nasser's diplomatic skills is shown in the way he handled the opposing axis of Kings Hussein and Faisal in the first two summits. Before the first summit in January 1964, Nasser met King Hussein privately and discussed with him the possibility of resuming diplomatic relations. Nasser's main motivation behind this initiative was to crack the Kings' alliance in order to isolate King Faisal, his main rival and adversary in inter-Arab politics. In July 1964, therefore, only two months before the second meeting, Nasser dispatched Field Marshall Amer to Jordan to offer King Hussein the immediate resumption of relations between the two countries if Hussein would agree to withdraw his support from the Yemeni Imam and recognise the Egyptian backed republican regime. As this was the period of 'Arab solidarity', such an offer would have the effect of increasing Hussein's popularity without undermining his political position.[1] Hussein, therefore, duly obliged by recognising the republican government in Sana'. The resulting erosion in the Kings' axis, however, was a factor leading to Faisal's later acceptance of a ceasefire in the Yemen, and Hussein's endorsement of the decision to establish the Palestinian Liberation Organisation, both arrived at during the second Summit meeting.[2]

The skill of the Egyptian leadership in handling diplomatic activity was evident as early as 1955. Although the main response to the Baghdad Pact was channelled through a vigorous propaganda campaign, this was reinforced by effective manoeuvering in the diplomatic sphere aimed at isolating the Iraqi government. Egypt's initial diplomatic reply to the Baghdad Pact was the sponsorship of an emergency meeting of the Arab League in Cairo aimed at censuring the Iraqi government. Later, Egypt concluded its own bilateral treaties with Syria and Saudi Arabia, and this was followed in January 1957 with the 'Treaty of Arab Solidarity' which joined Egypt with Saudi Arabia, Jordan and Syria in a political pact deemed to last for a period of ten years. This pact, at least for the time being, successfully isolated Iraq from the rest of the Arab states, and as such, was designed to complement Egypt's propaganda efforts aimed at secluding the Iraqi leaders from their own domestic environment.

The preceding utilisation of the Arab League as an instrument of Egyptian diplomacy was not a solitary event. Egypt effectively used its centrality in the Arab League to pass resolutions aimed at constraining the policies of rival Arab governments. While carrying no real operational value such as sanctions, the significance of these resolutions lay in their psychological impact on the Arab public, which was derived from the League's position as the only existing, albeit limited, symbol of Arab unity. Thus, in the wake of the rupture between Nasser's Egypt and Kassem's Iraq over the activities of the Communist parties in Iraq and Syria, the Political Committee of the League adopted the following resolutions:

> It is necessary for Arab countries to adhere to the policy of non-alignment and non-subservience . . .

> The Committee denounces foreign influence, from whatever source it may come, which aims at disuniting the Arabs and encroaching upon their rights to handle their own affairs . . .

> The Committee appeals to the Iraqi government to be at one with the Arab countries in adhering to the resolutions adopted at this session . . . [3]

The perceived Egyptian manipulation and domination of the League led, on many occasions, to the refusal of other Arab states to participate in the activities of the League. For example, Tunisia joined the League in October 1958 but withdrew its membership barely a year later, accusing Egypt of imposing her will over the League. In April 1959, Iraq boycotted the thirteenth session of the League's cultural committee because of the Secretariat's alleged impartiality in convening the meeting in Cairo after it had already been agreed that the meeting should be held in Baghdad. For the same reasons, Iraq refused to attend the Arab Foreign Ministers Conference in Casablanca in August of the same year, and it announced its intention to boycott the next meeting scheduled to be held in Cairo. During the period of Nasser's presidency, there were frequent accusations from various Arab quarters that Egypt's leaders tended to impose their will on a supposedly 'multi-state' organ. One Iraqi paper accused the League of being a tool of Egyptian policy 'which controls its machinery and directs it according to its own whims and ambitions'.[4] Another insisted that Egypt 'seemed to regard the League almost as a branch of its Foreign Ministry'.[5] In similar tones, the Tunisian radio explained Bourguiba's decision to boycott the League in September 1966 as a response to Egypt's domination of the organisation.[6] Even as late as 1968, the Tunisians were accusing the Egyptian decision-makers of harbouring hegemonial designs on the League.[7] To these accusations, the Egyptians were adamant in denying any such manipulations. As evidence, Nasser pointed out that 'all the victories of this republic have been achieved outside the League.'[8] Indeed, in 1966 *al-Ahram* complained that the League had become dominated by an alliance of Jordan, Tunisia and Saudi Arabia.[9] Nevertheless, it is clear that Egypt channelled much of her diplomatic activity through the League. However, the periods characterised by the radicalisation of Egyptian policy tended to precipitate a general de-emphasis of the League's role and its importance. In 1962, for instance, the National Charter declared that the League was an institution of 'limited utility' as it could not 'serve the noble and ultimate objective of Arab unity',[10] and in 1966 *al-Ahram* described the League's meeting as a 'facade'.[11]

From the above discussion, a distinction must be drawn between the negative and positive uses and effects of diplomacy. On the one hand, the diplomatic instrument was utilised primarily for negative purposes such as using the Arab League to censure rival Arab governments, as was the case with Iraq in 1959. Such manipulation proved, in the long run, to be counter-productive as it only led to the eventual isolation of Egypt itself after the explosion at Shtoura in August 1962. On the other hand, however, the series of summit conferences of 1964 and 1965 yielded many positive achievements, particularly the two peace conferences over the Yemen, the establishment of the Palestinian Liberation Organisation, and the co-operation over the river Jordan crisis. Similarly, it was through Nasser's vigorous diplomatic intervention in September 1970 that the bloody Jordanian civil war was terminated. It is also evident that the effectiveness of diplomacy was highest in the periods of moderation, whereas in the phases of confrontation, diplomacy became secondary to other instruments such as propaganda, clandestine activities and the use of physical coercion.

PROPAGANDA

Propaganda can be defined as the deliberate attempt by the government of one state to influence the values and opinions of the population of another state through the means of mass communications, so that the behaviour of those influenced will correspond to that desired by the

communicating government.[12] Unlike Diplomacy, therefore, the target
is the population, which means that the governments are bypassed. In
other words, the direction of political communication in the case of
propaganda is between government A and population B and vice
versa. A further distinction between the two instruments can be
discerned from the nature of the interaction between the government
and population of each state. An effective propaganda campaign tends
to induce intensive interaction within the recipient state between the
government and its own population. The nature of diplomatic method,
characterised by the participation of a very small group of decision-
makers, and with its emphasis on secrecy, renders the interaction
between the government and its own population less intensive (see
Fig. 7).

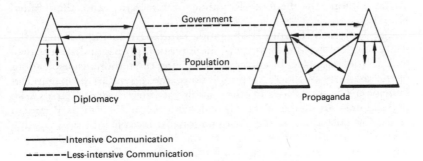

FIG. 7 Diplomacy and Propaganda

What induced the Egyptian leadership to utilise propaganda as a
primary instrument of Egypt's foreign policy was probably a rational
definition of the prevailing Arab situation on the one hand, and a
correct assessment of Egypt's capabilities, particularly in the fields of
culture and communications, on the other hand. As far as the Arab
world was concerned, the rate of illiteracy was (and still is) very high.
This made the radio the most effective medium for reaching a large
number of people. Moreover, the traditional social values of Arab
societies led to a universal scarcity of Western-type social pastimes such
as theatres, dance halls and clubs which tended to focus much of the
social activity in the Arab world on the radio. Finally, the advent of
the transistor radio made it possible to reach an audience hitherto unattainable because of the lack of electricity. The assessment of Egypt's
own capability centred on her status as the leading cultural centre in
the Arab world which allowed her to utilise a variety of radio programmes such as songs, plays, poetry, as well as news, in order to
ensure maximum impact.[13]

The Egyptian leadership seemed to have correctly perceived these factors, for as early as 1953 the military junta was beginning to study means of effectively employing the potential utility of propaganda for the achievement of Egypt's foreign policy objectives in the Arab world.[14] In July 1953, the 'Voice of the Arabs' started its transmissions to the Arab world, and a year later its daily transmission time was increased by four hours. The emphasis on radio propaganda was gradually increased over the years, until in 1963 Cairo was broadcasting in twenty-four languages and its rate of transmission had reached a staggering 755 hours per week. Thus, by the early sixties, propaganda had been established as a major instrument of Egyptian foreign policy in the Arab world. This trend continued so that by 1970 Cairo's broadcasts were relayed in thirty-four languages, and in terms of transmission hours, Egypt was surpassed only by the United States, the Soviet Union, the Federal Republic of Germany and the United Kingdom.

The analysis of Egypt's propaganda campaign during our period of study suggests that the strategy of the Egyptian propagandists was twofold. In the first place, by correctly perceiving the nationalist aspirations of the majority of the Arab populations, the Egyptian propagandists endeavoured to create in the minds of their targets (the Arab populations) an image of the United Arab Republic and its President as the sole custodians of the 'Arab nationalist movement', thus positing Nasser as an alternative leader to the indigenous leadership of the various Arab states. As such, Radio Cairo, Radio Damascus (between 1958 and 1961) and the Voice of the Arabs constantly reminded their audiences that it was the Egyptian elites rather than their own indigenous leaderships who were the defenders of 'their freedoms, their interests and their nationalism'. President Nasser, too, was consistently eulogised as 'the symbol of Arab nationalism [which represented] immediate unity and quick progress'.[15] By contrast, rival leaders whose policies contradicted those of Egypt were presented as the representatives of corrupt privileged minorities whose political survival entirely depended on the support of the 'imperialist powers', and who, as a consequence, became the bastions of a 'reactionary' movement aimed at hindering the progress of the 'Arab nation'. This contrast between the supposedly enlightened and universally accepted Egyptian regime and the allegedly corrupt and coercive regimes of Egypt's antagonists was heavily emphasised in Egyptian broadcasts. Thus, for example, in an analysis of the Saudi budget of 1966, an Egyptian broadcaster drew the inevitable conclusion:

In Egypt, the expenditure of the President and the President's office in the current fiscal year amounts to the equivalent of only 34 million Saudi riyals, while in Saudi Arabia, the allocation for Faisal and his

Royal Household amount to six times the allocations for the Presidency of Egypt, i.e. over 181 Saudi riyals. In Egypt, the expenditure of the Ministry of Interior amounts to the equivalent of 353 million riyals, and here we must bear in mind that Egypt has a population of over 28 millions. In Saudi Arabia, the expenditure of the Ministry of Interior in the new budget amounts to 684 million riyals, i.e. twice the budget of the Egyptian Ministry of Interior in the same year. And we must bear in mind that Saudi Arabia has only a third of the population of Egypt.[16]

The second strategy of Egypt's propaganda was directed at creating and encouraging domestic upheavals and turmoil. This was done either by manipulating ethnic or socioeconomic cleavages in the target country or by highlighting the alleged instability, and prophesying the imminent collapse of the political structure of these states. In this context, the broadcasts usually alleged that it would be merely a matter of days before the inevitable pro-UAR revolution would occur. Moreover, this alleged revolutionary orientation in the target country was usually presented as a universal phenomenon. In other words, it was not only some of the people who were supposedly rebelling; rather it was the entire population which was on the revolutionary march. Such a treatment was meant to encourage the listener to join the allegedly 'rolling bandwagon'.

In their efforts to ferment political unrest, the Egyptian propaganda machine tended to pay particular attention to the armed forces of the other Arab states, which were usually depicted as suffering from ideological fragmentation and leadership disputes. In 1967, for example, Radio Cairo contended that a power struggle was raging within the Saudi royal family over the leadership of the Tribal Guard.[17] Within this context, suggestions of nepotism and favouritism were used in order to create discontent in the ranks of these armies. Particularly effective in this sense was the allegation that such favouritism was aimed at ethnic minorities at the expense of the Arab majority. For example, utilising the Turkish descent of Nuri al-Said, the Prime Minister of Iraq, in 1958 the 'Voice of the Arabs' declared:

> You brethren of the Iraqi Arab army are well aware that the government of Nuri al-Said disperses the [Iraqi] officers and prevents them from holding high rank in the Iraqi army. They are replaced by Turkoman officers to ensure the subjugation of the Iraqi army and to force it to be loyal to imperialist obligations.[18]

Techniques

Propaganda has been defined as the deliberate attempt by a government to influence the values, attitudes and opinions of the citizens of another state. The success of propaganda, therefore, would ultimately depend on the effectiveness of the message transmitted by the communicator. According to the particular situation, the message might be rational or it might be emotional. Probably due to the high level of illiteracy in the Arab world, Egyptian propaganda tended to follow the latter pattern.[19] Nevertheless, whatever their type or pattern, propaganda messages are delivered through a variety of techniques. In this case, the Egyptian propagandists concentrated mainly on four major techniques in communicating their messages to the Arab populations. These were: (1) transfer, (2) testimonial, (3) name-calling and (4) bandwagon.[20]

(*1*) *Transfer:* This technique attempts to 'identify one idea, person, country or policy with another to make the target approve or disapprove it'.[21] Given the historical experiences, and consequently the predominant perceptual pattern, of the majority of the Arab populations, the most effective method of undermining a leader's position in any Arab state was to identify and associate him with 'imperialism'. Thus, one of the main techniques of the Egyptian propagandists was to depict Egypt's and Nasser's political opponents in the Arab world as the 'lackeys of colonialism' or the 'agents of imperialism'. Typical of these efforts was a broadcast by the 'Voice of the Arabs' which reminded its Iraqi listeners that Fadhil al-Jamali, the Foreign Minister of pre-republican Iraq 'has no right to speak on any of the affairs of Iraq, because he speaks on behalf of imperialism'.[22] In the same vein, Radio Cairo in 1966 volunteered the following advice to the Arab kings: 'Let Hussein ask himself: did imperialism save his grandfather, Abdulla, from his end at the hands of the people? . . . let Faisal ask his Brother Saud: did imperialism stand by him when he failed to ensure the interests of the imperialists? Imperialism can never protect a king or an agent.'[23]

The analysis of Egypt's radio broadcasts during our period of study further indicates that the Egyptians considered Britain as the major 'imperialist' power in the area. This was probably due to Britain's historical position in the Arab world as an imperialist power, its involvement in the Suez crisis, and until 1968, its continuing colonial status in the Arabian Peninsula. Moreover, the identification of Britain as the 'imperialist power' gave the abstract nature of the term 'imperialism' a central and substantive focus. The utilisation of 'British imperialism' by the Egyptian propagandists was poignantly effective in countries which had traditional and existing ties with Britain. This was particularly true of the Hashemite kingdoms of Iraq and Jordan. Thus, referring to the founder of the Hashemite dynasties, Cairo Radio insisted that 'the Arab revolt was led by a man chosen by British imperialism to lay the foundations of the British Empire in the Arab countries. This man was the Sharif Hussein, supported by a British spy called Lawrence.'[24] A further interesting example of the propagandists' concentration on the perceived Arab alienation from Britain is a broadcast by the 'Voice of the Arabs' on Samir al-Rifai, a Prime Minister of Jordan. Particularly significant is the number of times the word 'British' is used in such a short passage. The broadcast alleged that Rifai

> ... began life as a petty official in the *British* Governors office in Palestine. On the transfer of the *British* Governor, he went with him to Amman where he was appointed by the *British* envoy as an overseer in the *British* military airport workshop. Due to his closeness to the *British*, he was appointed as an interpreter to the *British* High Commissioner in Amman. Through the *British*, he became Secretary to the Jordanian Cabinet.[25] [My italics.]

Another technique which was frequently resorted to by the Egyptian propagandists was that of associating Egypt's political opponents with Israel. The highly charged emotional responses which 'Israel' and 'world Zionism' engendered in the Arab world facilitated their certain utilisation by the Egyptian propagandists. The most usual method used was to link the policies of Arab leaders with the 'interests' and 'ambitions' of Israel in the area. Thus, in the immediate aftermath of the abortive Shawaf revolt in Iraq in March 1959, the rupture between the UAR and Iraq was explained by Radio Damascus in the following terms:

> Israel does not want Arab unity to be achieved nor the Arab case to succeed and be victorious. Abd al-Karim Kassem and the Communists want the same. Israel does not want the UAR to have good relations with the Iraqi Republic or co-operation between them. The Communists and Kassem's government want the same. All these aims, decisions and accusations are in harmony in the propaganda of Baghdad, the Communists and Israel.[26]

Finally, while attempting to emphasise the alleged association of Egypt's political opponents with 'imperialism', 'Israel' or 'world Zionism',[27] the Egyptian propaganda machine spared no effort to contrast this congruence of interests with the mutual antagonism existing between the 'imperialists' or the 'Zionists' and Egypt's 'progressive' regime. Within this context, the hostility of the Western news media towards President Nasser and the Egyptian government was successfully utilised by Egyptian radio as proof of Egypt's continuous struggle against the 'imperialists' and the 'Zionists'.

(2) *Testimonial:* In this technique, the propagandist 'uses an esteemed person or institution to endorse or criticize an idea or political entity. [In other words], the target is asked to believe something simply because some "authority" says it is true.'[28] In their propaganda campaigns, the Egyptians relied on two distinct types of such 'authorities'.

These can be classified as 'the indigenous authorities' and 'the independent authorities'.

Within the former context, the Egyptian propagandists employed the services of important political refugees from the target country. It was reasoned that the messages transmitted by these prominent individuals to their own people would significantly supplement the effort to reorient the political dispositions of that country's indigenous population. Thus, there was undoubted benefit for the Egyptian regime when no less a figure than King Saud's own brother Prince Talal commented on Radio Cairo that the revolution in the Yemen was 'one of the chief reasons for the instability of the throne and the deterioration of the internal situation in Saudi Arabia'.[29] Similarly, a Jordanian officer who had defected to Egypt told the listeners of 'the Voice of the Arabs' in February 1967 that Jordan had become 'a great prison simmering with revolt against Hussein and his agent government'.[30] The same technique was frequently used in the cases of Iraq, Jordan, Tunisia and the Yemen.

As far as the second category was concerned, the Egyptian propagandists frequently utilised the views of prominent individuals who, although not citizens of the target country, nevertheless, because of the prestige attached to their person or position, increased the credibility of the propagandist's message. Thus, the 'Voice of the Arabs' reminded its listeners that the 'President of the Republic of India says that Abd al-Nasser is the symbol of the awakening spirit in the Arab world and that the Arab nationalism which Nasser represents, is a symbol of immediate independence, unity and quick progress.'[32] In another instance, Radio Cairo proudly declared that, at a rally in Libya, Colonel Qadhafi had introduced Nasser as 'the pioneer of Arab nationalism and the leader of the Arab struggle'.[33] Using the same method to emphasise a different point, Cairo Radio reinforced its own repeated appeals to the Jordanian people to overthrow King Hussein and his regime by referring to a statement made by Anthony Nutting, 'the former British Minister of State',[34] in August 1958 which allegedly advised the British government to withdraw its support from Hussein.

Perhaps the best illustration of this method's techniques occurred in June 1958 during the Lebanese civil war. President Chamoun's insistence on Lebanese 'independence' had contained a mainly implicit, but sometimes explicit, fear of Arab unity with its implications of a Moslem domination over the Christian communities in the Arab world generally, and in the Lebanon specifically. To counteract President Chamoun's 'message' to the Arab Christians, the Egyptian propagandists needed the 'testimonial' of a person whose 'prestige' or 'attributes' would add credibility to Egypt's 'counter-message' directed at the Christian communities of Lebanon and the Arab world. In this sense, the most obvious candidate would be someone who could be perceived as representing the views not only of Egypt's substantial Christian community but also of the church as a whole. Thus, a senior Coptic priest declared on the 'Voice of the Arabs':

> Chamoun claims to be the protector of Christianity. We can never agree that the protector of Christianity should be an underling of imperialism. We can never agree that the protector of Christianity should be someone who has been rejected by the Christians, because we believe in our Arab nationalism.[35]

(*3*) *Name-calling:* This technique aims at illiciting a favourable yet uncritical response from the target by attaching an emotive label to a government or a particular leader. The success of this technique will invariably depend on the congruity of the 'label' with the prevalent perceptual patterns of the audience. Given the prevailing quest for progress in the Middle East of the fifties and sixties and the almost obsessive motivation 'to catch up with the West', it is not surprising that the Egyptian propagandists utilised the terms 'reactionary' and 'feudalist' with all their derogatory connotations of 'moving backwards' to describe the anti-Egypt leaders of the Arab world. Kings Saud and Faisal of Saudi Arabia, Nuri al-Said of Iraq, King Hussein of Jordan, President Bourguiba of Tunisia, President Chamoun of Lebanon and President Qudsi of secessionist Syria were all called reactionaries or feudalists (or both) at one time or another during our period of study.

On a less general level, personal 'labels' were invented for specific leaders in order to highlight their supposed 'failings' and 'inadequacies'. This was designed to make them the objects of mistrust, suspicion and derision by their own people, thus invariably undermining their credibility as capable and trustworthy leaders. Probably the most widely-used of all such labels was the one first coined by Nasser himself, and later extensively used by the UAR radio, which described the Iraqi leader as 'Iraq's kassem', meaning in Arabic the 'divider of Iraq'.[36] This nomenclature related to Kassem's alleged efforts to encourage domestic conflicts and cleavages in order to perpetuate his own political position. As such, he was presented as an 'unjust' ruler trying to divide his people for the sake of personal ambitions. Kassem was also frequently ridiculed as an irrational and stupid man whose limited mental capacities led him to interpret events in simplistic, even imaginary, terms. Thus, five days before his overthrow, the 'Voice of the Arabs' derisively declared:

> Kassem, the Don Quixote, announces that he is going to stand by the government of Syria, if it is exposed to any aggression; Kassem, the Don Quixote, threatens the UAR with hell and many other big things if the UAR does not leave him alone to oppress Iraq and serve the aims of imperialism.[37]

The Egyptian propagandists used the same technique with other Arab leaders. Using the physical stature of King Hussein as a point of reference, Egyptian radio frequently identified the Jordanian monarch as the 'little King'. The function of this particular label was to create in the minds of the 'targets' a correlation between Hussein's small physique and his stature as a leader. In the case of King Saud, it was a much more straightforward identification process. The excesses of the King and the medieval political and social structure of Saudi Arabia earned the King the label of the 'immoral feudalist'. The contrast between Saud's personal life-style and his proclaimed role as the protector of Islam's holiest shrine, the Kaaba, made him extremely vulnerable to Cairo's attacks on him and his leadership. Thus in vicious, yet poignant terms, the 'Voice of the Arabs' reminded 'His Majesty' that 'the glory of Islam cannot be defended from within the perfumed palaces or from behind the silk curtains of the Hareem bedrooms.'[38]

(*4*) *Bandwagon:* This technique plays on people's tendency to 'belong' or to be in 'accord' with the majority. It utilises the individual's usual desire to be 'one of the crowd'. The technique 'implies that the target is in a minority – if he opposes the substance of the message – and should join the majority. Or, if the target is sympathetic to the propagandist, this technique will reinforce his attitudes by demonstrating that he is on the "right side" along with everybody else.'[39]

This technique was widely used by the Egyptian propagandists. Most broadcasts which carried messages supporting Egyptian policymakers and their ideals, or attacking rival Arab leaders or governments, contained such phrases as 'everyone knows . . .', 'you all believe . . .', 'all people share . . .', and so forth. These phrases were usually made the focus of the 'message' conveyed in order to add weight to its content.[40] For example, explaining the animosity of Egypt's leaders towards the rulers of Iraq, Jordan and Lebanon in March 1958, the 'Voice of the Arabs' claimed that 'everyone in the Arab nation feels today that traitors and imperialist collaborators must be eliminated so that real freedom and unity can be established in the Arab homeland.'[41] Or, in addressing King Hussein after the Iraqi revolution, Radio Cairo enquired, 'Do you know what the entire world knows about the reality of the throne on which you sit? It is an imaginary throne guarded by the forces of occupation against the Jordanian people and army.'[42] Similarly, in replying to the rulers of Saudi Arabia, who accused Egypt's leaders of atheistic orientations, the 'Voice of the Arabs' addressed an 'open letter' to Prince Faisal, the then Prime Minister of Saudi Arabia, which began 'Your Highness knows, as the sons of the Arabian Peninsula and other brothers of the Arab nation know, that you are one of those who least adhere to the teachings of Islam and the tradition of the Prophet . . .'[43]

Effects

It has already been argued that as early as 1955, the Egyptian leaders had begun to consider propaganda as a potentially effective method of achieving Egypt's policy objectives. In the following twelve years, propaganda, as a primary instrument of foreign policy, became a major factor in the political interactions amongst the units of the Middle Eastern regional system. There can be no doubt that in many instances, propaganda was an important determining factor in the development of events. A salient example in this case was the role Egyptian propaganda played in dissuading the Jordanian government from joining the Baghdad Pact in December 1955–January 1956. Cairo propaganda effectively reinforced the hostility felt by the majority of the Jordanian people towards the Pact by depicting the Pact as 'covert colonialism', by attacking the Jordanian leaders as 'agents of Imperialism', and by inciting the Jordanian population to overthrow their 'pro-British' leaders. The demonstrations, strikes and rioting that followed were instrumental in bringing two governments down and eventually forcing the Jordanian government to refrain from joining the Pact. While the basic reason for the turmoil was the Jordanians' residual antagonism to the Pact, the role of propaganda in this case was to ferment, encourage and perpetuate the violent outbursts of popular hostility to the Pact.

The response of the other Arab states to Egyptian propaganda indicates that the leaders of these states acknowledged and appreciated the role of propaganda as a significant factor in inter-Arab political interactions. Fadhilal-Jamali, a Prime Minister of pre-republican Iraq, later insisted that the 'Voice of the Arabs' played a 'primary role in bringing down the Iraqi monarchy'.[44] It is also interesting that Iraq's official withdrawal from the Baghdad Pact on March 24, 1959 followed a week of intensive propaganda campaigns by the UAR's radios.

The operational reaction of the Arab governments to Egypt's propaganda campaigns took a negative and a positive form. On the negative side, through the obstruction of the communication channel, they hoped to prevent the 'message' from reaching the 'target'. This they tried to do by jamming the UAR radio stations. For example, as early as 1954, the Iraqis had installed six jammers in Baghdad, Basrah, Mosul and Kirkuk. The same technique was later used by the Jordanians, and the Saudis banned listening to Cairo, 'Voice of the Arabs' and Sana' radios.

Going on the offensive, the anti-Egypt Arab leaders and governments retaliated with their own propaganda campaigns against Egypt. Indeed, their attacks on the 'rulers of Egypt' were often verbally more vicious than those of Egypt. Two discernible strategies seem to have been employed by Egypt's antagonists. In the first place, they counteracted Egypt's nationalist appeals by deriding her nebulous and recently acquired 'Arab' pretentions. Thus, for example, Jordanian Radio reminded its listeners that 'Gamal Abd al-Nasser, who is new to Arabism, began trying to teach a lesson in nationalism and liberation to the Arab kings who have been shouldering the mission for generations.'[45] An important part of this strategy was to undermine the credibility of Egypt's proclaimed Arab orientations by frequent references to her pharonic past.[46] Secondly, anti-Egypt propaganda utilised the junta's early rejection of the two-party 'democratic' model of government and the dominant position of 'Colonel' Nasser in the decision-making process to highlight the allegedly 'dictatorial' and 'oppressive' nature of Egypt's 'police state'. For example, Radio Baghdad declared in June 1958, that 'hundreds of good politicians and honest men are in the prisons of Egypt. Nobody in Egypt is allowed to ask about their 'crimes' and fate. Their only fault is that they refused to bow their heads to oppression.'[47] Furthermore, according to the anti-Egypt regimes, Nasser's rule was not only oppressive, but it was also Communist. Thus Cairo Radio's calls for 'Arab nationalism' were described by the opposing broadcasters as 'communist calls for socialism [designed] to tame the peoples of the area with rifle and lash into submission to the foreigner'.[48] Indeed, the emphasis on the alleged 'dictatorial' and 'Communist' characteristics of the Egyptian political system constituted a major argument of the anti-Egypt propagandists.

Ferocious as it was, the anti-Egypt propaganda, however, did not match the effectiveness of Egypt's propaganda machine, partly because of Egypt's supremacy in the fields of culture and communication, and partly because Egypt's 'Arab nationalist', 'anti-Western' appeals fitted neatly within the prevalent perceptual patterns of the majority of the Arab populations. In this case, the perceived 'dependence' of most of Egypt's rivals in the Arab world on Western powers added credibility to Egypt's 'messages'. On the other hand, the emphasis of Egypt's rivals on Nasser's oppressive rule lacked authenticity in the face of his obvious popularity in Egypt and the Arab world. This is not to suggest that Egypt's propaganda was free of shortcomings. An obvious failing was its lack of consistency due to the shifts in Egyptian foreign policy from an activist revolutionary orientation to a static *status quo* posture and vice versa. Nevertheless, on the whole there can be no doubt that propaganda was an extremely effective instrument of Egyptian foreign policy in the Arab world. Finally, the resort to propaganda by Egypt and her Arab rivals contributed to a substantive change in the style of conducting international relations in the Arab world. Whereas in the pre-1953 period, decision-makers emphasised the role of secret diplomacy, the fifties and sixties saw the gradual utilisation by all states of propaganda as a primary instrument of foreign policy in the area. It was only after the war of June 1967, and the subsequent fundamental changes in the Arab political situation, that propaganda began to lose much of its pre-1967 significance.[49] Indeed, by 1970, propaganda had ceased to constitute an effective instrument of Egypt's foreign policy in the Arab world.

CULTURAL ACTIVITIES

The cultural instrument can be defined as 'the selective presentation by a government of aspects of the social system within which it operates for transmission to a foreign population, with the official acquiescence of the recipient government, and for the purpose of creating a commonwealth of shared attitudes, images and goals between the two countries'.[50] This instrument is distinguishable from propaganda in one important aspect. Whereas in propaganda the government of state A transmits the 'message' directly to the population of state B, in the cultural instrument the 'message' flows from government A to population B via the government of B. In this lies the crucial difference, for unlike propaganda the cultural instrument allows the recipient government the opportunity to reject, alter or modify the message (see Fig. 8).

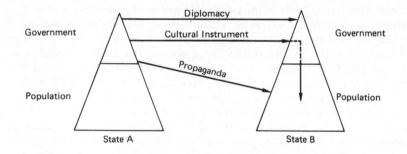

FIG. 8 Diplomacy, the Cultural Instrument and Propaganda

The leaders of revolutionary Egypt had always considered cultural activities as an important instrument of Egyptian policy. As early as 1962, Egypt had established twenty-three cultural centres in foreign countries: eight centres in the Arab world, five in Africa, six in Asia, three in Europe and one in South America.[51] Moreover, 'cultural agreements' were considered by the Egyptian leadership as an important part of their international transactions with other states. For example, in the wake of the Iraqi coup of 1958, the UAR Minister of Education Kamal al-Din Hussein arrived in Baghdad and signed a cultural agreement with the Iraqis which provided 'for full co-operation of the two countries in the fields of science, education and culture'.[52] However, the main thrust of the cultural instrument as utilised by Egypt in the Arab world concentrated on the following activities: the delegation of Egyptian teachers to Arab countries, the admission of Arab students to Egyptian educational institutions, and the export of Egyptian films, books, newspapers and periodicals to the various Arab countries.

Egyptian teachers in Arab countries contributed to the achievement of Egypt's objectives in the Arab world in two ways. In the first place, they became, in a sense, the 'evidence' for Egypt's proclaimed cultural and demographic supremacy, and as such, enhanced its perceived leadership of the Arab world. More importantly, they were placed in a position of great moral and ideological influence over a highly impressionable, yet in terms of future considerations, an extremely significant section of society.

With all its population problems, Egypt could still boast the most numerous and best qualified middle class in the Arab world. Moreover, the emphasis placed by the Egyptian leadership on the rapid expansion of secondary and university education produced a surplus of educated personnel who could not be absorbed by the country's economic, social and educational institutions. This, of course, happened at a time when other Arab countries were adopting as their primary goal the rapid social progress of their populations. However, the achievement of this goal was constrained in these countries by the chronic shortage of qualified personnel, particularly in the field of education. The late fifties and early sixties, therefore, witnessed an influx of Egyptian teachers into Arab countries, so that between the years 1954 and 1965, the number of Egyptian teachers in Arab countries increased from 580 to 4032.[53] During this period, the number of Egyptian teachers delegated to all developing countries increased from 624 to 5173.[54] However, 1965 was the peak year for the delegation of Egyptian teachers abroad, since by 1970 the number had slumped to 3973.[55] This was probably due to the increasing level of education in the recipient countries themselves, and to the greater demand for teachers in Egypt's own educational system.

Referring to our definition at the beginning of this section, it is interesting to note the control of the recipient government over the cultural instrument. Iraq is, probably, the most pertinent case. The decrease of Egyptian teachers from 136 in 1956 to 63 in 1958 corresponded with the increasing hostility between Egypt and the Iraqi monarchy. The 1958 revolution in Iraq dramatically increased the numbers of delegated Egyptian teachers to 449. However, by April 1959, as a result of the progressive worsening of relations, which culminated in the UAR's involvement in the abortive Shawaf coup, all the Egyptian teachers had returned home from Iraq.[56]

The training of Arab students in Egypt's educational institutions constituted the second aspect of Egypt's cultural instrument. Aware of the importance of this medium as a vehicle for inculcating future elites with

Egypt-oriented values, the government encouraged foreign students, particularly those from the newly independent developing countries, to acquire their education in Egypt's schools, colleges and universities. Thus, in the academic year 1966–7, the number of foreign students reached the impressive figure of 34,516 (see Table 14). Out of these, nearly 70 per cent originated from Arab countries.

TABLE 14
Non-Egyptian Students Studying at UAR Institutions

Year	Arab Students		Total Foreign Students	
	Universities	Total	Universities	Total
1961–2	6,439	13,517	6,874	20,878
1962–3	8,296	14,477	8,930	22,514
1963–4	10,295	18,945	10,808	27,975
1964–5	11,092	21,549	12,745	32,154
1965–6	14,093	24,745	15,045	33,415
1966–7	12,126	23,734	17,178	34,516

Source: UAR, *Statistical Yearbook, 1964* [in Arabic], p. 304; *1965*, p. 181; *1966*, p. 199; *1967*, p. 192.

The last three categories of Egypt's cultural instrument in the Arab world concerned the despatch of films, books, newspapers and periodicals to the Arab countries. It was hoped, no doubt, that these activities would contribute to the achievement of Egypt's foreign policy goals in the Arab world by influencing the psychological environment of the populations of these countries. On a general level, the Egyptian films, books and newspapers were meant to acquaint the 'target' with Egyptian values, norms, goals and aspirations. More specifically, they would sometimes contain an explicit or an implied 'message' designed to enforce, modify or alter the orientations or behaviour of the 'target'. The significant point here is that, due to the lack of capabilities, the other Arab countries could not challenge Egypt's supremacy in these fields. The comparative classification of relevant data, pertaining to the imports and exports of films, books, newspapers and periodicals (see Tables 15, 16 and 17) clearly shows, without the need for further comment, Egypt's complete ascendancy over her Arab rivals in the fields of cinema and publishing.[57]

From the preceding discussion of the cultural instrument, two points emerge. The first point relates to the existence of an important definitional distinction between propaganda and the cultural instrument. It is clear that only with the concurrence of the recipient government could the cultural instrument be effectively utilised, and as such, only in an atmosphere of friendship and an acknowledged congruence of

TABLE 15

Egypt's Imports and Exports of Films to the Countries of the Arab League
('000 kilograms)

	1957		1961		1966		1970	
	Imports	*Exports*	*Imports*	*Exports*	*Imports*	*Exports*	*Imports*	*Exports*
Syria	0.0	1.1	0.0	1.2	0.5	1.0	0.0	0.0
Iraq	0.2	0.9	0.0	0.0	0.0	1.5	0.0	0.5
Jordan	0.3	1.1	0.1	0.4	0.0	1.0	0.0	1.0
Lebanon	1.4	2.0	0.6	0.9	4.0	6.0	4.0	2.0
Saudi A.	0.0	0.0	0.0	0.0	0.0	0.0	0.0	5.0
Algeria	0.0	0.0	0.0	0.0	0.0	0.5	0.0	1.0
Libya	0.0	1.4	0.0	1.3	0.0	1.0	0.0	1.0
Others	0.0	3.5	0.0	5.0	0.0	7.0	0.0	7.0
Total	1.9	10.0	0.7	8.8	4.5	18.0	4.0	17.5

TABLE 16

Egypt's Imports and Exports of Books to the Countries of the Arab League
('000 kilograms)

	1957		1961		1966		1970	
	Imports	*Exports*	*Imports*	*Exports*	*Imports*	*Exports*	*Imports*	*Exports*
Syria	6.7	36.3	0.2	6.1	0.0	27.0	0.0	0.0
Iraq	0.3	210.0	0.4	124.8	0.0	229.0	0.0	114.0
Jordan	0.5	29.3	0.6	9.5	0.0	72.0	0.0	26.0
Lebanon	93.9	285.7	46.4	385.1	84.0	492.0	150.0	317.0
Saudi A.	0.3	356.9	0.2	324.9	0.0	228.0	0.0	74.0
Algeria	0.0	25.0	0.0	8.1	1.0	97.0	4.0	124.0
Libya	0.4	163.2	0.0	239.2	0.0	660.0	0.0	597.0
Others	2.7	314.6	1.2	579.7	0.0	446.0	0.0	915.0
Total	104.8	1,421.0	49.0	1,677.4	85.0	2,251.0	154.0	2,167.0

values and goals would cultural activities be employed as an instrument
of a state's foreign policy. The second point that emerges from the preceding discussion is Egypt's complete supremacy in the Arab world in
the fields of education and culture. Thus, in the competition for value
inculcation amongst the Arab states, the directional flow was heavily
weighted in favour of Egypt. This means that while their indigenous
population underwent minimal exposure to external values, the Egyptian leaders ensured that their own goals and aspirations would have
maximum impact on the Arab populations. It is probably for this
reason that cultural activity constituted such an important instrument
of Egyptian foreign policy.

TABLE 17

Egypt's Imports and Exports of Newspapers and Periodicals to the Countries of the Arab League

('000 kilograms)

	1957		1961		1966		1970	
	Imports	Exports	Imports	Exports	Imports	Exports	Imports	Exports
Syria	8.5	154.9	27.8	84.0	0.0	46.0	1.2	230.0
Iraq	0.0	9.4	0.5	14.7	0.3	197.0	10.0	101.0
Jordan	0.9	31.8	0.3	16.7	11.0	115.0	10.3	69.0
Lebanon	54.0	144.4	37.5	108.9	323.0	250.0	263.0	99.0
Saudi A.	0.6	104.6	0.9	71.4	0.0	0.0	0.0	0.0
Algeria	0.0	0.4	0.0	0.0	2.0	56.0	1.3	81.0
Libya	0.0	23.7	0.0	17.9	0.0	144.0	15.0	309.0
Others	0.5	29.6	3.6	100.6	13.5	457.0	117.0	648.0
Total	64.5	498.8	70.6	414.2	349.8	1,265.0	417.8	1,537.0

Source: Data for the Tables 15–17 come from various editions of the UAR, *Annual Statement of Foreign Trade*, Cairo: Central Agency for Public Mobilisation and Statistics.

CLANDESTINE ACTIVITIES

Clandestine activities can be defined as the unauthorised political and/or quasi-military penetration by one government into the affairs of foreign societies in order to achieve political objectives. The primary and most widely used clandestine activity is subversion. This can be defined as 'a rebellious activity inside a country [which is] organised, supported and/or directed by a foreign power, using for its own purposes the disaffected members of society'.[58] However, other activities fall within the conceptual boundary of this category. The creation of political scandals, the offering of bribes to officials, the distribution of underground leaflets and newspapers, the recruitment and subsidy of agents and informants, are all unauthorised activities undertaken by one government for the purpose of achieving its objectives in the 'target' country.

Obviously, analysts find it difficult to ascertain, with any degree of certainty or objectivity, the utility of this instrument to the achievement of a state's foreign policy. Very occasionally, if at all, do governments admit to specific acts of subversion in foreign countries. Consequently, the alleged utilisation of this instrument by a government usually emanates from the 'target' country in the form of 'accusations'. However, due to the nature of the instrument, such accusations are rarely satisfactorily substantiated or documented. This problem is relevant to this particular study, since all available data on Egypt's use of subversion and other clandestine activities come from rival Arab countries. Nevertheless, there is enough evidence to suggest that clandestine activity constituted an important, if not a major, instrument of Egyptian foreign policy. Humphrey Trevelyan relates that he was once told by Nasser: 'I tell my intelligence service that the only revolutions which succeed in the Middle East are those we don't make.'[59]

Throughout the period of Nasser's leadership, Egypt was being continuously accused by rival Arab governments of engaging in subversive activities against these governments. Fadhil al-Jamali claimed that 'Egyptian intelligence' played an important part in the disintegration of the Iraqi monarchy.[60] King Hussein, too, has frequently accused the Egyptian authorities of attempting to overthrow his regime. Salih Alial-Saadi, the Iraqi delegate, informed President Nasser during the March 1963 unity talks that the Iraqis had proof that 'certain groups' operating from Cairo were working to undermine the Baathist regime.[61] Similarly, the secessionist Syrian leaders produced at the Arab League meeting at Shtoura in August 1962 a long list of Egyptian 'agents' working in Syria.[62] However, the most substantiated accusations were those relating to the activity of the UAR in Iraq, particularly its involvement in the abortive coups of Rashid Ali al-Gaylani in December 1958 and Abd al-Wahab al-Shawaf in March 1959.

The evidence of the UAR's involvement in the Gaylani affair came from Rashid Ali's two main accomplices, Mubdir al-Gaylani and Abd al-Rahim al-Rawi.[63] They testified in the 'People's Court' that they had established contact with the Counsellor at the UAR embassy at an early stage and that they had been promised arms supplies and financial assistance. The weapons were to be supplied from the town of Susa in Syria on the border with Iraq. If needed, the UAR would use its air force to drop further arms supplies to the rebels inside Iraq. Moreover early in December, the UAR embassy paid Gaylani 10,000 Iraqi dinars in a current account at the Baghdad branch of the Banque Nationale Pour la Commerce et l'Industrie.[64] Although the Egyptian press denied the UAR involvement, there can be no doubt that in this case the UAR embassy was an active participant in the affair.

The UAR has also been conclusively implicated in the abortive Shawaf revolt. The trials of the primary conspirators in the 'People's Court' clearly prove the UAR's involvement.[65] However, the most damning evidence came seven years later in an article written by the leading civilian member of the abortive coup, Mahmoud al-Durra.[66] Durra admitted that on the night of the revolt, March 7, he and another plotter took an army lorry to the Syrian border and brought back a small Syrian radio station. The station was used the next morning to broadcast the first communiqué, composed by Durra, to the people of Mosul. However, too weak to reach other parts of Iraq, the radio station was abandoned and the communiqué was taped and broadcast through Damascus Radio to the Iraqi people throughout Sunday March 8. Durra further suggested that 'there was a prior understanding between the revolutionary officers and the UAR's authorities that a squadron of UAR planes would be used for the protection of the revolutionary base in Mosul from the air. . . A reason for the non-implementation of this agreement could be the time factor (i.e. the speed with which the coup had collapsed).'[67]

Although the UAR authorities usually reacted with extreme indignation to any suggestions relating to the alleged participation of the UAR in clandestine activities, there is enough evidence to suggest that this instrument was frequently resorted to by the UAR leadership in an effort to achieve their foreign policy objectives. Within this context, subversion and other clandestine activities seem to have been particularly effective in situations of intensive intra-state as well as inter-state conflict. Consequently, this instrument was specifically directed at states undergoing domestic turmoil and upheavals such as Iraq in 1958–9 and again during the 1963 Baathist rule, Jordan after the Iraqi revolution, Lebanon in May–June 1958, and post-secession Syria. On the other hand, the relatively minimal utility of this instrument to the Egyptian leaders in their bitter struggle with other 'enemies' of Egypt, such as Tunisia and Saudi Arabia, suggests that they correctly perceived the low-level domestic conflict existing within these two countries.

THE THREAT AND USE OF FORCE

This instrument relates to the efforts of one government to affect a desirable orientation in the policies of another government through the use, or threat, of physical coercion. In terms of cost-benefit evaluation, this instrument is used usually only as a last resort – when the objective pursued is perceived to be significant for the maintenance of the foreign policy system as a whole and when all other instruments have failed to achieve the desired objective. The threat or use of force is utilised either to support a perceived friendly regime against domestic rebels or foreign intervention, or to help a rebellious movement against a perceived antagonistic regime. In the case of Egypt, force was used twice as an instrument of foreign policy – in the wake of the Syrian secession and in the immediate aftermath of the partially successful Yemeni coup. Both these cases have already been adequately dealt with in previous sections of this study.[68] Suffice it to say here that the main feature of both operations was the perceived significance of the causal situation to the foreign policy system of Egypt. The Syrian secession and the Yemeni civil war were both perceived in 'progress versus reaction' terms; both were seen as an effort to isolate Egypt strategically and politically from the area; both were viewed as a challenge to Egypt's prestige and leadership in the Arab world; both were interpreted as empirical proof of the increasing power of forces determined to bring about the downfall of the Egyptian regime itself; and finally (and probably crucially) both cases were erroneously perceived as requiring only limited and short-term interventions for the purpose of achieving the leadership's desired objectives. As such, in terms of cost-gain evaluation and due to the impotence of other instruments to affect the desired result, the Egyptian leadership, in these two cases, resorted to the use of military intervention as an instrument of foreign policy.

CONCLUSION

This chapter has dealt with a number of methods which the Egyptian decision-makers utilised for the purpose of achieving their foreign policy objectives. The analysis has been primarily illustrative and explanatory in character. The concluding section, however, will attempt to abstract from this specific, one-country study, a number of assumptions relating to the use by a government of its foreign policy instruments. These assumptions will be posited as 'general hypotheses' which can be empirically tested in future studies for the purpose of theory-building. In this particular case, the abstracted hypotheses are:

Hypothesis 1: A state which is committed to expansionary goals and/or ideological principles but which lacks military or economic capabilities will utilise propaganda and/or clandestine activities as its primary instruments of foreign policy.

Hypothesis 2: In a situation where the 'target' country suffers from acute political, ideological and/or socio-economic cleavages, the decision-makers of the communicating country will adopt clandestine activities and/or propaganda as their primary instrument of foreign policy.

Hypothesis 3: The instrument of physical coercion will be utilised only when the objective pursued is deemed by the decision-makers to be particularly crucial for the maintenance of the foreign policy system as a whole, and when all efforts to use other instruments have been either exhausted or deemed inoperative in the specific case.

Hypothesis 4: In terms of the perceived cost-benefit calculus, and depending on the level of inter-state conflict (low or high), diplomacy and propaganda are the most widely used instruments of foreign policy.

As has been indicated, these hypotheses, relating to the instruments of foreign policy, have been abstracted from this specific study of Egypt's foreign relations with the countries of the Arab world for the purpose of theory-building. The achievement of this objective can be realised only when these hypotheses are rigorously applied to, and tested against, comparable studies of other states. The type of results arrived at will indicate whether these hypotheses can be treated as valid components of a partial theory of state behaviour.

13 The New Era: Egypt's Foreign Policy Under Sadat

One of the main features of Egypt's political system during 1954–70 was the intensely personalised presidency of Gamal Abd al-Nasser which stamped that era with a distinctive style that obviously could not be emulated or repeated. Thus, with the death of the Chief Executive on September 28, 1970, an entire page of Egypt's history came to an abrupt end. Due to Nasser's charismatic authority and the consequent lack of an independently legitimate institutional structure,[1] most observers predicted that systemic dislocation would soon follow the demise of the towering leader. Yet six years later, the regime of Nasser's successor, Anwar al-Sadat, has proved not only secure but also capable of persisting in spite of certain trends in its domestic and foreign policy that ran against the tenets of Nasserite ideology. In the Arab sphere, the policy of President Sadat, while seemingly similar to that of Nasser during 1967–70, has exhibited subtle differences in emphasis which indicate basic shifts in the underlying elements of the policy. To analyse and explain these elements, and to facilitate comparison with the Nasserite era, the foreign policy model, which has served as the methodological infrastructure of this study, will be utilised in this chapter to explore the setting, the actors, the attitudes and the processes of Egypt's Arab policy under President Sadat.

CAPABILITIES AND CONSTRAINTS

The External Environment
In the global system, both superpowers have endeavoured to decrease the level of hostility and polarisation by consciously pursuing policies of crisis management rather than crisis escalation. This is evident from the several SALT meetings, the various summit conferences between the leaders of the two superpowers, and the diplomatic activities undertaken by both parties during the October 1973 war in order to confine the conflict to the regional system.[2]

The detente at the global level, however, did not preclude superpower competition at the regional level. Both superpowers continued to safeguard their political and strategic interests in the area through massive injection of military and economic aid. In the case of Egypt, client–patron relations have significantly changed from that under President Nasser. Apart from a temporary respite during 1973, Egyptian–Soviet relations have progressively worsened since President Sadat expelled some 21,000 Russian advisers from Cairo in July 1972 as a result of the Soviet unwillingness to supply Egypt with modern offensive weapons. On the other hand, the United States, through the imaginative diplomacy of its Secretary of State, Henry Kissinger, has witnessed a dramatic upsurge in its fortune in the area. After nearly two decades of bitter inter-state hostility, US–Egyptian relations became overtly cordial in the wake of the October war, to the extent that President Nixon was given a triumphant tour of the country in 1974.

These changes in the intrusive activities of the global system acted both as a capability for, and a constraint on, the formulation and implementation of Egypt's foreign policy. The Egyptian-induced break in Soviet–Egyptian relations earned the unequivocal approval of the conservative, yet oil-rich states of the Arab world. Virulently anti-Communist, these states, particularly Saudi Arabia, proceeded to extend massive financial aid to Egypt to further decrease Egypt's dependence on the Soviet Union. Domestically, too, the expulsion of the Soviet advisers was enthusiastically greeted by an Egyptian public that had become resentful of the seemingly pervasive Russian presence. Moreover, this increase in public support came at a time when the President's popularity at the mass level was at a low ebb in view of his inability to fulfill the promise of making 1971 'the year of decision' regarding Arab–Israeli relations. Finally, the improvement of relations with the United States allowed the Egyptian leadership to make political demands on the one power which possessed the capability for inducing Israel to make meaningful concessions.

On the other hand, however, the paralysis in Egyptian–Soviet relations has deprived Egypt of the capability to manipulate the competitive nature of the bi-polarised global system. As present relations stand, Egypt does not possess the option which it put to good use in the early sixties – that of playing one superpower against the other. This is certainly evident from the fact that the Egyptian leadership has found it extremely difficult to replace Soviet economic and military assistance with American aid. In this respect, the Egyptian decision-makers seem to have underestimated the influence of the pro-Israel American Congress on the implementation of United States foreign policy.[3] Moreover, while gaining the support of the conservative Arab elements, Sadat's seemingly anti-Soviet orientations have equally alienated the 'radical' and 'leftist' forces inside Egypt and in the Arab world generally. These have tended to perceive Sadat's policies as a flagrant reversal of the Nasserite socialist, anti-imperialist crusade.

It is important to note, however, that whatever their perception of Egyptian policies, whether they have approved or disapproved of them, the Arabs have continued to accord Egypt a position of centrality which has enhanced its capabilities. For example, in announcing its decision to cease its attacks on the Egyptian regime in May 1975, the Libyan radio explained: 'We are convinced that Egypt is the heart of Arabism, and has constantly made sacrifices for the Arab nation. It is also the rock on which the ambitions of the enemies of this nation were wrecked.'[4] Moreover, Heikal contends that in the course of the deliberations over the timing of the October 1973 operations, General Yusif Shakur, the Syrian Chief of Staff, told General Ahmad Ismael, Egypt's War Minister: 'If Damascus falls it can be recaptured; if Cairo falls the whole Arab nation falls.'[5] While not necessarily imposing an obsequious posture on the other Arab states, such perceptions have tended to strengthen Egypt's hand in inter-Arab diplomatic and political bargaining.

The Domestic Environment

Demographically, Egypt has remained the most densely populated state in the Arab world. Apart from its obvious utility for the industrial and military potential of the country, the sheer size of the population in comparison with other Arab countries has significantly contributed to Egypt's persisting centrality in the Arab world. Table 18 clearly shows the considerable gap between the size of Egypt's population and those of the other Arab states. Moreover, Egypt's population has continued to grow by about 2.5 per cent annually, and the total increase during 1971–5 has amounted to 9.7 per cent.

Egypt's large population contains a correspondingly large and well qualified middle-class sector. As has been discussed, the enormous efforts expended by the Nasserite leadership to expand education at

TABLE 18
Populations of Egypt and the other Arab States, 1971–5
(millions)

	Asian Arabs[a]	African Arabs[b] Excluding Egypt	Egypt	Total Arab	% of Egypt to Total
1971	37.1	53.4	34.2	124.7	27
1972	39.4	55.7	34.9	130.0	27
1973	41.1	56.7	35.7	133.5	27
1974	42.0	58.4	36.6	137.0	27
1975	43.5	60.2	37.5	141.2	27

[a] Iraq, Jordan, Kuwait, Lebanon, Saudi Arabia, Syria, YAR, PDRY.

[b] Algeria, Libya, Morocco, Sudan, Tunisia.

Source: IISS, *The Military Balance, 1971–1972*, pp. 27–33; *1972–1973*, pp. 29–36; *1973–1974*, pp. 31–40; *1974–1975*, pp. 31–40; *1975–1976*, pp. 30–9; also United Nations, *Demographic Yearbook*, 1973, pp. 101–107.

the secondary and university level tended to produce a surplus of educated personnel who could not be absorbed by the country's economic, social and educational institutions. This trend has continued in the present period in which almost all of those concerned with educational planning agree that university graduates are far too many for the country's needs.[6] Consequently, many of these graduates have been dispatched to teach and work in the educational institutions of Arab and other developing countries. The consequent ability of the Egyptian teachers to inculcate the future elites of these countries with Egypt-oriented values has constituted an important capability of Egypt's foreign policy.

The high growth rate of Egypt's population has also had inbuilt disadvantages. To begin with, it has continued to outstrip the increase in agricultural land and production, thus adversely affecting the man–land ratio. More generally, it has significantly compounded the problems of Egypt's structurally fragile economy, in which the efforts to achieve an equitable growth has been retarded not only by the scarcity of basic raw materials and currency-earning commodities, but also by the country's rapidly increasing population.

The continuing weakness of the Egyptian economy can be clearly discerned from an examination of Egypt's trade balance with foreign countries (see Table 19). As has already been shown, Nasser's efforts to industrialise the country were beginning to bear fruit by 1970. In that year, Egypt's exports succeeded in decreasing the country's deficit to a manageable $22 million. This trend has certainly continued during the present period, and in fact, as a result of the consistent improvement in Egypt's export drive, the trade balance in 1973 showed a healthy surplus of $211 million. However, due to the severe world inflation, which exposed the economy's basic fragility, and to the massive defence expenditure, the value of Egypt's imports in 1974 registered a staggering 160 per cent increase over the 1973 level. Consequently, even with

TABLE 19
Egypt's Trade Balance, 1970–4
($ million)

	Exports	Imports	Balance
1970	762	784	−22
1971	789	920	−131
1972	825	899	−74
1973	1,117	906	+211
1974	1,516	2,348	−832

Source: United Nations, *Monthly Bulletin of Statistics*, June 1975, pp. 112–13.

exports reaching the record value of $1516 million, Egypt's trade balance in 1974 showed a deficit of $832 million. Moreover, this upward trend shows no sign of receding in the near future. In fact Egypt's economic plight has reached such alarming proportions that it now finds itself needing more than $1000 million a year in foreign currency just to feed her population, leaving nothing for capital investment.[7]

As indicated above, the adverse economic situation has been aggravated by Egypt's phenomenal spending on her armed forces. Egypt's defence expenditure as a percentage of her Gross National Product has risen from 13.5 in 1967 to a crippling 34.1 in 1975.[8] According to the director of the Central Bank of Egypt, the country has spent, or has borrowed in order to spend, no less than $25,000 million on military equipment and operations during the period 1967–75.[9] Military spending on this scale has necessitated corresponding sacrifices in other sectors of the economy, and as such it has emphasised the subservience of domestic consideration to the primary Egyptian foreign policy objective of 'eradicating the traces of Israeli aggression'. The economic variable can therefore be posited as a primary determinant of Egypt's decision to accept American mediation in the Arab–Israeli conflict in the wake of the October 1973 war.

While it has unquestionably constituted a huge burden on the country, Egypt's defence expenditure has had, nevertheless, one redeeming feature, in the sense that, as Table 20 clearly illustrates, it has maintained Egypt's military centrality in the Arab world. The interesting aspect here is that Egypt's defence expenditure has consistently amounted to nearly three times as much as the combined total expenditure of Iraq, Syria and Jordan, the next three Arab states in military ranking.

In its impact on Arab perceptions, the quantity of Egypt's military hardware has constituted an undoubted capability for Egypt. Arab public and leaders alike have continued to accept Egypt's military

TABLE 20
Defence Expenditure of Selected Arab Countries, 1971–5
($ million)

	1971	*1972*	*1973*	*1974*	*1975*
Iraq	237.2	237.2	338.0	803.0	803.0
Syria	176.0	206.5	216.0	460.0	668.0
Jordan	90.4	90.4	119.2	142.0	155.0
Total	503.6	534.1	673.2	1,405.0	1,626.0
Egypt	1,495.0	1,510.0	1,737.0	3,117.0	6,103.0

Source: IISS, *The Military Balance, 1971–1972*, pp. 27–33; *1972–1973*, pp. 29–36; *1973–1974*, pp. 30–8; *1974–1975*, pp. 31–40; *1975–1976*, pp. 31–40.

leadership in the Arab world and to regard Egypt's armed forces as the backbone of the Arab 'struggle' against Israel. Thus, according to Heikal, the Syrian Chief of Staff General Shakur told General Ismael, the Egyptian War Minister during the final preparations for the October war: 'If there is failure on the Egyptian front, it will be the end of the Arabs, which means the end of Syria. If there is failure on the Syrian Front this would not be the end. It is on Egypt that all our hopes are pinned.'[10] It is probably this high regard for Egypt's military capability which can best explain the bitterly hostile response of the Palestinians to the Egyptian–Israeli disengagement agreement of September 1975.

The Egyptian–Israeli accord, however, clearly illustrates that, as far as the Egyptians were concerned, the economic cost of Egypt's defence expenditure far outweighed its political benefits of enhancing Egypt's centrality in the Arab world. Egypt's military spending, coupled with the country's burdensome overpopulation, and the paucity of its basic raw materials and currency-earning commodities, have made Egypt almost totally dependent on foreign aid for economic survival and solvency. Thus, for example, during August 1974, Egypt received $300 million in grants-in-aid from Saudi Arabia, $21 million in long-term loans and $63 million in short-term loans from France, and $1285 million in credits and assistance from the International Bank for Reconstruction and Development.[11] In November of the same year, Prime Minister Abd al-Aziz Hegazi toured the countries of the Arabian Peninsula and secured in the process funds totalling $2500 million from Saudi Arabia, Qatar, United Arab Emirates, Bahrain and Kuwait.[12] Indeed, between 1967 and 1975, Saudi Arabia alone extended aid to Egypt totalling $2600 million.[13] Moreover, by mid-1975, Egypt's indebtedness to the West, including short-term borrowing, had amounted to something like $3000 million, while East bloc loans for civilian projects had amounted to the equivalent of at least $1000 million.[14] This debt has been largely paid in exports of cotton, which have reduced the hard-currency-earning capacity of the country.

As has been indicated before, heavy dependence on foreign aid can constitute a clear constraint on the recipient's foreign policy. It can be utilised by the donor state as a possible weapon if it wishes to induce a specific reorientation in the foreign policy of the recipient country. Thus, for example, the Soviet Union's refusal to grant President Sadat's request for a long-term moratorium on the repayment of Soviet credits occurred in the wake of the increasing rapport between Egypt and the United States. Similarly, the United States' decision in the spring of 1975 to freeze temporarily an Israeli request for $3000 million in aid constituted a crucial contributing factor to Israel's acceptance of the interim agreement in September 1975.

Foreign aid can also be a constraining influence on the recipient's foreign policy without it being consciously pursued by the donor state. Whatever the attitude of the donors, the recipient decision-makers will always need to take foreign aid into their consideration when formulating their policies. For example, it could be argued that Egypt's campaign to blame the Soviet Union for Palestinian hostility to the interim agreement[15] could be at least partly attributed to Egyptian efforts to placate the pro-Palestinians, yet virulently anti-Soviet, Saudi government.

In their effort to rectify the deteriorating economic situation, the present Egyptian leadership has increasingly resorted to liberalising the Nasserite economic structure. Since the October war, the Egyptian government has pursued an 'open door' policy designed to encourage Arab and Western investment in Egypt as a means of stimulating the stagnating economy and increasing hard currency reserves. In July 1975, the National Assembly effectively reversed Nasser's nationalisation measures of 1960–2 by allowing foreign banks to resume operations in Egypt, by easing import and export restrictions, and by decentralising the public sector.[16] While the long-term results of these measures cannot yet be assessed, it is nevertheless apparent that Sadat's 'open door' policy has not halted (indeed some would argue that it has actually stimulated) Egypt's spiralling inflation. This assumption seems to be confirmed by Table 21, which shows that during the six years spanning July 1967–June 1973 the consumer price index rose by 29.3 points in the rural areas and 18.9 points in the urban areas. However, the following fifteen months witnessed increases of 23.4 and 19.4 points in the two areas, respectively. The steepest rises were recorded in foodstuffs and beverages, whose price index during the period January 1973–September 1974 advanced by 19.8 points in the rural areas and 29.0 in the urban areas.[17] These rises occurred in spite of a government

TABLE 21
The Consumer Price Index, 1967–74
(1966–7 = 100)

	Rural Area	*Urban Area*
1967–8	101.8	102.0
1968–9	105.6	106.1
1969–70	113.5	109.2
1970–1	117.9	113.6
1971–2	117.6	116.3
1972–3	129.3	118.9
Jan 1974	141.0	129.0
Sept 1974	152.7	138.3

Source: National Bank of Egypt, *Economic Bulletin*, vol. 28, no. 1, 1975, pp. 120–1; Central Bank of Egypt, *Economic Review*, vol. 14, no. 4, 1974, pp. 213–15.

subsidy of $1475 million in 1974, designed to protect the Egyptian consumer from the rocketing world commodity prices. As usual, therefore, those at the lower end of the economic scale have been the hardest hit.

The worsening economic situation has naturally resulted in much social discontent, particularly among industrial workers whose inadequate $30 a month wage packets have been further eroded by the soaring inflation. A number of strikes, demonstrations and riots have thus occurred during 1974 and 1975, which have manifested the growing impatience of this most 'Nasserite' sector of society with the economic and social policies of the present leadership. For example, on January 1, 1975, workers from the Helwan iron and steel complex rioted in downtown Cairo chanting: 'Ya batal al-Ubur, feen al-futur?' which translates to 'hero of the [Canal] crossing, where is our breakfast?'[18] Sadat responded to the demonstrations by announcing reallocations from the hard currency budget for imports of essentials like meat, tea, sugar and cheap cotton fabrics.

The demands of the rioting crowd, however, reflected a more general malaise than the mere concern over the rising cost of living. Chanting such slogans as 'Sadat, your government are thieves and you are blind', and 'We work full-time and the government robs the country full-time,'[19] the demonstrating workers and their student sympathisers were communicating to the leadership their disillusionment with the country's entire social structure. In present day Egypt, and particularly in Cairo, mass transport, sewage systems, water supplies, telephone communications, roads, hospitals and similar services are painfully inadequate. Government and bureaucratic corruption is rampant, and the gap between the rich few and the poor masses has, if anything, become greater as a result of the 'liberalisation measures'. As such, until some way is found to overcome Egypt's massive social and economic problems, the Egyptian leadership will need to continue to be sensitive to the demands of this highly vociferous pressure group.

Generally, however, the strictly authoritarian nature of Egypt's political system has tended to seriously diminish the power and independence of pressure groups, a situation which is readily apparent in the case of the Egyptian press. While President Sadat has consistently declared that his foremost concern has been to 'liberate the press from the yoke of censorship',[20] in reality the freedom of the press to question, probe or criticise has been rigidly controlled. Editorial comment in all the papers has tended to mirror the leadership's current attitudes towards the Soviet Union, the Nasser era, the public sector, the liberalisation measures, Arab unity, Libyan hostility and so forth. Yet on the policies of the present leadership, the press have been generally far more restrained and cautious. For example, while the press were obviously 'free' to claim in February 1974 that Nasser's sequestration measures turned 'once peaceful Egypt into a gruesome theatre of torture, unprecedented in the darkest years of the Middle Ages',[21] six months later, the most muted innuendoes about the state of Egypt's economy were immediately condemned by Sadat and resulted in his decision to reorganise the press.[22] In another instance, the first copy of a new publication, *Horiyah* [Freedom], was banned in April 1974 because it criticised United States policies, and in February 1974, Heikal was dismissed from his post at *al-Ahram* for gently cautioning against too much dependence on the United States. Thus, whatever the claims of the present leadership, the Egyptian press have continued to be completely subservient to the wishes and dictates of the decision-making elite. As a result, the Egyptian papers have been inclined to overlook all domestic and foreign policy issues deemed embarrassing to the current leadership. For example, the huge anti-Sadat demonstrations staged by students of Cairo University in January 1972 were largely ignored by the press. Instead, the papers gave prominence to a telegram of support sent to the President by the Alexandria students.[23] Similarly, the letter in support of Israel, which was signed by seventy-six United States senators in May 1975, failed to appear in any of the Arabic-language Egyptian papers. The letter was later published only after a strong protest from members of the National Assembly.[24] Therefore, by endorsing and applauding rather than questioning and criticising, the Egyptian press have constituted a foremost capability for the Sadat regime.

The religious community as a group have also formed an important segment of Sadat's power base. Unlike their support of Nasser in his inter-Arab quarrels, the religious community of the al-Azhar institution have used their moral authority to cement Sadat's domestic position. For example, in the wake of the student unrest in January 1973, the President of al-Azhar sent a message to Sadat expressing 'absolute support for your excellency's vigilant and wise leadership . . . may God grant you success, guide your steps on the right path, and keep you as support for the homeland, Islam and Arabdom.'[25] The al-Azhar University followed its president's initiative by asking everyone to 'rally round the leadership of Sadat whom God has entrusted with guiding the ship of state through rough seas'.[26] In the traditionally devout and conservative Moslem society of Egypt, such pronouncements held undoubted benefits for the Egyptian leaders.

INSTITUTIONS AND PROCESSES

In Nasser's Egypt, the legitimacy of the political system was not dependent upon any institutional or legal imperatives, but on the charismatic authority of the Chief Executive. Naturally, therefore, the political structure left by Nasser was geared towards maintaining a strong presidency which would possess the power to make formal decisions without much intrusion from the other institutions. On the other hand, however, no person in Egypt possessed enough prestige to be able to immediately fill the role left by the departing leader. Consequently, upon the death of President Nasser, a sort of collective leadership emerged comprising the new President, Anwar al-Sadat, his two Vice-Presidents, Ali Sabri and Hussein Shafei, Prime Minister Mahmoud Fawzi, and other important figures such as Sha'arawi Juma'a, the Interior Minister, and Muhammed Fawzi, the War Minister. In this configuration, Sadat was the first among equals but his power base was not necessarily stronger than that of his competitors.

The Principal Decision-Maker

Mitigating against the permanency of a collective leadership in Egypt, however, was Nasser's own legacy, which was reinforced by a political culture emphasising the predominance of a strong central authority. As such, with the passage of time, a power struggle between the various competing interests was bound to occur. The struggle was initiated by those in the collective leadership who were becoming alarmed by Sadat's increasing tendency to take unilateral decisions. By May 1971, the President was, indeed, pursuing strong leadership from the top. For example, the decision to join Libya and Syria in the Federation of Arab Republics was taken by Sadat alone without any consultations. By this time, it was becoming clear that Sadat's perceptions of the role of the Chief Executive in the decision-making process differed little from that of his predecessor. Within this context, Sadat declared in the May Day speech in 1971: 'When the people elected me President of the Republic this was actually a solemn agreement between me and the people to preserve and strengthen national unity in preparation for the battle of destiny.'[27] This perception was certainly not shared by the other members of the collective leadership, each of whom considered himself to be the rightful heir to the mantle of Nasser. The conflict reached its climax in mid-May 1971 when the anti-Sadat faction within the leadership unsuccessfully attempted to oust him from the presidency. As a result of the abortive coup, Sadat succeeded in eliminating from the political power structure some of his most powerful rivals. This group included Ali Sabri, Sha'arawi Juma'a and General Muhammed Fawzi, in addition to Sami Sharaf, the Minister for Presidential Affairs, Hilmi al-Said, Minister of Power, Sa'ad Zaid, Minister of Housing, Muhammed Faiq, Minister of Information, Abd al-Muhsin Abu al-Nur, the Secretary-General of the Arab Socialist Union, Dhiya al-din Daud, member of the ASU's Supreme Executive Committee, and Labib Shuqair, the President of the National Assembly. Also the heads of the two intelligence services were replaced and more than 100 senior officers were dismissed from these services and from the police. Similarly, about forty army officers of varying ranks were purged. Many senior officials of the Ministry of Information were replaced and the heads of Egypt's radio and television stations were retired. With these measures, Sadat's position in the governmental structure was finally consolidated.

However, Sadat had yet to establish a broad power base among the people. To this end, he initiated a series of support-winning policies designed to strengthen his mass popularity. The first such measure was Sadat's proclamation that 1971 would be the year of decision – a year in which the stalemate produced by the 'no peace, no war' situation in the Arab–Israeli conflict would be broken. For reasons still unclear, though, the 'year of decision' failed to materialise, and as a result, Sadat's credibility was undermined. However, his dramatic expulsion of over 21,000 Soviet personnel from Egypt in July 1972 increased his prestige in the country, particularly amongst the armed forces. His newly-acquired esteem was institutionalised in March 1973 when in a cabinet reshuffle, Sadat appointed himself Prime Minister and Military Governor-General. This process of consolidation was completed with Egypt's successes in the October war, which were largely attributed to the courage, cunning and decisiveness of President Sadat. The cumulative effect of these 'achievements' meant that Sadat no longer needed to continually proclaim his allegiance to the memory and principles of President Nasser, an allegiance typified by the following statement in November 1971: 'We find ourselves without his [Nasser's] presence among us, and his mind, organization and leadership – although his thoughts, principles and attitudes remain as an inexhaustible treasure for us forever.'[28] In the aftermath of the October war, Sadat finally emerged from the shadow of his towering predecessor to establish himself as the principal decision-maker in his own right.

On acquiring this new status, Sadat began to enact measures designed to modify the ideological, economic and political foundations upon which the Nasser legacy was based. In the domestic sector, he embarked upon an economic 'liberalization' programme which included opening the Egyptian economy to foreign investment and encouraging the emergence of a vigorous private sector designed to operate parallel to, and in competition with, the pervasive public sector. These measures were obviously completely antithetic to the fundamental tenets of Nasserism.

In foreign policy, one of the major departures from the Nasserite past has been Sadat's rapprochement with the United States, a move primarily resulting from Sadat's belief that the Americans alone held the key to peace in the Middle East. Moreover, as his rapport with the United States increased, his relations with the Soviet Union witnessed a corresponding decline. Indeed, the extent of this deterioration in Soviet–Egyptian relations could not have been thought possible at the time of Nasser's death.

The Subordinate Institutional Structure

Sadat's leadership has differed from Nasser's not only in substance but also in style. With the consolidation of his authority, Sadat has exhibited a far greater tendency to delegate administrative duties to his chief lieutenants. Thus, cabinet members have participated more actively in the execution, and sometimes even the formulation, of Egypt's policies. For example, it was Premier Abd al-Aziz Hegazi who, on a tour of the Arab Gulf states in November–December 1974, secured funds totalling $2500 for Egypt's economic and monetary requirements.[29] Similarly, on two separate occasions during 1975, Vice-President Husni Mubarak visited a number of Arab capitals in an effort to rally Arab support for Egypt's interim agreement with Israel. It is noteworthy that during his tours, Mubarak made a series of important policy statements.

The appointment of General Mubarak to the vice-presidency emphasises the close association between the presidency and the defence establishment. Under Sadat, the military have continued to occupy the central position in the decision-making process which they had filled during the Nasser era. This was particularly true after the October war when the prestige and influence of Marshall Ahmad Ismael, who represented the military's interests in the cabinet, was second only to that of Sadat's. However, unlike the independent decision-making power which accrued to Marshall Abd Al-Hakim Amer in the mid-sixties, Sadat seems to have successfully kept the military under firm presidential control. This can be discerned, for example, from Sadat's unilateral decision to dismiss the popular Minister of War, General Muhammed Sadeq, in October 1972, along with the Deputy Minister of War, the Commander of the Navy, the General commanding the central military area, and the Director of Intelligence. The catalyst for this summary purge was apparently a difference of opinion between Sadat and the army's hierarchy over the president's conception of a limited war with Israel.[30] Presidential control of the military is also evident from Sadat's sudden announcement in December 1973 of his decision to dismiss the army's highly respected Chief of Staff, General Saad Shazli, who earlier had been eulogised as one of the heroes of the October war.

The rest of the institutional structure has remained subordinate to the presidency, particularly in the foreign policy sector. The Arab Socialist Union, Egypt's sole political party, along with the National Assembly, the country's parliament, have continued to function primarily as mobilisational and legitimising agents for the executive branch. Despite Sadat's repeated proclamations that the ASU, for example, was to be the 'source of all power',[31] the organisation's subordinate status has changed very little since the Nasser era. However, it must be remembered that the power relationship between the presidency and these two organisations is inversely proportional. In other words, the degree of the subservience of the ASU and National Assembly to the presidency is primarily dependent on the relative strength of the latter institution at any given time. Thus, for example, during the presidency's weakest periods, the National Assembly in December 1972 was able to criticise the government 'for asserting that a plan to prepare the country for war had been completed while facts indicated the contrary'.[32] Yet even in this rare outbreak of criticism, the discontent of the National Assembly was wholly directed at the Prime Minister, Aziz Sidqi, rather than at President Sadat himself. Generally, therefore, the records of both the ASU and the National Assembly have indicated the tendency to mirror and confirm presidential decisions.

Because the entire institutional structure is dependent for its momentum upon presidential direction and control, the durability of the decision-making process will continue to be determined by the strength of the presidency. Whereas the authority of Nasser's presidency lay in his charismatic relationship with the Egyptian people, a relationship which could, and did, endure defeat, Sadat has yet to establish a charismatic authority in Egypt. The legitimacy of President Sadat is based not on charisma, but on a functional relationship with the people which is dependent on continued 'successes' in the foreign and domestic sectors. There can be no doubt that this consideration has constituted an important determinant in the formulation of such decisions as the expulsion of the Soviet advisers, the October war, the liberalisation of Egypt's economy, the opening of the Suez Canal, and the interim agreement with Israel.

VALUES AND IMAGES

As has been shown, Sadat's legitimacy in the period immediately following Nasser's death did not stem from any independently derived legal and/or institutional imperatives, but from his long association and his perceived comradeship with the late President. Therefore, until he could establish his own independently derived authority, the successor of the departing leader could deviate very little from such cherished Nasserite principles as anti-imperialism, Arabism and the leadership of the Arab revolutionary struggle. Indeed, in a major speech to the ASU in November 1970, Sadat dutifully reiterated these principles with the same vigour and emphasis of his predecessor. On anti-imperialism, Sadat promised that 'all efforts, manpower, and economic resources will be mobilized until victory against Zionism and imperialism is achieved.'[33] On Arabism, he reminded his listeners that 'the fact that we belong to the Arab nation both historically and by common destiny (impels us) to work to unite Arab action.'[34] Moreover, efforts at such unity, Sadat insisted, 'impose on our people the duty of leading, and serving as the vanguard in, the Arab revolutionary role'.[35] Whether he genuinely believed in them or not, Sadat, at the time of these pronouncements, could not but emphasise to the nation his total and unequivocal adherence to the memory and principles of the late President.

However, as his domestic power and authority increased, Sadat began to gradually modify the Nasserite principles according to certain precepts he held of the global and regional systems. Within this context, the extremely broad parameters of Nasser's anti-imperialist struggle was narrowed by Sadat into an exclusively anti-Zionist campaign. Indeed, Nasser's vehement anti-Western orientation has been almost totally reversed. This is particularly true in the case of the United States, which had constituted the major focus of Nasser's anti-imperialist campaign, but which now seems to have replaced the Soviet Union as Egypt's trusted ally. Similarly, as Egyptian attitudes towards the Eastern bloc grew more ambivalent, Egypt's relations with the Western community as a whole, including the West European countries, became overtly warm and cordial. This transformation at the global level induced a modification in Egyptian attitudes at the regional level, as a result of which the pro-Western, conservative Arab regimes, who had formed Nasser's major regional enemies, became Sadat's main allies and supporters.

Egypt's Arab involvement has also reflected a change in its attitude towards Arab nationalism. As had been shown, this value was espoused by Nasser after the creation of the Baghdad Pact in 1955, reaching its zenith in the period following the establishment of the UAR and the subsequent collapse of the pro-West Iraqi monarchy in 1958. The organic unity of all the Arab people in South-West Asia and North Africa has formed the main operational manifestation of Arab nationalism. However, the existence of various environmental constraints on the achievement of this aspirational goal has resulted in certain scepticism regarding the viability of the goal of Arab unity. The Arab world has thus witnessed a major debate between the 'aspirationists' who adhered to Arab nationalism and advocated immediate Arab unity, and the 'pragmatists' who emphasised state nationalism (e.g. Egyptian as opposed to Arab) and prescribed domestic consolidation. This conflict between 'realism' and 'vision' was eloquently described by Heikal in these terms:

> History is a struggle between reality and paradise. Man fights his reality and aspires to an ideal about which he dreams. This is the story of mankind's history from beginning to end. The problem is that some people accept the reality and forget paradise, while others go to paradise and forget reality. . . The relation between the two is one of struggle, and without a struggle, we will be abandoning history.[36]

As his domestic power base grew stronger, Sadat began to gradually shift Egypt's attitudinal position regarding the Arab world towards an increasing emphasis on Egyptian affairs. Egypt's ideological orientation became progressively more inward-looking, thus exhibiting a clear 'Egypt-first' attitude. As such, Sadat's earlier adherence to 'Arab unity' in the period following Nasser's death had, by 1972, become subordinate to the value of 'Egyptian patriotism', a concept hardly utilised in the Nasser era. Thus, in a speech made in July 1972, Sadat declared that in the forthcoming 'battle' with Israel, 'Egyptian patriotism and Arab nationalism will, if necessary, be alone in the field. This imposes on us an organized program of action regarding Egyptian patriotism, and to safeguard it with domestic unity.'[37] This attitude grew even more pronounced in the post-1973 period. After the enormous human and material cost of the October war, the Egyptians felt that they had made enough sacrifices for the Arab cause, and that the time had come for them to turn their attention towards domestic reconstruction. Thus, replying to the Syrian accusation that he had abandoned the Arab cause by signing the interim agreement with Israel, Sadat unequivocally asserted that his first responsibility was to Egypt.[38] Such a statement is, indeed, a far cry from Nasser's often repeated assertion that his, and Egypt's, responsibility was to the Arab nation as a whole. Indeed, the support given by the Egyptians to Sadat's attitude towards the Arab world indicates that such value transformation is not confined to the leadership alone but that it reflects the orientation of Egyptian society as a whole.

One factor which has remained constant throughout the leaderships of Nasser and Sadat has been the Egyptian elite's perception of their leading role in the Arab world. As has been shown, this view is supported not only by the objective dimensions of Egypt's geographic, demographic and military capabilities, but also by the perceptions of the Arab elites generally. There can be no doubt, for example, that Qadhafi's almost fanatical desire to unite Libya and Egypt was motivated not only by his strong ideological commitment to Arab unity, but also by his belief that Egypt's capabilities would enhance his own claim to the leadership of the Arab world. It is within this context that Qadhafi allegedly made his famous assertion that whereas he was a leader without a country, Egypt was a country without a leader.[39]

Sadat's adherence to the principle of Egypt's regional centrality has reflected the conviction that the interests of the Arab world are inexorably linked to the continued strength and well-being of Egypt. This orientation is clearly discernible from the unilateral nature of some of Egypt's decisions in the regional and international systems. Thus, Sadat's extreme indignation at Syrian and Palestinian hostility to Egypt's interim agreement with Israel indicates that the Egyptian leadership had expected their policies to be met with wholehearted and unequivocal support, presumably because these policies were supposed to advance the ultimate interests of the Arab world.[40] Similarly, during the preparation for and the execution of the October war, the Egyptian leaders tended to take unilateral decisions that reflected a certain hegemonial attitude towards their Syrian allies. Thus, although the Egyptians promised to give the Syrians five days notice of D-Day, so that the Syrians would have time to empty the oil refinery at Homs, the choice of October 6 as D-Day was transmitted to the Syrians only on October 3. Despite the protestations of General Shakur, the Syrian Chief of Staff, the date stood.[41] Later on during the war, the Egyptian conditions for the cessation of fighting, as outlined by Sadat's speech to the National Assembly on October 16, were made without any prior consultation with President Asaad. The Syrian President subsequently reminded his Egyptian comrade-in-arms that he had the right to know Sadat's proposals before hearing about them in a radio broadcast.[42] Furthermore, Sadat's unilateral acceptance of the ceasefire on October 22 was made in spite of Syria's vigorous protestations. Indeed, the first time the Syrians heard about Egypt's decision was at the Security Council when the Egyptian representative announced his government's acceptance of the ceasefire.[43] It seems that an important determinant of Egyptian–Syrian relations during the war was the conviction of the Egyptian leaders that it was Egypt who bore the major responsibility for the overall planning and conduct of the war, and that Syria was a decidedly junior partner.

Running parallel to the regime's assertion of Egypt's continued centrality in the Arab world has been a corresponding emphasis on Egypt's 'prestige' and the 'dignity' of her people. Like Nasser before him, Sadat's adherence to these two principles has probably stemmed from his sensitivity to the perceived ignominy of Egypt's long history of subservience to foreign domination. Indeed, in the pre-October war period, these two values constituted crucial determinants of Sadat's foreign policy. In a speech to air force pilots in November 1971, Sadat declared that all hopes for a peaceful solution with Israel 'had come to an end, and nothing remains but to fight to regain our land, honour and dignity.'[44] While other, perhaps more important, considerations were also involved in Sadat's decision to wage the October war, the humiliating presence of Israeli troops on Egyptian soil constituted a crucial psychological impetus. As is the case with most authoritarian leaders, Sadat's perception of his own prestige became synonymous with that of Egypt. Thus, responding to General Dayan's declared plans for a new Israeli post in the Gaza strip called Yamit, Sadat said: 'every word spoken about Yamit is a knife pointing at me personally and at my self-respect.'[45] However, Egyptian achievements in foreign affairs since 1952, which culminated in the successes of October 1973, have somewhat diminished the prominence of 'prestige' as a value of Egypt's foreign policy. In the post-1973 period, the Egyptian leadership seems to have adopted the attitude that Egyptian prestige and dignity are better served by concrete achievements than by repeated emphasis in leaders' rhetoric.

POLITICAL OBJECTIVES

As has been argued, the dependence of Sadat's legitimacy, in the period immediately following on Nasser's death, on his long association with the departing leader impelled the new President to advocate Nasser's principles regarding the Arab world. Thus, during that initial period Sadat continued Nasser's pursuit of the goal of Arab unity. However, with his gradual emergence from the shadows of his predecessor, Sadat proceeded to modify this goal according to his own evaluation of the operative environmental constraints. The history of the 'Federation of Arab Republics' (FAR) clearly illustrates the relationship between Sadat's consolidation of his domestic power base and the corresponding modification in his ideological commitment to the goal of Arab unity.

At the beginning of November 1970, Sadat agreed with Numeiry of Sudan and Qadhafi of Libya to establish a union amongst the three countries. In announcing the 'historic' event, Sadat insisted that the agreement formed 'a real, solid nucleus for organized Arab unity. It [was] not an axis or a bloc in the Arab world [but] a nucleus of three states whose systems were homogeneous.'[46] Further consultations during the following months led to Sudan's withdrawal from the plan for 'domestic considerations' and to Syria's inclusion in the agreement. This resulted in the establishment, in April 1971, of the FAR comprising Egypt, Syria and Libya. Apart from other considerations, Sadat agreed to join the FAR in order to cement his internal position by exhibiting his adherence to Nasser's principles. Yet, ironically, it was this agreement which exposed the fragility of Sadat's domestic power base by inducing the May 1971 anti-Sadat movement. Indeed, Sadat's domestic position was so weak that Heikal was compelled to come to his rescue by declaring in *al-Ahram* that in agreeing to the FAR, Sadat had merely subscribed to the wishes of President Nasser.[47] However, after the failure of the anti-Sadat movement and the consequent elimination of almost all of his political rivals, Sadat's domestic power gradually increased throughout 1971 and 1972. This process was further stimulated by his enactment of support-winning measures such as his decision to expel the Soviet advisers in July 1972. As Sadat's internal popularity increased, his need to evoke the Nasserite legacy for the purpose of political entrenchment decreased, and consequently, his enthusiasm for the FAR witnessed a corresponding decline. On the other hand, Qadhafi had become, by this time, so alarmed with Sadat's growing ambivalence towards the FAR, that he decided to dispatch, in July 1973, some 30,000 Libyans on a 2000-kilometer 'holy march' to

Cairo to present Sadat with a document written 'in the blood of Libyan citizens' demanding the immediate union of the two countries.[48] The ensuing fiasco only reinforced Sadat's alienation from the FAR and the Libyan leader, and with Sadat's emergence as the undisputed leader of Egypt in the wake of the October war, future plans of the federation were unceremoniously shelved by the Egyptians.

The gradual abandonment of the goal of 'organic unity' corresponded with the growing decline in the importance of 'Arab nationalism' as a value of Egypt's foreign policy. The post-1973 emergence of 'Egyptian patriotism' as the primary value of the Egyptian decision-makers, which was reinforced by their evaluation of the benefits Egypt could receive from the massive Arab wealth, led to the adoption of 'Arab solidarity' as Egypt's major objective in the Arab world. The tenets of this objective were elaborated by Sadat in a speech in April 1975, when he advocated a program of Arab action 'that would *voluntarily* combine *all* the Arab powers with no exception for the sake of total Arab advancement and Arab security [my italics]'.[49] Despite his break with Qadhafi over the FAR and his occasional denunciation of the Baath party and the PLO, Sadat has vigorously pursued the objective of 'Arab solidarity', particularly in the post-1972 period. Thus, Egypt's relations with the majority of the Arab states have grown in cordiality, and consequently, in contrast to the Nasser era, the intra-Arab environment has generally become tranquil and co-operative. Not only has the pursuit of this objective brought Egypt political benefits, as witnessed by the unified Arab action (with the exception of Libya) during the October war, but it has also contributed to the influx of massive Arab economic aid to Egypt. As such, Egyptian policies in the Arab world have tended to reflect an economic as well as a political rationale.

ECONOMIC OBJECTIVES

In a lecture to the National Bank of Egypt in 1974, Dr Abd al-Muneim al-Qaissouni, who between 1954 and 1968 filled a variety of Cabinet posts relating to economic affairs and planning, unofficially yet clearly outlined the general tenets of Egypt's economic objectives in the Arab world. Qaissouni argued that because the October war was partly responsible for the huge increases in oil revenues, the surplus Arab countries should therefore 'feel indebted in part to the deficit countries particularly those in the front line, and that they should feel duty bound to assist them in rebuilding their infrastructure and in making up for lost time and also to enable them to develop.'[50] More specifically, Qaissouni contended that 'some of the deficit countries, particularly those directly involved in the conflict with Israel, have voiced the opinion that a major portion of the sums received by them from other Arab countries should take the form of aid or donations.'[51]

While not so direct, the official Egyptian policy statements and Egypt's actual diplomatic interaction in the Arab world have tended to affirm the general thesis of Qaissouni's argument. In April 1975, Sadat declared that 'Arab wealth has become the driving force which could best serve the economic and social structure of the *entire* Arab world [my italics]'.[52] To this end, the Egyptian leadership has initiated a series of measures such as the economic liberalisation laws, which have been designed to encourage the oil-rich Arab states to invest their surplus wealth in Egypt.[53] One major such investment occurred in January 1974, when Saudi Arabia, Kuwait, Qatar and Abu Dhabi joined Egypt in forming a $400 million company to build a 207-mile oil pipeline from Suez to Alexandria.

Egypt has also been effectively utilising her 'front-line' status to secure massive aid from the oil-rich Arab states. There can be no doubt that, in contrast to the Nasser era, the rich Arab states have come to feel 'duty bound' towards helping the confrontation states, especially Egypt. For example, in the wake of the dramatic and huge increases in oil revenues, the capital of the Kuwait Fund For Arab Economic Development was increased, in March 1974, from $680 million to $3400 million.[54] Egypt, therefore, has become a consistent recipient of Arab aid. In January 1974, Kuwait agreed to finance projects amounting to $700 million,[55] and in December it contributed a further $1300 million to help finance housing projects, the development of hydro-electric power, maritime transport, tourism and industry.[56] In November of the same year, Egypt's Prime Minister Abd Al-Aziz Hegazi secured funds totalling $1200 million from Saudi Arabia, Qatar, the United Arab Emirates and Bahrain,[57] and in July 1975, Saudi Arabia donated a further $600 million, while Kuwait gave $500 million.[58] The primacy of Egypt's economic objective is clearly discernible from Egypt's diplomatic moves in the Arab world after signing the interim agreement with Israel. Sadat's first activity after the conclusion of the agreement was to dispatch his Vice-President, General Husni Mubarak, to Saudi Arabia and Syria to explain the accord to Egypt's two most important allies. In Saudi Arabia, General Mubarak delivered a detailed message to King Khalid from Sadat, and held a series of discussions with the King and other members of the Saudi leadership in Taif. Indeed, the Egyptians openly maintained that Saudi Arabia's approval of the agreement had been obtained before Dr Kissinger embarked upon his mission. This reflects the importance attached by the Egyptian leaders to the financial and economic powers of Saudi Arabia. Moreover, the itinerary of Mubarak's tour served to emphasise the shift in Egyptian priorities from regional involvement to domestic reconstruction: although President Asaad had constituted Sadat's ally and 'brother-in-blood' during and after the October war, the first Arab leader to hear the details of the Sinai accord was not the Syrian

President but King Khalid, the foremost contributor of foreign aid to
Egypt.

INSTRUMENTS

As has been indicated, the choice of the method of policy implementation will be determined by the pursued objective and the existence or
non-existence of capabilities. Obviously, some instruments tend to be
better suited to the implementation of certain objectives than others.
Thus, depending on its capabilities at any given time, a state pursuing
expansionary goals and revolutionary objectives will usually resort to
such methods of implementation as propaganda, clandestine activities,
and/or the threat and use of force. On the other hand, a state pursuing
status quo objectives will normally utilise the method of diplomatic
interaction as its primary instrument of foreign policy. In this there
exists a continuous process of interaction between capabilities, values,
objectives and instruments.

We have seen that after his first uncertain year Sadat gradually
adopted 'Egyptian patriotism' as the major value of Egypt's foreign
policy. Consequently, and particularly after 1971, he began to pursue
the objective of 'Arab solidarity', which emphasised the continuation
of the *status quo* in inter-Arab relations. As such, the Sadat period,
which has coincided with the general deradicalisation of inter-Arab
politics, has witnessed the primacy of diplomatic interaction over the
other instruments of foreign policy.

Due to the highly centralised nature of the Egyptian decision-making
process, diplomatic activity has been usually conducted by either the
President himself or by one of his chief lieutenants. Utilising Egypt's
prestige as a regional leader, the Egyptian leadership has assumed the
role of the primary conciliator in the Arab world. Indeed, the services
of the Egyptian leaders have been frequently utilised to mediate in
disputes involving such regional actors as Iraq, Syria, Kuwait, Iran,
Jordan and the PLO. Apart from his intense antipathy towards Libya's
Qadhafi, the Egyptian President has certainly tried to remain on good
personal relationship with the other Arab heads of state. This is particularly true of the post-October 1973 period, in which Sadat has consciously endeavoured to communicate Egypt's policise and objectives to
the other Arab leaders. Thus, in order to explain the sudden normalisation of US–Egyptian relations following Kissinger's visit to Cairo in
November 1973, Sadat, in January 1974, embarked upon a diplomatic
offensive in the Arab world which included visits to Saudi Arabia,
Syria, Kuwait, Qatar, Abu Dhabi, Algeria and Morocco. Later that
year in the Rabat summit conference, Sadat and Faisal were the prime
manipulators behind the conference's major resolution, which recognised the PLO as the 'sole, legitimate representative of the Palestinian
people over any liberated Palestinian territory'.[59] In May 1975, in

order to explain Egypt's position after the temporary suspension of Kissinger's peace mission, and to mediate in the Iraqi–Syrian Euphrates dispute, Sadat visited Kuwait, Iraq, Syria and Jordan. In the case of Iraq and Jordan, this was the first such visit by an Egyptian head of state. In a general comment on the tour, Sadat declared: 'we have consolidated our Arab solidarity and our viewpoints about the immediate future. I conveyed the whole picture to them to find out their views, and we reached full agreement.'[60] Indeed, to reach any sort of agreement with the militant Iraqis over the Arab–Israeli conflict, Sadat needed considerable diplomatic skill and political acumen. This personal quality has reinforced Egypt's changing attitudes, values and goals, which altogether have made diplomatic interaction the primary instrument of Egypt's foreign policy in the Arab world.

CONCLUSION

In attempting to draw broad comparisons between the Nasser and Sadat eras, the authoritarian nature of the political system and the personalised characteristics of its decision-making process inevitably focuses the attention of the analyst on the leaders themselves, their aspirations, their concepts of leadership and their achievements.

After the reshuffle of the press which occurred in the wake of press criticisms of Kissinger's abortive peace efforts in March 1975, one re-shuffled editor described the paradox between Sadat's political aspirations and the realities of his regime in these terms:

> Sadat wants to grant political freedoms without political parties or opposition . . . he wants to 'de-Nasserize' under the slogan of 'continuing the Nasser revolution', to restore capitalism with a socialist label, to have unified, co-ordinated Arab action, but determined by himself, and to have a 'free' press uniformly expressing the views of his regime. The only way Sadat could maintain the shaky balance between the dream and reality was to lock up the opposition and muzzle the press.[61]

This quote perceptively illustrates Sadat's dilemma. The conservative background, social orientations and political style of Sadat instinctively propels him towards a Western-type social and economic order. However, lacking the charismatic authority of Nasser, Sadat's efforts to achieve his political aspirations are constrained by the continuing persistence of his predecessor's ideological and political imperatives and social direction. Indeed, as one of Nasser's main lieutenants, Sadat is himself inculcated with the general tenets of Nasserite ideology. Whether Sadat can succeed in completely extricating both Egypt and himself from the Nasserite past is open to conjecture. What is certain, however, is that this goal will not be achieved by the efforts to undermine Nasser's legacy through wholesale, anti-Nasser press campaigns.

It can be achieved only by the consolidation of Sadat's own authority, which itself is dependent upon the people's continued perception of him as a successful and meritorious leader.

Sadat's perceived 'successes', however, will need to be different from Nasser's. The late President concentrated on achieving largely foreign policy political objectives which were relevant to that particular phase in the development of Egypt's national, anti-imperialist 'struggle'. Such goals as Egypt's independence, Arab unity, and the affirmation of Egypt's role as a regional leader were pursued by Nasser in order to emphasise the final emergence of Egypt's national identity. Whether he objectively achieved these political goals is unimportant; what is relevant is that he was perceived to have achieved them. The October war was Sadat's contribution to this process of political achievements, and as a result, his popularity in Egypt received a tremendous boost. However, the changing environmental situation in the post-1973 period has necessitated a shift in priorities from foreign policy successes to domestic social and economic reconstruction. It is on the achievement of this goal that the legitimacy and permanency of Sadat's political order will depend. The irony for Sadat is that it is far more difficult to achieve concrete economic goals that it is to fulfil intangible political promises.

Notes

CHAPTER 1

1. T. Y. Ismael, *The UAR in Africa: Egypt's Policy Under Nasser*, Evanston, Illinois: Northwestern University Press, 1971, p. 7.
2. Boutrous Boutrous-Ghalli, *Azamat al-Diblomasiya al-Arabiya* [The Crisis of Arab Diplomacy], Cairo: Dar al-Kitab al-Jadid, 1969, p. 183.
3. Philip K. Hitti, *A Short History of the Near East*, London: Van Nostrand Company Inc., 1966, p. 26.
4. Vladmier B. Lotski, *Tarikh al-Aqtar al-Arabiya al-Hadith* [History of the Modern Arab States], Moscow: Progress Books, 1971, pp. 126–7.
5. George Antonious, *The Arab Awakening: The Story of the Arab National Movement*, London: Hamish Hamilton, 1938, p. 25.
6. *Ibid.*, pp. 24–5; see also Sydney N. Fisher, *The Middle East: A History*, New York: Alfred A. Knopf, 1959, p. 282.
7. Lotski, *op. cit.*, pp. 142–4; Fisher, *op. cit.*, p. 283.
8. Quoted in T. Y. Ismael, *op. cit.*, pp. 15–16.
9. Consult Patrick Seale, *The Struggle for Syria*, London: Oxford University Press, 1962, pp. 16–18.
10. Pierre Rondot, *The Changing Patterns of the Middle East*, London: Chatto and Windus, 1961, p. 79. Note also that Prince Faisal demanded independence for 'the Arabic-speaking people of Asia' only. *Ibid.*
11. The domestic power struggle within Egypt between Nahas Pasha and King Farouk, in which both sought to bolster their positions by bidding for the title of the 'Leader of the Arabs', was another factor in the creation of the Arab League. See Seale, *op. cit.*, pp. 20–1.
12. For the significant parts of Nuri's plan, see Muhammed Khalid, *The Arab States and the Arab League: A Documentary Record*, vol. II, Beirut: Khayyats, 1962, pp. 9–12.
13. For a brief analysis of the establishment of the League, see Majid Khadduri, 'Towards Arab Union', *American Political Science Review*, XL, February 1946, pp. 90–100. See also Robert W. Macdonald, *The League of Arab States: A Study in the Dynamics of Regional Organisation*, Princeton, New Jersey: Princeton University Press, 1965, pp. 33–43.
14. See, for example, A. G. Chejne, 'Egyptian Attitudes towards Pan-Arabism', *Middle East Journal*, vol. 11, no. 3, summer 1957, pp. 253–8.

CHAPTER 2

1. *Daily Telegraph*, July 11, 1955.
2. P. J. Vatikiotis, 'The Foreign Policy of Egypt', in R. C. Macridis, ed., *Foreign Policy in World Politics*, London: Prentice–Hall Inc., 1962, p. 336.
3. *Sunday Times*, June 24, 1962.
4. Erskine B. Childers, *The Road to Suez*, London: Macgibbon and Kee, 1962, pp. 120–1.
5. British Broadcasting Corporation, *Summary of World Broadcasts*: Part IV, *The Middle East*, London, January 12, 1954, p. 4. (Hereafter cited as *SWB*.)
6. *SWB*, January 15, 1954, p. 3.

7. *Ibid.*, July 21, 1954, p. 4.
8. *Al-Ahram*, March 10, 1955.
9. G. Lenczowski, 'The Objects and Methods of Nasserism', *Journal of International Affairs*, vol. 19, no. 1, January 1965, p. 66.
10. Two divergent views can be found in Maxime Rodinson, *Israel and the Arabs*, Harmondsworth: Penguin Books Ltd, 1970, pp. 65–71; and John Kimche, *The Second Arab Awakening*, London: Thames and Hudson, 1970, pp. 102–4.
11. Robert Stephens, *Nasser: A Political Biography*, London: Allen Lane, The Penguin Press, 1971, p. 157.
12. Humphrey Trevelyan, *The Middle East in Revolution*, London: Macmillan and Co. Ltd, 1970, pp. 27–8.
13. Seale, *op. cit.*, p. 236; Trevelyan, *op. cit.*, p. 28; Stephens, *op. cit.*, p. 159.
14. Charles D. Cremeans, *The Arabs and the World: Nasser's Arab Nationalist Policy*, London: Frederick A. Praeger, 1963, p. 145.
15. The Republic of Egypt, *The Constitution of the Republic of Egypt*, Cairo: Ministry of Information, 1956.
16. Anthony Eden, *Full Circle*, London: Cassell, 1960, p. 335.
17. N. Frankland and V. King, eds, *Documents on International Affairs, 1956*, London: Oxford University Press, 1959, pp. 69–70.
18. For the story of the collusion, consult Anthony Nutting, *No End of a Lesson: The Story of Suez*, London: Constable, 1967.
19. Walter Laqueuer, *The Road to War*, Harmondsworth: Penguin Books, 1968, p. 36.
20. Quoted in P. J. Vatikiotis, 'Dilemmas of Political Leadership in the Arab Middle East: The Case of the UAR', *American Political Science Review*, vol. 55, no. 1, March 1961, p. 108.
21. P. E. Zinner, ed., *Documents on American Foreign Relations, 1957*, New York: Harper and Brothers, 1958, p. 201.
22. Childers, *op. cit.*, p. 313.
23. G. A. Lipsky, *et al.*, *Saudi Arabia*, New Haven, Connecticut: Hraf Press, 1959, p. 201.
24. George Kirk, *Contemporary Arab Politics: A Concise History*, London: Methuen, 1961, pp. 110–20.
25. H. B. Westerfield, *The Instruments of American Foreign Policy*, New York: Thomas Y. Crowell Company, 1963, p. 479.
26. Dwight D. Eisenhower, *The White House Years:* Vol. II, *Waging Peace*, New York: Doubleday, 1965, p. 197.
27. Seale, *op. cit.*, p. 303.
28. Stephens, *op. cit.*, p. 271.
29. *Al-Ahram*, October 23, 1961.
30. Quoted in Seale, *op. cit.*, p. 311.

CHAPTER 3
1. UAR, *The Provisional Constitution of the United Arab Republic*, Cairo: Ministry of Information and National Guidance, 1958.
2. United Arab Republic, Information Department, *President Gamal Abd al-Nasser's Speeches and Press Interviews, 1958*, Cairo: n.d., p. 27 (hereafter cited as *Nasser's Speeches*).
3. For full text, see *ibid.*, pp. 28–45.
4. See Seale, *op. cit.* for a detailed account of this rivalry.
5. *SWB*, February 3, 1958, p. 7.
6. For a comprehensive analysis of the impact of the UAR's formation on Lebanese society and of the crisis that followed, see Fahim Qubain, *Crisis in Lebanon*, Washington: Middle East Institute, 1961.
7. See Charles Malik's speech in the United Nations Security Council of June 6, 1958. *UN Doc. S/PV. 823*, June 6, 1958, pp. 1–43. This document can be found

in Qubain, *op. cit.*, pp. 181–96.

8. *UN Doc. S/PV. 834*, pp. 1–13; Qubain, *op. cit.*, pp. 201–10.
9. *UN Doc. S/4069*, July 30, 1958, p. 21; Qubain, *op. cit.*, pp. 144–5.
10. *UN Doc. S/4085*, August 14, 1958, p. 15; Qubain, *op: cit.*, p. 145.
11. Eisenhower, *op. cit.*, p. 270.
12. *SWB*, July 26, 1958, pp. 7–9.
13. See Majid Khadduri, *Republican Iraq: A Study in Iraqi Politics since the Revolution of 1958*, London: Oxford University Press, 1969, pp. 113–17; also Uriel Dann, *Iraq Under Qassem: A Political History, 1958–1963*, pp. 69–107.
14. *SWB*, November 6, 1958, p. 6.
15. *Al-Ahram*, November 28, 1958.
16. Childers, *op. cit.*, p. 349.
17. See below, p. 178.
18. *Al-Akhbar* (Beirut), December 14, 1958.
19. *Nasser's Speeches*, 1958, pp. 353–5.
20. *Al-Ahram*, January 27, 1959.
21. *SWB*, March 11, 1959, p. 11; March 12, 1959, p. 10.
22. *Nasser's Speeches, 1959*, pp. 126–33.
23. *Ibid.*, p. 149; see also *SWB*, March 19, 1959, p. 10.
24. *SWB*, March 18, 1959; p. 9.
25. Quoted in Benjamen Shwadran, *The Power Struggle in Iraq*, New York: Council for Middle Eastern Affairs Press, 1960, p. 50.
26. *Al-Thawra* (Baghdad), November 16, 1959.
27. *Ibid.*, March 28, 1959.
28. Stephens, *op. cit.*, p. 343.
29. *Ibid.*, p. 333; *al-Ahram*, November 17, 1961.
30. Malcolm Kerr, *The Arab Cold War, 1958–1970*, London: Oxford University Press, 1971, p. 34.
31. *SWB*, October 3, 1961, ME/758/A/5.
32. *Al-Ahram*, March 31, 1961.
33. *SWB*, June 27, 1961, ME/675/A/1–3.
34. *Al-Ahram*, July 5, 1961.
35. *The Times*, September 21, 1961; see also *SWB*, October 4, 1961, ME/759/A/10.

CHAPTER 4

1. *Nasser's Speeches, 1961*, p. 243.
2. *Ibid.*, pp. 261–2.
3. *Ibid.*, pp. 293–4.
4. *Ibid.*, p. 296.
5. *Al-Ahram*, November 3, 1961.
6. *Ibid.*, November 24, 1961.
7. *Nasser's Speeches, 1961*, pp. 258–86.
8. *Ibid.*, pp. 285–6.
9. United Arab Republic, *The Charter*, Cairo: Information Department, 1962.
10. For an explanation of 'Political Culture', see Gabriel Almond and G. Bingham Powell, Jr, *Comparative Politics: A Developmental Approach*, Boston: Little Brown, 1966, pp. 50–72.
11. UAR, *The Charter*, p. 35.
12. *Ibid.*, p. 40.
13. *Ibid.*, p. 21.
14. *Ibid.*, p. 22.
15. *Ibid.*, p. 79.
16. *SWB*, October 4, 1961, ME/759/A/12; *al-Jumhuriya*, October 30, 1961; see also *Nasser's Speeches, 1961*, pp. 347–61.
17. *Nasser's Speeches, 1962*, p. 45.

18. Tom Little, *Modern Egypt*, London: Ernest Benn Ltd, 1967, p. 199.
19. Interview with *Look* magazine on March 4, 1968, reported in *The Times* of March 5, 1968.
20. *Al-Ahram*, October 19, 1962.
21. *Nasser's Speeches, 1962*, pp. 258–9.
22. David Holden, *Farewell to Arabia*, New York: Walker and Company, 1967, p. 99.
23. Manfred, W. Wenner, *Modern Yemen*, Baltimore: Johns Hopkins Press, 1967, p. 196.
24. Nasser's speech on January 9, 1963, *Arab Political Documents, 1963*, Beirut: American University Press, 1967, p. 8.
25. *Nasser's Speeches, 1962*, p. 260.
26. *Al-Ahram*, November 16, 1962.
27. *Ibid.*, December 24, 1962.
28. Edgar O'Ballance, *The War in the Yemen*, London: Faber and Faber, 1971, p. 97.
29. UAR, *Mahadhir Jalsat Mubahathat al-Wuhda*, Cairo: National Printing and Publishing House, 1963, p. 574 (hereafter cited as *Mahadhir*).
30. *Ibid.*, p. 124.
31. *Ibid.*, p. 7.
32. *Ibid.*, p. 20.
33. *Ibid.*, p. 217.
34. *Ibid.*, p. 53.
35. *Ibid.*, p. 77.
36. *Al-Ahram*, May 17, 1963.
37. Full text in *Nasser's Speeches, 1963*, pp. 118–56.
38. *Al-Ahram*, December 27, 1963; *Rose al-Yusif*, December 17, 1963.
39. *Nasser's Speeches, 1963*, p. 311.
40. *The Times*, September 15, 1964.
41. UAR, *Majmouat Khutab Wa Tasrihat Wa Bayanat al-Rais Gamal Abd al-Nasser* [Nasser's Speeches, Interviews and Statements], Cairo: Maslahat al-Isti'Lamat, n.d., vol. 5, p. 368 (hereafter cited as *Khutab*).
42. *Ibid.*, vol. 5, p. 373.
43. *The Times*, August 25, 1965.
44. *Al-Ahram*, October 30, 1965.
45. *The Times*, December 9, 1965; December 22, 1965.
46. *SWB*, February 22, 1966, ME/2097/A/3–4.
47. Peter Mansfield, *Nasser's Egypt*, London: Penguin Books, 1969, p. 76.
48. *The Times*, December 22, 1965.
49. *Khutab*, vol. 5, p. 501; see also *SWB*, February 25, 1966, ME/2097/A/7.
50. *The Times*, December 22, 1965.
51. *Egyptian Gazette*, February 8, 1966; *Khutab*, vol. 5, p. 488.
52. *New York Times*, May 5, 1966.
53. *Al-Ahram*, April 29, 1966.
54. *SWB*, July 25, 1966, ME/2221/A/15.
55. *Al-Ahram*, August 26, 1966.
56. The best account of the chain of events immediately preceding the war of June 1967 can be found in Stephens, *op. cit.*, pp. 466–92.

CHAPTER 5

1. Nasser's speech on November 23, 1967, quoted in American University of Beirut, *Arab Political Documents, 1967* [in Arabic], Beirut, n.d., p. 718 (hereafter cited as *APD*).
2. The Institute for Strategic Studies, *The Military Balance, 1967–1968*, London: 1967, p. 50.
3. *Al-Ahram*, October 6, 1967.
4. This is confirmed by President Sadat in an interview with the *New York Times* as

quoted in *USSR And The Third World*, London: Central Asian Research Centre, vol. II, no. 1, p. 31.

5. *Al-Ahram*, June 30, 1967.
6. *Ibid.*, June 21, 1967.
7. Yair Eyron, *The Middle East: Nations, Super-powers and Wars*, London: Paul Elek, 1973, pp. 81–3.
8. *SWB*, June 14, 1967, ME/2490/A/14.
9. As quoted in *SWB*, June 30, 1967, ME/2504/A/1.
10. *SWB*, September 4, 1967, ME/2559/A/2.
11. *Ibid.*
12. *APD, 1968*, p. 378.
13. Al-Fat'h means 'conquest', but it is also the acronym spelled backwards of Harakat al-Tahrir al-Filastinya [the Movement for the Liberation of Palestine].
14. See Evron, *op. cit.*, p. 99.
15. *APD, 1968*, p. 378.
16. *Al-Ahram*, August 16, 1968.
17. *SWB*, July 22, 1968, ME/2827/A/1.
18. *Al-Ahram*, August 12, 1968.
19. *SWB*, October 13, 1969, ME/3201/A/6.
20. *Ibid.*, December 29, 1969, ME/3264/A/10.
21. For an excellent discussion of Israel's 'deep-penetration bombing' of Egypt see Evron, *op. cit.*, pp. 111–17.
22. *APD, 1970*, p. 270.
23. *Al-Ahram*, May 22, 1970.
24. *Ibid.*, March 13, 1970.
25. *Ibid.*, March 20, 1970.
26. *Ibid.*, July 31, 1970.
27. Although some criticisms were voiced which led to Nasser's suspension of Palestinian broadcasts from Cairo.
28. *Al-Ahram*, October 16, 1970.
29. *Ibid.*, September 9, 1970.

CHAPTER 6

1. For example, Richard Snyder, H. W. Bruck and Burton Sapin, *Foreign Policy Decision Making: An Approach to the Study of International Politics*, New York: Free Press, 1962; Roy C. Macridis, ed., *Foreign Policy in World Politics*, 2nd ed., Englewood Cliffs, New Jersey: Prentice–Hall, 1962; James Rosenau, ed., *International Politics and Foreign Policy*, New York: the Free Press, 1961; Barry R. Farrell, ed., *Approaches to Comparative and International Politics*, Evanston, Illinois: Northwestern University Press, 1966; Joseph Frankel, *The Making of Foreign Policy: An Analysis of Decision-Making*, London: Oxford University Press, 1963.
2. K. J. Holsti, *International Politics: A Framework for Analysis*, Englewood Cliffs, New Jersey: Prentice–Hall, Inc., 1967, p. 21.
3. *Ibid.*, pp. 21–2.
4. The article appears in Rosenau, *op. cit.*, p. 15.
5. Joseph Frankel, 'Towards A Decision-Making Model in Foreign Policy', *Political Studies*, vol. 7, no. 1, March 1959, p. 1.
6. David O. Wilkinson, *Comparative Foreign Relations: Framework and Methods*, Belmont, California: Dickinson Pub. Co., 1969, p. 4.
7. M. Brecher, B. Steinberg and J. Stein, 'A Framework for Research on Foreign Policy Behaviour', *Journal of Conflict Resolution*, vol. 13, no. 1, March 1969, pp. 75–101.
8. *Ibid.*, p. 77.
9. *Ibid.*, p. 78.
10. In Farrell, *op. cit.*, pp. 27–92.

11. Brecher *et al.*, *op. cit.*, p. 79.
12. *Ibid.*, p. 79.
13. *Ibid.*
14. *Ibid.*, p. 80.
15. See C. R. Mitchell, 'Foreign Policy Problems and Polarized Political Communities: Some Implications of a Simple Model', *British Journal of Political Science*, vol. 1, no. 2, April 1971, p. 223.
16. Michael Brecher, *The Foreign Policy System of Israel: Setting, Images and Processes*, London: Oxford University Press, 1972.
17. Michael Brecher, *Decisions in Israel's Foreign Policy*, London: Oxford University Press, 1974; see also Michael Brecher, 'Images, Processes and Feedback in Foreign Policy: Israel's decision on German Reparations', *American Political Science Review*, vol. 67, no. 1, March 1973, pp. 75–102; and Michael Brecher, 'Inputs and Decisions for War and Peace: The Israeli Experience', *International Studies Quarterly*, vol. 18, no. 2, June 1974, pp. 131–77.

CHAPTER 7

1. See Morton A. Kaplan, 'Variants on Six Models of the International System', in James N. Rosenau, ed., *International Politics and Foreign Policy*, New York: the Free Press, 1969, pp. 296–303.
2. Except for Turkey and Iran, the northern tier states who experienced intensive superpower activity during this period.
3. The term is used by Cantori and Spiegel to denote 'politically significant participation of external powers in the international relations of the subordinate system', see Louis J. Cantori and Steven L. Spiegel, *The International Politics of Regions: A Comparative Approach*, Englewood Cliffs, N. J.: Prentice–Hall, 1970, p. 25.
4. The first conspicuous shift towards the Soviet Union emanated from the Syrian government formed in February 1955 in which Khalid al-Azm, a landowner with declared pro-Soviet leanings, held the Foreign and Defence portfolios.
5. Such as NATO, the Warsaw Pact, OAS, EEC, COMECON, Schuman Plan and the Council for Economic Mutual Assistance.
6. See David Horowitz, *From Yalta to Vietnam*, Harmondsworth, Middlesex: Penguin Books Ltd, 1969, pp. 82–3.
7. *Izvestia*, November 11, 1951.
8. See Cremeans, *op. cit.*, pp. 144–5.
9. Zinner, *op. cit.*, p. 201.
10. See Chapter 2, pp. 13–14.
11. See pp. 83–9.
12. See Kirk, *Contemporary Arab Politics*, pp. 110–20; also Westerfield, *op. cit.*, p. 479.
13. Childers, *op. cit.*, p. 313.
14. For example, the movement of the fleet immediately after the Iraqi coup in July 1958; see Nutting, *op. cit.*, p. 235; the fleet was also deployed during the Jordanian crisis of April 1957; see Royal Institute of International Affairs, *Documents on International Affairs, 1957*, p. 289. It is also a widely held belief that a major variable in the Syrian decision to withdraw its short-lived intervention in the civil war in Jordan in September 1970 was the ominous movements of the Sixth Fleet.
15. Like the troop landing in the Lebanon on July 16, 1958.
16. For a more detailed discussion, see Yair Evron, *The Middle East: Nations Superpowers and Wars*, London: Elek Books, 1973, pp. 192–207; Michael Brecher, *The Foreign Policy System of Israel: Setting, Images, Processes*, London: Oxford University Press, 1972, pp. 47–64; Leonard Binder, 'The Middle East as a Subordinate International System', *World Politics*, vol. 10, no. 3, 1958, pp. 408–29.
17. For example, Nuri al-Said and Abd al-Karim Kassem of Iraq, King Faisal of Saudi Arabia, and the Baath party in Syria and Iraq.
18. For example, Egypt's active role in the creation of the 'League of Arab States', its

persistent efforts to establish an Arab Common Market, and its initiatory role in convening the summit conferences.

19. See R. Hrair Dekmejian, *Egypt Under Nasser: A Study in Political Dynamics*, London: University of London Press, 1971, pp. 116–17; Malcolm H. Kerr, 'Egyptian Foreign Policy and The Revolution', in P. J. Vatikiotis, ed., *Egypt Since The Revolution*, London: George Allen and Unwin, Ltd, 1968, pp. 132–3.

20. See Stephens, *op. cit.*, p. 464.

21. *Mahadhir*, p. 74.

22. *Ibid.*, p. 37.

23. Quoted in Seale, *op. cit.*, p. 311.

24. *Al-Ahram*, September 9, 1962.

25. *Ibid.*, January 10, 1970.

26. While a 'fully geographic approach' should attempt a complete analysis of such elements as location and size, transportation and communication, natural resources, and population, this section will be limited to an analysis of Egypt's location only, as it was deemed organisationally preferable to study the other elements under different categories, such as the demographic economic factors.

27. Roy C. Macridis, *Foreign Policy in World Politics*, 3rd ed., Englewood Cliffs, New Jersey: Prentice–Hall, Inc., 1967, pp. 4–7.

28. Harold and Margaret Sprout, *Foundations of International Politics*, London: D. Van Nostrand, Inc., 1962, p. 288.

29. *Al-Ahram*, February 11, 1966.

30. G. A. Nasser, *The Philosophy of the Revolution with an Introduction by John C. Badeau and biographical sketch by John Gunther*, Buffalo, New York: Economica Books, 1959, p. 59.

31. Boutrous B. Ghalli, 'The Foreign Policy of Egypt', in J. E. Black and K. W. Thompson, eds, *Foreign Policies in a World of Change*, New York: Harper and Row, 1963, p. 320.

32. See Charles Issawi, *Egypt in Revolution: An Economic Analysis*, London: Oxford University Press, 1963, p. 163; also the index number for agricultural production in 1969–70 was 299 compared with a base of 100 in 1951–2: see UAR, *Statistical Handbook, 1952–1972*, Cairo: Central Agency for Public Mobilisation and Statistics, 1973, p. 24.

33. Kamil Bakri, *Al-Sukan wal Numui al-Iqtisadi fi Misr* [Population and Economic Growth in Egypt], Alexandria: Nabi' al-Fikr, 1969, p. 17.

34. For a fuller discussion of these problems, see Issawi, *op. cit.*, p. 298; also Marcien Rosciszewski, 'Population Growth and Economic Development in Egypt', in Wilbur Zelinsky *et al.*, eds, *Geography And A Crowding World*, London: Oxford University Press, 1970, pp. 332–47; also Glen T. Trewartha, *The Less Developed Realm: A Geography of its Population*, London: Wiley 1972, pp. 175–9.

35. UAR, *The Charter*, Cairo: Information Department, 1962, p. 53.

36. Quoted in Stephens, *op. cit.*, p. 8.

37. Sati al-Husri, *al-Uruba awalan* [Arabism first], Beirut: Dar al-Ilm Lil Malayeen, 1966, pp. 136–65.

38. See p. 130–131

39. *Al-Ahram*, November 3, 1961.

40. *Mahadhir*, p. 94.

41. National Bank of Egypt, *Economic Bulletin*, vol. 21, no. 1, 1968.

42. *Ibid.*, vol. 23, no. 1, 1970.

43. Marshall I. Goldman, *Soviet Foreign Aid*, London: Frederick A. Praeger, 1967, p. 492.

44. Patrick O'Brien, *The Revolution in Egypt's Economic System*, London: Oxford University Press, 1966, p. 154.

45. *Ibid.*

46. Mansfield, *op. cit.*, p. 165.

47. Ali Sabri, *Years of Socialist Transformation: an evaluation of the first Five-Years plan* [Arabic text], Cairo, 1966, p. 185, as referred to in Galal Amin, 'The Egyptian Economy and the Revolution', in P. J. Vatikiotis, ed., *Egypt since the Revolution*, London: Allen and Unwin, 1968, p. 44.
48. *Ibid.*, pp. 43–4.
49. Mansfield, *op. cit.*, p. 181.
50. See Bent Hansen and Girgis Marzouk, *Development and Economic Policy in the UAR* [Egypt], Amsterdam: North Holland Publications, Inc., 1965, pp. 189–205.
51. Malcolm Kerr, 'The United Arab Republic: The Domestic, Political and Economic Background of Foreign Policy', in R. Y. Hammond and S. S. Alexander, eds, *Political Dynamics in the Middle East*, New York: American Elsevier Publications, Inc., 1972, p. 208.
52. The Soviet Union figure comes from US, Department of State, Bureau of Public Affairs, *Communist States and Developing Countries: Aid and Trade in 1972*, RECS-10, Washington: June 1973; the United States figure comes from Robert S. Walters, *American and Soviet Aid: A Comparative Analysis*, Pittsburgh: University of Pittsburgh Press, 1970, p. 85. This amount covers the period 1954–68. However, since the bulk of US aid occurred between 1958 and 1966, this figure should closely approximate to the one relating to the period 1958–70.
53. Heikal, *op. cit.*, p. 141.
54. *New York Times*, May 5, 1966.
55. For a discussion of the importance of military expenditure on the ranking of a particular state in the international system, see David O. Wilkinson, *Comparative Foreign Relations: Framework and Methods*, Belmont, California: Dickenson Publishing Company, Inc., 1969, pp. 53–61.
56. *Al-Ahram*, September 27, 1963.
57. Additionally, the military aid received by Egypt exceeded that of the combined aid received by Iraq and Syria. Between 1954 and 1968, Egypt was the recipient of $1550 worth of military aid compared to $1157 received by the other two Arab states. See Walters, *op. cit.*, pp. 83–5.
58. *Al-Ahram*, March 31, 1961. See also on the same subject, *ibid.*, January 7, 1966.
59. *APD, 1968*, p. 376.
60. Nasser, *Philosophy of the Revolution*, pp. 76–7.
61. Quoted in Vatikiotis, *The Egyptian Army in Politics*, Bloomington, Indiana: Indiana University Press, 1961, p. 241.
62. Mahadhir, *op. cit.*, p. 409.
63. See *Majallat al-Azhar* [The al-Azhar Magazine], vol. 34, no. 1, June 1962, p. 2.
64. *Ibid.*, vol. 34, no. 6, January 1963, p. 574. See also J. H. Proctor, ed., *Islam and International Relations*, New York: Frederick A. Praeger, 1965, p. 142–3.
65. *Majallat al-Azhar*, vol. 39, no. 1, April 1967, p. 4; see also in this connection, *ibid.*, vol. 39, no. 2, May 1967, p. 135; vol. 37, no. 2, 3, September 1965, English section, p. 1.
66. See, for example, *Nasser's Speeches, April–June 1960*, p. 55.
67. *New York Times*, August 22, 1966; *Egyptian Gazette*, August 22, 1966.
68. Although, as has been mentioned already, a resurgence of their power necessitated further repression in 1965. See *SWB*, August 22, 1966, ME/2246/A/11–12; *Observer*, September 22, 1966.
69. *SWB*, December 31, 1963, ME/1440/i.
70. *Al-Ahram*, November 15, 1968.
71. *Ibid.*, December 20, 1968.
72. The paragraph draws heavily on Issawi, *op. cit.*, pp. 194–6; on O'Brien, *op. cit.*, pp. 69–77; and on Amin, *op. cit.*, pp. 42–6.
73. P. A. Reynolds, *An introduction to international relations*, London: Longmans, 1971, pp. 80–3.
74. G. K. Hirabayashi and M. F. al-Khatib, 'Communication and Political Aware-

ness in the Villages of Egypt', *Political Opinion Quarterly*, vol. 22, 1958–9, pp. 357–363.
75. A condition of 'Cognitive Dissonance' exists when incoming information conflicts with the expectations and desires held by people as a result of their beliefs, values and experiences. See Leon Festinger, *A Theory of Cognitive Dissonance*, Stanford, California: Stanford University Press, 1957.
76. *New York Herald Tribune*, May 24, 1957.

CHAPTER 8
1. See Gaetano Mosca, *The Ruling Class*, trans. H. Kahn, ed. A. Livingston, New York: McGraw–Hill, 1939, p. 50.
2. See Robert A. Dahl 'A Critique of the Ruling Elite Model', *American Political Science Review*, vol. 52, no. 2, June 1958, pp. 463–75.
3. Frankel, *op. cit.*, p. 10.
4. B. Boutrous-Ghalli, 'The Foreign Policy of Egypt', in *Foreign Policy in a World of Change*, ed. J. E. Black and K. W. Thompson, New York: Harper & Row, 1963, p. 320.
5. Frankel, *op. cit.*, p. 5.
6. Cremeans, *op. cit.*, p. 32.
7. Childers, *op. cit.*, p. 375. This is confirmed by Anwar al-Sadat in a speech on September 28, 1971 to the Arab Socialist Union, *SWB*, September 30, 1971, ME/3800/A/7–8.
8. See I. M. Husaini, *The Moslem Brethren*, Beirut: Khayats, 1956.
9. Little, *op. cit.*, p. 103.
10. Husaini, *op. cit.*, p. 131.
11. *APD, 1968*, p. 586.
12. E. Be'eri, *Army Officers in Arab Politics and Society*, London: Pall Mall Press, 1970, p. 8.
13. S. E. Finer, *The Man on Horseback: the Role of the Military in Politics*, London: Pall Mall Press, 1962, p. 11.
14. D. A. Rustow, 'The Military in Middle Eastern Society and Politics', in Sidney Fisher, ed., *The Military in the Middle East*, Columbus, Ohio: Ohio State University Press, 1963, p. 9.
15. See M. Negiub, *Egypt's Destiny*, London: Gollancz, 1955; A. es-Sadat, *Revolt on the Nile*, London, Wingate, 1957; and G. A. Nasser, *The Philosophy of the Revolution*, Buffalo, New York: Economica Books, 1959.
16. 1 Feddan = 1.038 acres.
17. *SWB*, September 16, 1952, pp. 26–30.
18. *Ibid.*, August 17, 1954, p. 22.
19. M. Weber, *The Theory of Social and Economic Organization*, trans. A. M. Henderson and Talcott Parsons, London: Oxford University Press, 1947, pp. 358–9.
20. H. C. Gerth and C. Wright Mills, *From Max Weber*, London: Routledge & Kegan Paul, 1970, p. 247.
21. For an elaboration of this orientation see D. D. Eisenhower, *The White House Years*, vols I, II, London: Heinemann, 1963, 1966.
22. Frankel, *op. cit.*, p. 9.
23. See D. N. Wilber, *United Arab Republic: Egypt*, New Haven, Connecticut: Hraf Press, 1969, p. 133; and P. J. Vatikiotis, *The Egyptian Army in Politics: Patterns for New Nations?*, Bloomington, Indiana; Indiana University Press, 1961, p. 227.
24. P. J. Vatikiotis, 'Foreign Policy of Egypt', in R. C. Macridis, *Foreign Policy in World Politics*, 2nd ed., London: Prentice–Hall, Inc., 1962, p. 340.
25. C. Issawi, 'Negotiation from Strength? A Reappraisal of Western–Arab Relations', *International Affairs*, vol. 35, no. 1, 1959, pp. 1–9. Issawi treats the 'West' in this article as a unified entity. He does this for two reasons: first, because Western countries appear capable of co-ordinating their policies to a degree that makes it

possible to speak of a 'Western' policy, and secondly, because Arabs generally perceive the West as a single unit.

26. P. L. Kendall, 'The Ambivalent Character of Nationalism Among Egyptian Professionals', *Public Opinion Quarterly*, 20, 1956, pp. 283–5. Even Nasser himself is said to have admitted that 'We Egyptians have lived for centuries under foreign domination, and that has given us a complex, an inferiority feeling . . .' Quoted in Wilton Wynn, *Nasser of Egypt: The Search for Dignity*, Cambridge, Massachusetts: Arlington Books., Inc., 1959, p. 59.
27. From John Badeau's introduction to G. A. Nasser, *op. cit.*, p. 14.
28. Anthony Nutting, *Nasser*, London: Constable and Company, Ltd, p. 194.
29. *Ibid.*, p. 176.
30. Cremeans, *op. cit.*, p. 33.
31. See J. Rosenau's writings on the necessity of a linkage theory, particularly his *The Scientific Study of Foreign Policy*, London: Collier–Macmillan, Ltd, 1971, pp. 307–38.
32. Vatikiotis, *op. cit.*, 1962, p. 341.
33. Nutting, *op. cit.*, pp. 425–6; Stephens, *op. cit.*, pp. 506–9.
34. Erikson's work is critically reviewed in Lucien W. Pye, 'Personal Identity and Political Ideology', in *Psychoanalysis and History*, ed. Bruce Mazlish, Englewood Cliffs, New Jersey: Prentice–Hall, 1963, pp. 150–73.
35. *Ibid.*, p. 158.
36. See Dekmejian, *op. cit.*, pp. 97–101.
37. *Al-Mussawar yuqadem Gamal Abd al-Nasser* [al-Mussawar introduces Jamal Abd al-Nasser], Cairo: 1957, p. 9.
38. Wilton Wynn, *Nasser of Egypt: The Search for Dignity*, Cambridge, Massachusetts: Arlington Books, Inc., 1959, pp. 19–20.
39. J. Joesten, *Nasser: The Rise to Power*, London: Odhams Press, 1960, p. 15.
40. *Sunday Times*, June 17, 1962.
41. Joesten, *op. cit.*, p. 15.
42. *Akher Sa'a* [Cairo], July 23, 1958.
43. *Sunday Times*, June 17, 1962.
44. *Egyptian Gazette*, January 29, 1958.
45. *The Times*, December 6, 1956.
46. *Sunday Times*, June 24, 1962.
47. Majid Khadduri, *Arab Contemporaries: the role of personalities in politics*, London: Johns Hopkins University Press, 1973, p. 58.
48. *SWB*, July 25, 1961, ME/699/A/14.
49. Dekmejian, *op. cit.*, p. 182.
50. Nutting, *op. cit.*, p. 410.
51. *Ibid.*
52. Stephens, *op. cit.*, pp. 342–3.
53. *Al-Ahram*, July 22, 1959; see also *ibid.*, February 3, 1967.
54. See, for example, *al-Ahram*, November 15, 1968; also Naji Alloush, 'Political Factors in the Military Defeat' [in Arabic], *Dirasat Arabiya*, vol. 4, no. 1, November 1967, pp. 22–31; Stephens, *op. cit.*, pp. 358–62.
55. *Al-Ahram*, April 5, 1968.
56. *Time* magazine, May 16, 1969, p. 31.
57. Nutting, *op. cit.*, pp. 224–5.
58. Stephens, *op. cit.*, p. 416. This revelation was conveyed to Stephens by Numaan.
59. Good discussions of this episode can be found in Stephens, *op. cit.*, pp. 512–15; Nutting, *op. cit.*, pp. 428–30. For a colourful, yet rather unreliable account see Amos Perlmutter, *Egypt: The Praetorian State*, New Brunswick, New Jersey: Transaction Books, 1974, pp. 181–4.
60. See B. Boutrous-Ghalli, *op. cit.*, 1969, pp. 15ff.
61. Frankel, *op. cit.*, p. 26.

62. *New York Times*, May 5, 1955.
63. Don Peretz, 'Democracy and the revolution in Egypt', *Middle East Journal*, vol. 13, 1959, p. 33; and P. J. Vatikiotis, *The Egyptian army in Politics: Pattern for New Nations?*, Bloomington, Indiana: Indiana University Press, 1961, p. 105.
64. *SWB*, July 23, 1960, ME/392/A/8.
65. Leonard Binder, 'Political Recruitment and Participation in Egypt', in J. Palombara and M. Weiner, eds, *Political Parties and Political Development*, Princeton, New Jersey: Princeton University Press, 1966, pp. 236–9.
66. Vatikiotis, *op. cit.*, 1961, p. 106.
67. Nasser's interview with the *Sunday Times*, June 24, 1962.
68. *Al-Ahram*, July 2, 1959.
69. *Egyptian Gazette*, May 9, 1966.
70. *Al-Ahram*, June 3, 1960.
71. *Ibid.*, July 2, 1959.
72. *SWB*, July 24, 1959, ME/86/A/28.
73. Dekmejian, *op. cit.*, p. 62.
74. *Ibid.*, p. 147.
75. *Al-Ahram*, February 11, 1966.
76. Binder, *op. cit.*, 1966, p. 227.
77. *SWB*, June 14, 1960, ME/358/A/9.
78. Dekmejian, *op. cit.*, p. 152.
79. Naji Alloush, 'Political Factors in the Military Defeat' [in Arabic], *Dirasat Arabiya*, vol. 4, no. 1, November 1967, pp. 25–6.
80. *Al-Ahram*, April 12, 1968; see also *ibid.*, November 11, 1968.
81. Ahmad Hamrush, *Rose al-Yusif*, July 24, 1967.
82. Except perhaps for a brief period spanning the years 1963–7 when the defence establishment seems to have established a measure of independence from Nasser's control.

CHAPTER 9

1. Kenneth E. Boulding, *The Image*, Ann Arbor, Michigan: University of Michigan Press, 1956.
2. See Ole Holsti, 'The Belief System and National Images: A Case Study', *Journal of Conflict Resolution*, vol. 6, 1962, pp. 244–52.
3. Frankel, *op. cit.*, p. 106.
4. George J. Graham, *Methodological Foundations for Political Analysis*, Waltham, Massachusetts: Xerox College Publishing, 1971, p. 72.
5. Anwar al-Sadat takes the view that ideology is the product of the people's 'own historical experience': *al-Ahram*, June 9, 1961.
6. Michael Brecher, *The Foreign Policy System of Israel: Setting, Images, Processes*, London: Oxford University Press, p. 12.
7. For a further elaboration of the functional roles of ideology, see Karen Dawisha, 'The Roles of Ideology in the Decision-Making of the Soviet Union', *International Relations*, vol. 4, no. 2, November 1972, pp. 156–76.
8. *Al-Ahram*, December 17, 1958.
9. Al-Jumhuriya al-Arabiya al-Muttahida, *Majmuat Khutab wa Tasrihat wa Bayanat al-Rais Gamal Abd al-Nasser* [Nasser's speeches, Arabic text], vol. 5, July 1964– June 1966, Cairo: Maslahat al-Isti'lamat, n.d., p. 46 (hereafter cited as *Khutab*); see also *ibid.*, vol. 2, p. 54.
10. *SWB*, July 28, 1956, p. 15.
11. *Nasser's speeches, 1962*, p. 260; *1963*, pp. 34–5; *al-Ahram*, December 24, 1962.
12. For example, Dekmejian, *op. cit.*, pp. 108–15; Cremeans, *op. cit.*, pp. 140–54; Little, *op. cit.*, pp. 157–76; Nutting, *op. cit.*, pp. 74–167; Stephens, *op. cit.*, pp. 140–197; for an opposing view, see Kimchie, *op. cit.*, pp. 86–122.
13. *Al-Ahram*, September 7, 1967.

14. See Salah Bitar's opinion on the matter in Stephens, *op. cit.*, p. 343.
15. *Al-Ahram*, December 15, 1958; *Khutab*, p. 62; *New York Herald Tribune*, June 16, 1958.
16. *APD, 1968*, pp. 375–6.
17. *SWB*, April 14, 1970, ME/3352/A/2; see also *al-Ahram*, March 13, 1970.
18. *SWB*, June 12, 1967, ME/2488/A/2.
19. *Al-Ahram*, July 3, 1961; July 5, 1961; *Akhbar al-Yawm*, July 8, 1961.
20. *SWB*, March 18, 1959, p. 1.
21. *Khutab*, vol. 1, pp. 62, 83, 172; *Al-Ahram*, April 7, 1962; *Daily Telegraph*, July 11, 1955; *Khutab*, vol. 5, pp. 146, 368, 488.
22. *Al-Ahram*, April 13, 1962; *SWB*, July 30, 1960, ME/398/A/3.
23. See David Easton, *A Framework for Political Analysis*, London: Prentice–Hall International, Inc., 1965, p. 50.
24. See among others Mansfield, *op. cit.*, pp. 55–60; Stephens, *op. cit.*, pp. 140–277; Rodinson, *op. cit.*, pp. 77–90; Cremeans, *op. cit.*, pp. 137–59; Dekmejian, *op. cit.*, pp. 39–47.
25. Hisham Sharabi, *Nationalism and Revolution in the Arab World*, London: D. Van Nostrand Co., Ltd, 1966, p. 96.
26. Nasser, *op. cit.*, p. 62.
27. *Khutab*, vol. 1, p. 247.
28. *Mahadhir*, p. 94.
29. See, for example, *Khutab*, vol. 1, p. 41; *New York Times*, November 5, 1959; *Observer Foreign News Service*, November 20, 1958.
30. Tareq Ismael, *The UAR in Africa: Egypt's Policy under Nasser*, Evanston, Illinois: Northwestern University Press, 1971, pp. 102–6; see also *al-Ahram*, April 16, 1958; *Rose al-Yusif*, December 22, 1958; *al-Ahram*, January 10, 1959; *The Charter*, p. 103.
31. *Al-Ahram*, October 23, 1961.
32. *SWB*, September 29, 1961, ME/755/A/9.
33. *Ibid.*, February 25, 1966, ME/2097/A/2. Nasser also insisted that Egypt was 'duty bound' to come to Syria's assistance against the threat of an Israeli attack in May 1967: see *SWB*, February 17, 1968, ME/2698/A/6.
34. *Khutab*, vol. 1, p. 62.
35. *Ibid.*, p. 462.
36. Nasser, *op. cit.*, pp. 61, 78. See also Heikal's exposition on the subject: *al-Ahram*, January 19, 1968.
37. See pp. 76–7.
38. For example, Abd al-Karim Zuhur's opinions in *Mahadhir*, p. 75.
39. *Khutab*, vol. 1, pp. 183–4, 415–16.
40. *Nasser's Speeches, January–March, 1960*, p. 106.
41. UAR, *The Charter*, p. 15. See also *al-Ahram*, August 19, 1966.
42. Stephens, *op. cit.*, pp. 289–90; Nutting, *op. cit.*, pp. 235–40.
43. *Al-Ahram*, October 19, 1962.
44. *Ibid.*, October 13, 1961.
45. *Ibid.*, January 18, 1963.
46. *Ibid.*, March 31, 1963.
47. *Ibid.*, February 16, 1970.
48. *Ibid.*, March 13, 1970.
49. *Ibid.*, August 12, 1966.
50. Quoted in Stephens, *op. cit.*, p. 343.
51. *Sunday Times*, November 10, 1968.
52. *APD, 1968*, p. 378.
53. *SWB*, April 21, 1970, ME/3358/A/6.
54. *Ibid.*, July 25, 1961, ME/699/A/1–2.
55. See Wilton Wynn, *Nasser of Egypt*, Cambridge, Massachusetts: Arlington Books, Inc., 1959, p. 63.

56. *Nasser's Speeches, 1962,* pp. 275–6.
57. *Ibid. January–March, 1960,* pp. 147–8.
58. *Sunday Times,* August 19, 1956.
59. Trevelyan, *op. cit.,* p. 55.
60. *Khutab,* vol. 5, p. 104; see also *ibid.,* p. 279; and *al-Ahram,* February 24, 1967.
61. *SWB,* July 28, 1956, p. 11.
62. Charles O. Lerche, Jr, quoted in Abdul A. Said, *Theory of International Relations,* Englewood Cliffs, New Jersey: Prentice–Hall International, Inc., 1968, p. 1; also Robert J. Lieber, *Theory and World Politics,* Cambridge, Massachusetts: Winthrop Publishers, Inc., 1972, p. 2.
63. *Ibid.*

CHAPTER 10

1. See Frankel, *op. cit.,* p. 112; also John W. Burton, *World Society,* London: Cambridge University Press, 1972, p. 127.
2. Frankel, *op. cit.,* pp. 136–9; K. J. Holsti, *International Politics: A Framework For Analysis,* Englewood Cliffs, New Jersey: Prentice–Hall, 1967, pp. 175–6.
3. *SWB,* August 15, 1961, ME/176/A/9.
4. *Egyptian Gazette,* January 29, 1958.
5. *SWB,* February 10, 1958, p. 1. This is evident from the discernible contrast between Nasser's speeches in the pre-unity period and in the post-unity period.
6. *Khutab,* p. 23, p. 411; *New York Times,* November 5, 1959; *Observer Foreign News Service,* November 20, 1958; Be'erie, *op. cit.,* pp. 179–80.
7. For example, *SWB,* March 27, 1958, p. 1; March 31, 1958, p. 2; April 16, 1958, pp. 1–2; April 17, 1958, pp. 7–8; May 3, 1958, p. 1; May 13, 1958, pp. 2–3; May 25, 1958, p. 1.
8. See, for example, *Khutab,* pp. 1–192.
9. For example, *SWB,* July 26, 1958, pp. 7–9; Dann, *op. cit.,* p. 78; George M. Haddad, *Revolutions and Military Rule in the Middle East: The Arab States,* part I: *Iraq, Syria, Lebanon and Jordan,* New York: Robert Speller and Sons, Publishers, Inc., 1971, p. 108; Benjamin Shwadran, *The Power Struggle in Iraq,* New York: Council for Middle Eastern Affairs Press, 1960, p. 23.
10. For example, *SWB,* August 5, 1958, p. 1; August 8, 1958, p. 2; August 15, 1958, p. 2; August 24, 1958, p. 3; September 3, 1958, p. 2.
11. *Ibid.,* August 9, 1958, p. 8; August 8, 1958, p. 10.
12. *Al-Ahram,* November 17, 1961; *Khutab,* p. 175.
13. See Evron, *op. cit.,* pp. 23–5; Karl Deutsch, *The Nerves of Government: Models of Political Control and Communication,* London: Collier–Macmillan, Ltd, 1963, pp. 91–4; John Burton identifies the term as 'Classification and Memory', see *Systems, States, Diplomacy and Rules,* London: Cambridge University Press, 1968, pp. 63–5.
14. As early as January 1958, Nasser told a group of American journalists 'the door is open to other countries who may wish to join the two united countries.' *Nasser's Speeches, 1958,* p. 363. It is important to note, however, that the quest for comprehensive unity was mainly expressed in terms of hopes and expectations. For example, *Egyptian Gazette,* January 29, 1958; *Khutab,* pp. 1, 22–3, 48, 74–5, 138, 144; *SWB,* February 10, 1958, p. 2; *The Charter,* p. 47.
15. *Khutab,* p. 175.
16. *Ibid,* p. 455.
17. For example, contrast the relative tranquillity of the domestic situation in Lebanon and Jordan during this period with the turmoil of the earlier phase.
18. *Al-Ahram,* March 31, 1961.
19. See pp. 33–4.
20. *New York Times,* October 16, 1962.
21. *Guardian,* July 18, 1966.
22. See for example, *Nasser's Speeches, 1961,* pp. 349–54; also Stephens, *op. cit.,* p. 341.

23. *Al-Ahram*, December 29, 1961.
24. UAR, *The Charter*, p. 78.
25. *Ibid.*, p. 79.
26. *Al Ahram*, October 19, 1962; see also Nasser's interview with the Lebanese newspaper *al-Muharir*, April 2, 1963.
27. See pp. 37–40. Heikal insists that 'it was the unity of aim, without any previous knowledge which made Abd al-Nasser stand with al-Sallal and his popular revolution.' *Al-Ahram*, October 19, 1962.
28. *Ibid.*, July 26, 1963.
29. See Khalid Mohyddin's exposition of the same doctrine in Vatikiotis, ed., *op. cit.*, pp. 135–9.
30. See pp. 43–4.
31. *Nasser's Speeches, 1962*, p. 45.
32. *Khutab*, vol. 4, p. 447.
33. In six speeches delivered by Nasser during his visit to the Yemen in the spring of 1964, he made ninety-six direct and indirect references to British imperialism, nineteen references to 'reaction' generally, and only one oblique reference to Saudi Arabia.
34. *Khutab*, vol. 5, p. 501.
35. *Ibid.*, p. 592.
36. *Al-Ahram*, April 29, 1966.
37. Nasser's speech on December 22, 1966, *SWB*, December 26, 1966, ME/2351/A/12
38. See pp. 53–4.
39. Nasser's speech of April 15, 1968, *SWB*, April 17, 1968, ME/2746/A/2.
40. *Al-Ahram*, December 5, 1969.
41. Brecher, *op. cit.*, (1975).

CHAPTER 11

1. For example, Stephens, *op. cit.*, p. 270; Issawi, *op. cit.*, p. 307ff; Ismael, *op. cit.*, pp. 122ff.
2. There was no doubt in Nasser's mind that Egypt constituted the leading industrial power in the region. See his statement in *Life* magazine, July 14, 1959; also *Khutab*, p. 462.
3. Issawi, *op. cit.*, p. 308.
4. *Arab Observer*, September 3, 1962, p. 41.
5. Khadduri, *op. cit.*, p. 157.
6. *Al-Jumhuria*, December 8, 1958.
7. This section depends heavily on the study by Alfred G. Musrey, *An Arab Common Market: A Study in Inter-Arab Trade Relations*, London: Frederick A. Praeger, 1969, pp. 107–15.
8. Lebanon, in a direct reference to the Egyptian economy, demanded the abolition of all discriminatory legislation against the inter-state commercial activities of Arab nationals, and the provision for the free flow of capital and commodities across national borders as a preliminary step towards economic integration.
9. Musrey, *op. cit.*, p. 114.
10. See *SWB*, November 11, 1963, ME/1401/A/5; see also *al-Ahram*, May 19, 1961.
11. *SWB*, July 21, 1958, p. 7.
12. *Al-Hayat* (Beirut), January 10, 1959.
13. *Al-Ahram*, December 12, 1963.
14. See Nasser's interviews with the Lebanese *Kuli Shai'*, May 13, 1962, and with the Indian journalist Karanjia on September 29, 1959 in *Khutab*, p. 177; see also *Nasser's Speeches, 1958*, p. 298.
15. See also George K. Kardouche, *The UAR in Development: A Study in Expansionary Finance*, London: Frederick A. Praeger, 1966, p. 18.
16. It is interesting to note that while cotton constituted 64.7 per cent of Egypt's total

exports in 1961, it had slumped to 39.7 per cent in 1969. On the other hand, the percentage of semi-finished and finished industrial products increased from 23.3 in 1961 to 43.6 in 1969. See National Bank of Egypt, *Economic Bulletin*, vol. 23, no. 1, 1970, pp. 25–9.

17. United Nations, *Yearbook of International Trade Statistics, 1972–1973*, New York: Department of Economics and Social Statistics, p. 238.
18. Vatikiotis, ed., *op. cit.*, p. 127.
19. Issawi, *op. cit.*, p. 309.
20. Consult UAR, *Annual Statement of Foreign Trade, 1958*, Cairo: Central Agency for Public Mobilisation and Statistics, 1960; *1959*, 1961; *1960*, 1963; *1961*, 1964.

CHAPTER 12

1. See pp. 43–4.
2. See Nutting, *op. cit.*, pp. 347–53.
3. *SWB*, April 9, 1959, p. 8.
4. *Al-Zaman* (Baghdad), February 11, 1960.
5. *Al-Akhbar* (Baghdad), September 1, 1962.
6. *SWB*, September 20, 1966, ME/2269/A/6–7.
7. *Ibid.*, September 5, 1968, ME/2865/A/2.
8. *Al-Ahram*, September 9, 1962.
9. *Ibid.*, September 15, 1966.
10. UAR, *The Charter*, p. 95.
11. *Al-Ahram*, September 15, 1966.
12. See also Terence H. Quatter, *Propaganda and Psychological Warfare*, New York: Random House, Inc., 1962, p. 27; also L. John Martin, *International Propaganda*, Minneapolis, Minnesota: University of Minnesota, 1958, pp. 10–18.
13. See A. Loya, 'Radio Propaganda of the United Arab Republic: An Analysis', *Middle Eastern Affairs*, vol. 13, no. 4, April 1962, pp. 98–110.
14. *Al-Ahram*, October 21, 1953.
15. *SWB*, April 29, 1960, ME/320/A/3.
16. *Ibid.*, October 24, 1966, ME/2298/A/5.
17. *Ibid.*, May 1, 1967, ME/2642/A/4.
18. *Ibid.*, May 3, 1958, p. 1.
19. Not always, however; for example, see the sophisticated argument in *SWB*, September 26, 1963, ME/1362/A/2, and contrast it with the frivolous terminology of the broadcast: *SWB*, September 19, 1963, ME/1356/A/2.
20. These categories are taken from Holsti, *op. cit.*, pp. 258–9.
21. *Ibid.*, p. 259.
22. *SWB*, May 13, 1958, pp. 2–3.
23. *Ibid.*, October 8, 1966, ME/2285/A/5.
24. *Ibid.*, March 15, 1958, p. 1.
25. *Ibid.*, November 1, 1960, ME/477/A/10.
26. *Ibid.*, March 13, 1959, p. 8. See also *ibid.*, September 5, 1966, ME/2256/A/4; October 6, 1966, ME/2283/A/3.
27. Cairo Radio, for example, described the Jordanian–Saudi cordiality in 1966 as 'an alliance of destiny and life linking imperialism, Israel, Faisal and Hussein': see *ibid.*, December 1, 1966, ME/2231/A/5.
28. Holsti, *op. cit.*, p. 259.
29. *SWB*, October 19, 1962, ME/1077/A/1.
30. *Ibid.*, February 4, 1967, ME/2383/A/1.
31. See, for example, *ibid.*, April 1, 1959, p. 10; November 6, 1959, ME/175/A/5; October 16, 1962, ME/1074/A/1; November 14, 1962, ME/1099/A/6; March 31, 1958, p. 4; March 27, 1963, ME/1210/A/3; May 7, 1966, ME/2155/A/2.
32. *Ibid.*, April 29, 160, ME/320/A/3.
33. *Ibid.*, June 25, 1970, ME/3413/A/7. See also *ibid.*, July 22, 1966, ME/2220/A/2.

34. *Ibid.*, August 4, 1958, p. 3; see also *ibid.*, November 28, 1962, ME/1111/A/9; August 18, 1966, ME/2242/A/1.
35. *Ibid.*, June 2, 1958, p. 1.
36. *Khutab*, p. 353.
37. *SWB*, February 5, 1963, ME/1167/A/2.
38. *Ibid.*, April 2, 1962, ME/910/A/12.
39. Holsti, *op. cit.*, p. 259.
40. Sometimes, however, it was referred to casually so as to infer a matter of fact situation. See for example, *SWB*, April 16, 1958, pp. 1–2.
41. *Ibid.*, March 31, 1958, p. 2.
42. *Ibid.*, August 4, 1958, p. 7.
43. *Ibid.*, June 20, 1962, ME/974/A/3.
44. Fadhil al-Jamali, *al-Iraq al-Hadith* [Modern Iraq], Beirut: Dar al-Fikr, n.d., p. 17.
45. *SWB*, April 10, 1958, p. 7.
46. See, for example, *ibid.*, January 20, 1959, p. 7; March 11, 1959, p. 11; November 21, 1966, ME/2322/A/4.
47. *Ibid.*, June 28, 1958, p. 4.
48. *Ibid.*, May 28, 1966, ME/2173/A/5.
49. In January 1968, Heikal asserted that propaganda was counterproductive as it tended to cause much annoyance and boredom. *Al-Ahram*, January 12, 1968.
50. See Karen Dawisha, 'Soviet Cultural Relations with Iraq, Syria and Egypt, 1955–1970', *Soviet Studies*, vol. 27, no. 3, July 1975, p. 418.
51. *Al-Akhbar*, August 25, 1962.
52. *Al-Ahram*, October 28, 1958; see also *SWB*, October 30, 1958, p. 12.
53. UAR, *Statistical Handbook, 1952–1964* [in Arabic], Cairo: Central Agency for Public Mobilisation and Statistics, 1965, p. 138, and UAR, *Statistical Yearbook, 1952–1965*, Cairo: Central Agency for Public Mobilisation and Statistics, 1966, p. 182.
54. *Ibid.*
55. Arab Republic of Egypt, *Comparative Statistics of Education, 1961/62–1970/71*, Cairo: Ministry of Education, Department of Statistics, 1971, p. 68.
56. UAR, *Comparative Statistics of Education 1953/54–1961/62*, Cairo: Ministry of Education, Department of Statistics, 1962, pp. 114–15; see also Dann, *op. cit.*, p. 193.
57. Egypt's film industry is the only one of any consequence in the Arab world; see Mansfield, *op. cit.*, p. 145; and UNESCO, *Statistical Yearbook, 1963*, Paris: UNESCO, 1964, pp. 420–2; *1966*, pp. 449–51.
58. Holsti, *op. cit.*, p. 323.
59. Humphrey Trevelyan, *Diplomatic Channels*, London: Macmillan, 1973, p. 118.
60. Al-Jamali, *op. cit.*, p. 17.
61. *Mahadhir*, pp. 27–8.
62. Nutting, *op. cit.*, p. 314; *SWB*, August 14, 1962, ME/1020/A/3; August 27, 1962, ME/1031/A/2; August 30, 1962, ME/1034/A/7.
63. Republic of Iraq, *Mahkamat al-Shaab* [Proceedings of the Special Supreme Military Court], Baghdad: Ministry of Defence, 1959, vol. 5 (hereafter cited as *Mahkamat*).
64. *Ibid.*, vol. 5, pp. 185ff.
65. See *ibid.*, vols 18, 19.
66. Mahmoud al-Durra, 'The Mosul Revolt Seven Years Later' [in Arabic], *Dirasat Arabiya*, vol. 2, no. 6, April 1966, pp. 46–59.
67. *Ibid.*, pp. 58–9.
68. See pp. 33–40.

CHAPTER 13

1. This interpretation differs from the one forwarded by R. Hrair Dekmejian in his

book, *Egypt under Nasser*, London: University of London Press, 1971, pp. 4–9. I am confining my analysis to Weber's original definition of Charisma. See pp. 102–4.

2. For an incisive analysis of the October war as an illustration of crisis-management by the superpowers, see Coral Bell, 'The October Middle East War: A Case Study in Crisis Management during Detente', *International Affairs*, vol. 50, no. 4, October 1974, pp. 531–43.

3. For the extent of the Senate's pro-Israeli sympathies, see US Senate, Committee on Foreign Relations, *Emergency Military Assistance for Israel and Cambodia*, Washington: US Government Printing Office, 1973, pp. 127–32.

4. *SWB*, May 15, 1975, ME/4904/A/1. In January 1973, when his relations with President Sadat had already begun to get strained, President Qadhafi declared: 'Whoever humiliates Egypt humiliates the Arabs. Supporting Egypt means support for the Arabs.' *Ibid.*, January 6, 1973, ME/4187/A/2.

5. Mohammed Heikal, *The Road to Ramadan*, London: Collins, 1975, p. 31.

6. *Times Higher Educational Supplement*, February 14, 1975.

7. *New York Times Magazine*, June 1, 1975, p. 71.

8. IISS, *The Military Balance, 1968–1969*, p. 46; *1975–1976*, p. 32.

9. *New York Times Magazine*, June 1, 1975, p. 71.

10. Heikal, *op. cit.* (1975), p. 31.

11. *SWB*, August 20, 1974, ME/W789/A2–3.

12. *Egyptian Gazette*, November 11, 1974.

13. *International Herald Tribune*, July 22, 1975.

14. *Financial Times*, June 25, 1975.

15. *Guardian*, September 15, 1975; *The Times*, September 18, 1975; September 29, 1975.

16. *International Herald Tribune*, July 30, 1975.

17. Central Bank of Egypt, *Economic Review*, vol. 14, no. 4, 1974, pp. 215–16.

18. *Guardian*, January 13, 1975.

19. *Observer Foreign News Service*, January 7, 1975.

20. *Guardian*, May 29, 1975.

21. Quoted in the *Guardian*, February 28, 1974.

22. *Ibid.*, August 30, 1974.

23. *The Times*, January 22, 1974.

24. *Guardian*, May 29, 1975.

25. *SWB*, January 6, 1973, ME/4187/A/8.

26. *Guardian*, February 5, 1973.

27. *The Times*, May 12, 1971.

28. *SWB*, November 16, 1970, ME/3535/A/3.

29. *Egyptian Gazette*, November 25, 1974; December 4, 1974.

30. Heikal, *op. cit.* (1975), pp. 180–1; *International Herald Tribune*, November 27, 1972.

31. *SWB*, August 18, 1971, ME/3764/A/2.

32. *The Times*, December 11, 1972.

33. *SWB*, November 16, 1970, ME/3535/A/3.

34. *Ibid.*

35. *Ibid.*

36. *Al-Ahram*, July 7, 1973.

37. *SWB*, July 26, 1972, ME/4050/A/17.

38. *The Times*, September 10, 1975.

39. *Sunday Times*, January 14, 1973.

40. *Al-Ahram*, September 5, 1975.

41. Heikal, *op. cit.* (1975), pp. 29–30.

42. *Ibid.*, p. 231.

43. *Ibid.*, pp. 238–40.

44. *SWB*, November 23, 1971, ME/3846/A/1.

45. Heikal, *op. cit.* (1975), p. 205.
46. *SWB*, November 14, 1970, ME/3534/A/3.
47. *Al-Ahram*, May 7, 1971.
48. *Arab Report and Record*, no. 14, July 16–31, 1973, p. 321.
49. *Egyptian Gazette*, April 15, 1975.
50. Abd Al-Muneim al-Qaissouni, *International Economic Development with Special Reference to Egypt and the Arab World*, Cairo: National Bank of Egypt, 1974, p. 16.
51. *Ibid.*, p. 15.
52. *Egyptian Gazette*, April 15, 1975.
53. See Sadat's speech on January 2, 1975, in *SWB*, January 4, 1975, ME/4745/A/2–5.
54. *The Economist*, March 23, 1974, p. 86.
55. *Arab Report and Record*, no. 1, January 1–15, 1974, p. 25.
56. *Ibid.*, no. 23, December 1–15, 1974, p. 542.
57. *Egyptian Gazette*, November 25, 1974.
58. *International Herald Tribune*, July 22, 1975.
59. *SWB*, October 30, 1974, ME/4742/A/2.
60. *Ibid.*, May 20, 1975, ME/4908/A/1.
61. *Observer Foreign News Service*, March 25, 1975.

Bibliography

BOOKS

ANOUAR ABDEL-MALEK, *Egypt Military Society: The Army Regime, The Left, and Social Change under Nasser* trans. C. L. Markman, New York: Random House, 1968.

MICHAEL ADAMS, ed., *The Middle East: A Handbook*, London: Anthony Blond, 1971.

M. S. AGWANI, ed., *The Lebanese Crisis of 1958: A Documentary Study*, Bombay: Asia Publishing House, 1965.

GABRIEL ALMOND AND G. BINGHAM POWELL, JR, *Comparative Politics: A Developmental Approach*, Boston: Little Brown, 1966.

GEORGE ANTONIOUS, *The Arab Awakening: The Story of the Arab National Movement*, London: Hamish Hamilton, 1938.

KAMIL A. BAKRI, *al-Sukan wal Numu al-Iqtisadi fi Misr* [Population and Economic Development in Egypt], Alexandria: Nabi' al-Fikr, 1969.

ABD AL-RAHMAN AL-BAZZAZ, *On Arab Nationalism*, London: Embassy of the Republic of Iraq, 1965.

ELIEZER BE'ERI, *Army Officers in Arab Politics and Society*, London: Pall Mall Press, 1970.

WILLARD A. BELING, *The Middle East: Quest for an American Policy*, Albany, New York: State of New York University Press, 1973.

LEONARD BINDER, *The Ideological Revolution in the Middle East*, London: John Wiley and Sons, 1964.

——, 'Political Recruitment and Participation in Egypt', in J. La Palombara and Myron Weiner, eds, *Political Parties and Political Development*, Princeton, New Jersey: Princeton University Press, 1966, pp. 216–40.

KENNETH E. BOULDING, *The Image*, Ann Arbor, Michigan: University of Michigan Press, 1956.

BOUTROUS BOUTROUS-GHALLI, *Azamat al-Diblomasiya al-Arabiya* [The Crisis of Arab Diplomacy], Cairo: Dar al-Kitab al-Jadid, 1969.

——, 'The Foreign Policy of Egypt', in J. E. Black and K. W. Thompson, eds, *Foreign Policies in a World of Change*, New York: Harper and Row, 1963, pp. 319–50.

MICHAEL BRECHER, *Decisions in Israel's Foreign Policy*, London: Oxford University Press, 1974.

——, *The Foreign Policy System of Israel: Setting, Images and Processes*, London: Oxford University Press, 1972.

JOHN W. BURTON, *Systems, States, Diplomacy and Rules*, London: Cambridge University Press, 1968.

——, *World Society*, London: Cambridge University Press, 1972.

LOUIS J. CANTORI AND STEVEN L. SPIEGEL, eds, *The International Politics of the Regions: A Comparative Approach*, Englewood Cliffs, New Jersey: Prentice–Hall, Inc., 1970.

JAMES C. CHARLESWORTH, ed., *Contemporary Political Analysis*, London: Collier–Macmillan Ltd, 1967.

ERSKINE CHILDERS, *The Road to Suez*, London: MacGibbon and Kee, 1962.

MILES COPELAND, *The Game of Nations: The Amorality of Power Politics*, London: Weidenfeld and Nicolson, 1969.

CHARLES CREMEANS, *The Arabs and the World: Nasser's Arab Nationalist Policy*, London: Frederick A. Praeger, 1963.

URIEL DANN, *Iraq Under Qassem: A Political History, 1958–1963*, New York: Frederick A. Praeger, 1969.

R. HRAIR DEKMEJIAN, *Egypt under Nasir: A Study in Political Dynamics*, London: University of London Press, 1972.

——, *Patterns of Political Leadership: Lebanon, Israel, Egypt*, Albany, New York: State of New York University Press, 1975.

KARL DEUTSCH, *The Analysis of International Relations*, Englewood Cliffs, New Jersey: Prentice-Hall Inc., 1968.

——, *Nationalism and its Alternatives*, New York: Alfred A. Knopf, 1969.

——, *The Nerves of Governments: Models of Political Control and Communication*, London: Collier–Macmillan, Ltd, 1963.

DAVID EASTON, *A Framework for Political Analysis*, Englewood Cliffs, New Jersey: Prentice-Hall, Inc., 1965.

——, *A Systems Analysis of Political Life*, New York: John Wiley and Sons, Inc., 1965.

SIR ANTHONY EDEN, *Memories: Full Circle*, London: Cassell and Company, 1960.

DWIGHT D. EISENHOWER, *The White House Years:* vol. I, *Mandate for Change*, New York: Doubleday, 1963.

——, *The White House Years:* vol. II, *Waging Peace*, New York: Doubleday, 1965.

YAIR EVRON, *The Middle East: Nations, Super-Powers and Wars*, London: Elek Books, 1973.

RICHARD A. FALK AND SAUL H. MENDLOVITZ, eds, *Regional Politics and World Order*, San Francisco: W. H. Freeman and Company, 1973.

BARRY R. FARRELL, ed., *Approaches to Comparative and International Politics*, Evanston, Illinois: Northwestern University Press, 1966.

LEON FESTINGER, *A Theory of Cognitive Dissonance*, Stanford, California: Stanford University Press, 1957.

HERMAN FINER, *Dulles Over Suez*, Chicago: Quadrangle Books, 1964.

SAMUEL E. FINER, *The Man on Horseback: The Role of the Military in Politics*, London: Pall Mall Press, 1962.

SYDNEY N. FISHER, *The Middle East: A History*, New York: Alfred A. Knopf, 1959.

JOSEPH FRANKEL, *Contemporary International Theory and the Behaviour of States*, London: Oxford University Press, 1973.

——, *The Making of Foreign Policy: An Analysis of Decision-Making*, London: Oxford University Press, 1963.

W. J. GALLMAN, *Iraq Under General Nuri: My Recollections of Nuri al-Said, 1954–1958*, Baltimore: Johns Hopkins Press, 1964.

H. C. GERTH AND C. WRIGHT MILLS, *From Max Weber*, London: Routledge and Kegan Paul, 1970.

MARSHALL I. GOLDMAN, *Soviet Foreign Aid*, London: Frederick A. Praeger, 1967.

B. K. GORDON, *The Dimensions of Conflict in Southeast Asia*, Englewood Cliffs, New Jersey: Prentice-Hall, Inc., 1969.

GEORGE J. GRAHAM, *Methodological Foundations for Political Analysis*, Waltham, Massachusetts: Xerox College Publishing, 1971.

GEORGE M. HADDAD, *Revolutions and Military Rule in the Middle East: The Arab States*, part I: *Iraq, Syria, Lebanon and Jordan*, New York: Robert Speller and Sons, Publishers, Inc., 1971.

SYLVIA HAIM, *Arab Nationalism: An Anthology*, Berkeley, California: University of California Press, 1962.

P. Y. HAMMOND AND S. S. ALEXANDER, *Political Dynamics in the Middle East*, New York: American Elsevier Publishing Company, Inc., 1972.

BENT HANSEN AND GIRGIS A. MARZOUK, *Development and Economic Policy in the UAR* [Egypt], Amsterdam: North Holland Publications, Inc., 1965.

MOHAMMED HEIKAL, *Nasser: The Cairo Documents*, London: The English Library, 1972.

——, *The Road to Ramadan*, London: Collins, 1975.

PHILIP K. HITTI, *A Short History of the Near East*, London: D. Van Nostrand Company, Inc., 1966.

DAVID HOLDEN, *Farewell to Arabia*, New York: Walker and Company, 1967.

K. J. Holsti, *International Politics: A Framework for Analysis*, London: Prentice–Hall, 1967.

P. M. Holt, *Egypt and the Fertile Crescent, 1516–1922: A Political History*, Ithaca, New York: Cornell University Press, 1967.

——, *Political and Social Change in Modern Egypt*, London: Oxford University Press, 1968.

David Horowitz, *From Yalta to Vietnam*, Harmondsworth, Middlesex: Penguin Books, 1969.

Albert Hourani, *Arabic Thought in the Liberal Age, 1798–1939*, London: Oxford University Press, 1970.

J. C. Hurewitz, *Middle-East Politics: The Military Dimension*, London: Frederick A. Praeger, 1969.

——, ed., *Soviet–American Rivalry in the Middle East*, New York: Frederick A. Praeger, 1969.

Sati al-Husri, *Ara' wa Ahadith fi al-Qawmiya al-Arabiya* [Opinions and Conversations on Arab Nationalism], Beirut: Dar al-Ilm Lil Malayeen, 1956.

——, *Al-Uruba awalan* [Arabism First] Beirut: Dar al-Ilm Lil Malayeen, 1955.

Ishak M. Hussaini, *The Moslem Brethren*, Beirut: Khayats, 1956.

Tareq Y. Ismael, *Governments and Politics of the Contemporary Middle East*, Homewood, Illinois: Dorsey Press, 1970.

——, *The UAR in Africa: Egypt's Policy Under Nasser*, Evanston: Northwestern University Press, 1971.

Charles P. Issawi, *Egypt in Revolution: An Economic Analysis*, London: Oxford University Press, 1963.

Fadhil al-Jamali, *Al Iraq al-Hadith* [Modern Iraq], Beirut: n.p., n.d.

Joachim Joesten, *Nasser: The Rise to Power*, London: Odhams Press, 1960.

Roy E. Jones, *Analysing Foreign Policy: An Introduction to Some Conceptual Problems*, London: Routledge and Kegan Paul, 1970.

George K. Kardouche, *The UAR in Development: A Study in Expansionary Finance*, London: Frederick A. Praeger, 1966.

Mahmud Kamil, *Al-Dawlah al-Arabiya al-Kubra* [The Great Arab State], Cairo: Maktabat al-Dirasat al-Tarikhiya, n.d.

Malcolm H. Kerr, *The Arab Cold War: Gamal Abd al-Nasser and his Rivals, 1958–1970*, 3rd ed., London: Oxford University Press, 1971.

Majid Khadduri, *Arab Contemporaries: The Role of Personalities in Politics*, London: Johns Hopkins Press, 1973.

——, *Independent Iraq, 1932–1958*, 2nd ed., London: Oxford University Press, 1960.

——, *Political Trends in the Arab World: The Role of Ideas and Ideals in Politics*, London: Johns Hopkins Press, 1970.

——, *Republican Iraq: A Study in Iraqi Politics since the Revolution of 1958*, London: Oxford University Press, 1969.

Ahmad Khaki, *Falsafat al-Qawmiya* [The Philosophy of Nationalism], Cairo: al-Maktabah al-Ijtima'iya, 1962.

Lutfi al-Khauli, *Dirasat fi al-Waqi' al-Misri al-Mu'asir* [Studies in Contemporary Egyptian Politics], Beirut: Manshurat Dar al-Tali'ah, 1963.

Jon Kimche, *The Second Arab Awakening*, London: Thames and Hudson, 1970.

George E. Kirk, *Contemporary Arab Politics: A Concise History*, London: Methuen, 1961.

——, *A Short History of the Middle East*, London: Methuen, 1964.

Walter Laqueuer, *The Road to War*, Harmondsworth, Middlesex: Penguin Books, 1968.

Robert J. Lieber, *Theory and World Politics*, Cambridge, Massachusetts: Winthrop Publishers, Inc., 1972.

Tom Little, *Modern Egypt*, London: Ernest Benn, Ltd, 1967.

Vladmier B. Lotski, *A Modern History of Arab States* [in Arabic], Moscow: Progress Books, 1971.

KENNETT LOVE, *Suez: The Twice Fought War*, London: McGraw–Hill, 1969.

ROBERT W. MACDONALD, *The League of Arab States: A Study in the Dynamics of Regional Organization*, Princeton, New Jersey: Princeton University Press, 1965.

ROY C. MACRIDIS, ed., *Foreign Policy in World Politics*, 2nd ed., Englewood Cliffs, New Jersey: Prentice–Hall, Inc., 1962.

PETER MANSFIELD, *Nasser*, London: Methuen Educational Ltd, 1969.

——, *Nasser's Egypt*, revised edition; Harmondsworth, Middlesex: Penguin Books, 1969.

L. JOHN MARTIN, *International Propaganda*, Minneapolis, Minnesota: University of Minnesota Press, 1958.

BRUCE MAZLISH, ed., *Psychoanalysis and History*, Englewood Cliffs, New Jersey: Prentice–Hall, Inc., 1963.

SIR ROBERT MENZIES, *Afternoon Light: Some Memories of Men and Events*, London: Cassell and Company, Ltd, 1967.

GAETANO MOSCA, *The Ruling Class*, trans. H. Kahn, ed. A. Livingston, New York: McGraw–Hill, 1939.

ALFRED G. MUSREY, *An Arab Common Market: A Study in Inter-Arab Trade Relations*, London: Frederick A. Praeger, 1969.

HUSSEIN FAWZI AL-NAJJAR, *Wahdat al-Tarikh al-Arabi* [The Unity of Arab History], Cairo: n.p., n.d.

GAMAL ABD AL-NASSER, *The Philosophy of the Revolution with an Introduction by John C. Badeau and Biographical Sketch by John Gunther*, Buffalo, New York: Economica Books, 1959.

MOHAMMED NEGUIB, *Egypt's Destiny*, London: Gollancz, 1955.

F. S. NORTHEDGE, ed., *The Foreign Policies of the Powers*, London: Faber and Faber, 1968.

ANTHONY NUTTING, *Nasser*, London: Constable, 1972.

——, *No End of a Lesson: The Story of Suez*, London: Constable, 1967.

EDGAR O'BALLANCE, *The War in the Yemen*, London: Faber and Faber, 1971.

PATRICK O'BRIEN, *The Revolution in Egypt's Economic System*, London: Oxford University Press, 1966.

N. D. PALMER AND H. C. PERKINS, *International Relations*, Boston: Houghton Mifflin Company, 1969.

J. HARRIS PROCTOR, ed., *Islam and International Relations*, New York: Frederick A. Praeger, 1965.

ABD AL-MUNEIM AL-QAISSOUNI, *International Economic Development with Special Reference to Egypt and the Arab World*, Cairo: National Bank of Egypt, 1974.

TERENCE H. QUATTER, *Propaganda and Psychological Warfare*, New York: Random House, Inc., 1962.

FAHIM I. QUBAIN, *Crisis in Lebanon*, Washington: The Middle East Institute, 1961.

P. A. REYNOLDS, *An Introduction to International Relations*, London: Longmans, 1971.

JOSEPH H. DE RIVIERA, *The Psychological Dimensions of Foreign Policy*, Columbus, Ohio: Charles E. Merrill Books, 1968.

MAXIME RODINSON, *Israel and the Arabs*, Harmondsworth, Middlesex: Penguin Books, 1968.

PIERRE RONDOT, *The Changing Patterns of the Middle East*, London: Chatto and Windus, 1961.

JAMES ROSENAU, ed., *Domestic Sources of Foreign Policy*, London: Collier–Macmillan, Ltd, 1967.

——, ed., *International Politics and Foreign Policy*, New York: Free Press, 1961, 1969.

——, *The Scientific Study of Foreign Policy*, London: Collier–Macmillan, Ltd, 1971.

ANWAR AL-SADAT, *Revolt on the Nile*, London: Wingate, 1957.

ABDUL A. SAID, *Theory of International Relations*, Englewood Cliffs, New Jersey: Prentice–Hall, Inc., 1968.

PATRICK SEALE, *The Struggle for Syria: A Study in Post War Arab Politics, 1945–1958,*

London: Oxford University Press, 1965.

HISHAM SHARABI, *Governments and Politics of the Middle East in the Twentieth Century*, London: D. Van Nostrand Company, Inc., 1962.

——, *Nationalism and Revolution in the Arab World*, London: D. Van Nostrand Company Inc., 1966.

BENJAMEN SHWADRAN, *Jordan: A State of Tension*, New York: Council for Middle Eastern Affairs, 1959.

——, *The Power Struggle in Iraq*, New York: Council for Middle Eastern Affairs, 1960.

RICHARD SHYDER *et al.*, *Foreign Policy Decision-Makings: An Approach to the Study of International Politics*, New York: Free Press, 1962.

HAROLD AND MARGARET SPROUT, *Foundations of International Politics*, London: D. Van Nostrand Company Inc., 1962.

ROBERT STEPHENS, *Nasser: A Political Biography*, London: Allen Lane, Penguin Press, 1971.

RIADH TAHA, *Mahadhir Mubahathat al-Wuhda* [The Proceedings on the Talks on Unity], Beirut: Dar al-Taliah, 1963.

RAYMOND TANTER AND RICHARD ULLMAN, eds, *Theory and Policy in International Relations*, Princeton, New Jersey: Princeton University Press, 1972.

J. H. THOMPSON AND R. D. REISCHAUER, eds, *Modernization of the Arab World*, London: D. Van Nostrand Company, Inc., 1966.

GORDON H. TORREY, *Syrian Politics and the Military, 1945–1958*, Columbus, Ohio: Ohio State University Press, 1964.

HUMPHREY TREVELYAN, *Diplomatic Channels*, London: Macmillan, 1973.

——, *The Middle East in Revolution*, London: Macmillan, 1970.

GLENN T. TREWARTHA, *The Less Developed Realm: A Geography of its Population*, London: John Wiley and Sons, 1972.

P. J. VATIKIOTIS, *Conflict in the Middle East*, London: George Allen and Unwin, 1971.

——, *The Egyptian Army in Politics*, Bloomington, Indiana: Indiana University Press, 1961.

——, ed., *Egypt Since the Revolution*, London: Allen and Unwin, 1968.

——, *The Modern History of Egypt*, London: Weidenfeld and Nicolson, 1969.

WILLIAM WALLACE, *Foreign Policy and the Political Process*, London: Macmillan, 1971.

ROBERT S. WALTERS, *American and Soviet Aid: A Comparative Analysis*, Pittsburgh: University of Pittsburgh Press, 1970.

JAMES WARBURG, *Crosscurrents in the Middle East*, London: Gollancz, 1969.

MAX WEBER, *The Theory of Social and Economic Organization*, trans. A. M. Henderson and Talcott Parsons, London: Oxford University Press, 1947.

H. BRADFORD WESTERFIELD, *The Instruments of American Foreign Policy*, New York: Thomas Y. Crowell Company, 1963.

KEITH WHEELOCK, *Nasser's New Egypt: A Critical Analysis*, London: Stevens, 1960.

MANFRED WENNER, *Modern Yemen*, Baltimore: Johns Hopkins Press, 1967.

DONALD N. WILBER, *United Arab Republic*, New Haven, Connecticut: Hraf Press, 1969.

DAVID O. WILKINSON, *Comparative Foreign Relations: Framework and Methods*, Belmont, California: Dickenson Publishing Company, Inc., 1969.

WILTON WYNN, *Nasser of Egypt: The Search for Dignity*, Cambridge, Massachusetts: Arlington Books, Inc., 1959.

WILBUR ZELINSKY, *et al.*, eds, *Geography and a Crowding World*, London: Oxford University Press, 1970.

ARTICLES

I. ABU-LUGHOOD, 'International News in the Arabic Press: A Comparative Content Analysis', *Public Opinion Quarterly*, vol. 26, no. 4, Winter 1962, pp. 600–12.

S. ANDRIOLE *et al.*, 'A Framework for the Comparative Analysis of Foreign Policy Behaviour', *International Studies Quarterly*, vol. 19, no. 2, July 1975, pp. 160–98.

G. T. ALLISON, 'Conceptual Models and the Cuban Missile Crisis', *American Political*

Science Review, vol. 63, no. 3, September 1969, pp. 689–718.

N. ALLOUSH, 'Awamal Siyasiya Li al-Hazimah al-Askariya' [Political Factors of the Military Defeat], *Dirasat Arabiya*, vol. 4, no. 1, November 1967, pp. 22–31.

M. A. AZIZ, 'The Origins of Arab Nationalism', *Pakistan Horizon*, vol. 9, no. 1, March 1956, pp. 29–37.

J. S. BADENA, 'A role in Search of a Hero: A Brief Study of the Egyptian Revolution', *Middle East Journal*, vol. 9, no. 4, Autumn 1955, pp. 373–84.

N. BARBOUR, 'Impressions of the United Arab Republic', *International Affairs*, vol. 36, no. 1, January 1960, pp. 21–34.

P. BECHTOLD, 'New Attempts at Arab Cooperations: The Federation of Arab Republic, 1971–?' *Middle East Journal*, vol. 27, no. 2, Spring 1973, pp. 152–72.

A. BEN-TZUR, 'The Neo-Baath Party of Syria', *Journal of Contemporary History*, vol. 3, no. 3, July 1968, pp. 161–81.

L. BINDER, 'The Middle East as a Subordinate International System', *World Politics*, vol. 10, no. 3, April 1958, pp. 408–29.

M. BRECHER, B. STEINBERG AND J. STEIN, 'A Framework for Research on Foreign Policy Behaviour', *Journal of Conflict Resolution*, vol. 13, no. 1, March 1969, pp. 75–101.

A. G. CHEJNE, 'Egyptian Attitudes Toward Pan-Arabism', *Middle East Journal*, vol. 11, no. 3, Summer 1957, pp. 153–268.

R. A. DAHL, 'A Critique of the Ruling Elite Model', *American Political Science Review*, vol. 52, no. 2, June 1958, pp. 463–70.

A. I. DAWISHA, 'The Intervention in Yemen: An Analysis of Egyptian Perceptions and Policies', *Middle East Journal*, vol. 29, no. 1, Winter 1975, pp. 47–63.

——, 'The Transnational Party in Regional Politics: The Arab Baath Party', *Asian Affairs*, vol. 61, no. 1, February 1974, pp. 23–32.

K. DAWISHA, 'The Roles of Ideology in the Decision-Making of the Soviet Union', *International Relations*, vol. 4, no. 2, November 1972, pp. 156–76.

——, 'Soviet Cultural Relations with Iraq, Syria and Egypt, 1955–1970', *Soviet Studies*, vol. 27, no. 3, July 1975, pp. 418–42.

R. H. DEKMEJIAN, 'The UAR National Assembly: A Pioneering Experiment', *Middle Eastern Studies*, vol. 4, no. 4, July 1968, pp. 361–75.

M. AL-DURRA, 'Thwrat al-Mosul ba'ad Sabi' Sanawat' [The Mosul Revolution after Seven Years), *Dirasat Arabiya*, vol. 2, no. 6, April 1966, pp. 46–59.

H. ENAYAT, 'Islam and Socialism in Egypt', *Middle Eastern Studies*, vol. 4, no. 2, January 1968, pp. 141–72.

J. ENTELIS, 'Nasser's Egypt: The Failure of Charismatic Leadership', *Orbis*, vol. 18, no. 2, Summer 1974, pp. 451–64.

J. FRANKEL, 'Towards a Decision-Making Model in Foreign Policy', *Political Studies*, vol. 7, no. 1, March 1959, pp. 1–11.

M. A. HANZA, 'Egyptian Foreign Policy', *Pakistan Horizon*, vol. 6, no. 1, March 1953, pp. 29–35.

F. HARBISON, 'Two Centres of Arab Power', *Foreign Affairs*, vol. 37, no. 4, July 1959, pp. 672–83.

I. HARIK, 'The Single Party as a Subordinate Movement: The Case of Egypt', *World Politics*, vol. 26, no. 1, October 1973, pp. 80–105.

J. HEAPHEY, 'The Organization of Egypt: Inadequacies of a non-political model for nation-building', *World Politics*, vol. 18, no. 2, January 1966, pp. 177–93.

G. K. HIRABAYASHI AND M. F. AL-KHATIB, 'Communications and Political Awareness in the Villages of Egypt', *Public Opinion Quarterly*, vol. 22, 1958–9, pp. 357–63.

O. HOLSTI, 'The Belief System and National Images: A Case Study', *Journal of Conflict Resolution*, vol. 6, 1962, pp. 244–52.

A. HOURANI, 'Near Eastern Nationalism Yesterday and Today', *Foreign Affairs*, vol. 42, no. 1, October 1963, pp. 123–36.

C. ISSAWI, 'The Bases of Arab Unity', *International Affairs*, vol. 31, no. 1, January 1955, pp. 36–47.

——, 'Negotiations from Strength? A Reappraisal of Western–Arab Relations', *International Affairs*, vol. 35, no. 1, January 1959, pp. 1–9.

A. KELIDAR, 'The Struggle for Arab Unity', *The World Today*, 23(7), July 1967, pp. 292–300.

P. L. KENDALL, 'The Ambivalent Character of Nationalism among Egyptian Professionals', *Public Opinion Quarterly*, vol. 20, 1956–7, pp. 277–89.

M. H. KERR, 'Coming to terms with Nasser: attempts and failures', *International Affairs* vol. 43, no. 1, January 1967, pp. 65–84.

——, 'The Emergence of a Socialist Ideology in Egypt', *Middle East Journal*, vol. 16, no. 2, September 1962, pp. 127–44.

M. KHADDURI, 'Towards Arab Union', *American Political Science Review*, vol. 40, no. 1, February 1946, pp. 90–100.

G. LENCZOWSKI, 'The Objects and Methods of Nasserism', *Journal of International Affairs*, vol. 19, no. 1, January 1965, pp. 63–75.

S. H. LONGRIGG, 'New groupings among the Arab States', *International Affairs*, vol. 34, no. 3, July 1958, pp. 305–17.

A. LOYA, 'Radio Propaganda of the United Arab Republic: An Analysis', *Middle Eastern Affairs*, vol. 13, no. 4, April 1962, pp. 98–110.

J. MAJOR, 'The Search for Arab Unity', *International Affairs*, vol. 39, No. 4, October 1963, pp. 551–63.

C. R. MITCHELL, 'Foreign Policy Problems and Polarized Political Communities: Some Implications of a Simple Model', *British Journal of Political Science*, vol. 1, no. 2, April 1971, pp. 223–51.

G. MODELSKI, 'International Relations and Area Studies', *International Relations*, vol. 2, no. 3, April 1961, pp. 143–55.

C. H. MOORE, 'Authoritarian Politics in Uncorporated Society: The Case of Nasser's Egypt', *Comparative Politics*, vol. 6, no. 2, January 1974, pp. 193–218.

F. M. NAJAR, 'Islam and Socialism in the UAR', *Journal of Contemporary History*, vol. 3, no. 3, July 1968, pp. 183–99.

G. A. NASSER, 'The Egyptian Revolution', *Foreign Affairs*, vol. 33, no. 2, January 1955, pp. 199–212.

M. PALMER, 'The United Arab Republic: An Assessment of its Failure', *Middle East Journal*, vol. 20, no. 1, Winter 1966, pp. 50–67.

J. S. F. PARKER, 'The United Arab Republic', *International Affairs*, vol. 38, no. 1, January 1962, pp. 15–28.

D. PERETZ, 'Democracy and the Revolution in Egypt', *Middle East Journal*, vol. 13, no. 1, Winter 1959, pp. 26–40.

M. PERLMANN, 'Fusion and Confusion: Arab mergers and realignments', *Middle Eastern Affairs*, vol. 9, no. 4, April 1958, pp. 126–31.

A. PERLMUTTER, 'The Arab Military Elite', *World Politics*, vol. 22, no. 2, January 1970, pp. 269–300.

W. RANGE, 'An Interpretation of Nasserism', *Western Political Quarterly*, vol. 12, no. 4, December 1959, pp. 1005–16.

R. J. RATNAM, 'Charisma and Political Leadership', *Political Studies*, vol. 12, no. 3, October 1964, pp. 341–54.

N. SAFRAN, 'Arab Politics, Peace and War', *Orbis*, vol. 18, no. 2, Summer 1974, pp. 377–401.

P. J. VATIKIOTIS, 'Dilemmas of Political Leadership in the Arab Middle East: The Case of the United Arab Republic', *American Political Science Review*, vol. 55, no. 1, March 1961, pp. 103–11.

——, 'Egypt's Politics of Conspiracy', *Survey*, vol. 18, no. 2, Spring 1972, pp. 83–99.

D. WASSINGER, 'Land Reform in Egypt and its Repercussions', *International Affairs*, vol. 29, no. 1, January 1953, pp. 1–10.

W. ZARTMAN, 'Africa as a Subordinate State System in International Relations', *International Organization*, vol. 21, no. 3, Summer 1967, pp. 545–64.

PERIODICALS

al-Ahram (Cairo)
al-Akhbar (Cairo)
Akhbar al-Yawm (Cairo)
Akhir Sa'a (Cairo)
Arab Report and Record (London)
Egyptian Gazette (Cairo)
The *Guardian* (London)
al-Hayat (Beirut)
al-Jumhuriya (Cairo)
Majallat al-Azhar (Cairo)
al-Mussawar (Cairo)
al-Nahar (Beirut)
New York Herald Tribune (New York)
New York Times (New York)
The *Observer* (London)
Rose al-Yusif (Cairo)
Sunday Times (London)
al-Thawra (Baghdad)
Time magazine (New York)
The *Times* (London)
USSR and the Third World (London)

DOCUMENTS

American University of Beirut, Department of Political Studies and Public Admin-
istration, *Arab Political Documents*.
Arab Republic of Egypt, Ministry of Education, Department of Statistics, *Com-
parative Statistics of Education, 1961/62–1970/71*.
British Broadcasting Corporation, *Summary of World Broadcasts*, part IV: *The Arab
World, Israel, Greece, Turkey, Iran*.
Council on Foreign Relations, *Documents on American Foreign Relations*.
Iraq, Wizarat al-Irshad, *Speeches on Unity between Iraq and the United Arab Republic, 1963*.
al-Jumhuriya al-Arabiya al-Muttahida, *Mahadhir Jalsat Mubahathat al-Wuhda, 1963*.
al-Jumhuriya al-Arabiya al-Muttahida, Maslahat al-Isti'lamat, *Majmu'at Khutab wa
Tasrihat wa Bayanat al-Rais Gamal Abd al-Nasser*.
Royal Institute of International Affairs, *Documents on International Affairs*.
United Arab Republic, Information Department, *Arab Political Encyclopedia: Docu-
ments and Notes, 1961*.
United Arab Republic, Information Department, *The Charter*.
United Arab Republic, Ministry of Education, Department of Statistics, *Comparative
Statistics of Education, 1953/1954–1961/1962*.
United Arab Republic, Information Department, *President Gamal Abd al-Nasser's
Speeches and Press-Interviews*.
United Arab Republic, Ministry of Information and National Guidance, *The Provi-
sional Constitution of the United Arab Republic, 1958*.
United Arab Republic, Central Agency for Public Mobilisation and Statistics,
Statistical Handbook, 1952–1970.
United Nations, Department of Economic and Social Affairs, *Demographic Yearbook*.
United Nations, Department of Economic and Social Affairs, *Economic Developments in
the Middle East, 1957/1958, 1959/1961*.
United Nations, Department of Economic and Social Affairs, *Statistical Yearbook*.
United Nations, Department of Economic and Social Affairs, *Yearbook of International
Trade Statistics*.
United Nations, Security Council, *Official Records, 13th Year, 1958*.
UNESCO, *Basic Facts and Figures, 1961*.
UNESCO, *Statistical Yearbook*.
UNESCO, *Statistics of Students Abroad, 1962–1968*.

Index

Aflaq, Michel, 19
Ahmad, Imam (of Yemen), 35
al-Ahram, 16, 26, 27, 51, 161, 189, 197
Alexandria, Arab summit conference in (1964), 149
Alexandria Protocol, 4–5
Algiers, Arab summit conference in (1966), 46, 47
Amer, Marshal Abd al-Hakim, 21, 114, 116–17, 118, 120, 160, 192
Arab character, 52
Arab Common Market, 154–5, 158
Arab Economic Unity Council, 155
Arab–Israeli wars, *see* Sinai War (1956); June War (1967); October War (1973)
Arab League, 25, 33
   establishment of, 4–5
   Egypt's dominance in, 25, 161–2
   challenge to Egypt's dominance in, 36–7
   meeting in 'Shtoura', 37
Arab nationalism, 4, 117, 122, 127, 133–4, 192
   Egypt and, 4–5, 16
   and Islam, 89–90
   as a value of Egyptian foreign policy, 129–33, 193–4
   motivation for policies, 131
   limitation on policies, 131–2
   justification for policies, 132–3
Arab Oil Conference, 156
Arab socialism, 35
Arab Socialist Union (ASU)
   and press ownership, 92–3
   influence on decision-making, 120, 192–3
Arab solidarity, the objective of, 69, 160, 201
   adherence to, 30–1, 43–6, 53–9, 144–5, 148–9, 150–1, 198
   abandonment of, 36, 46
Arab world, 2
   Egypt primacy in, 1, 2
Arab unity, 21, 142–3, 148
   Nasser and, 21

redefinition of, 30, 36
   as a goal of Egypt's foreign policy, 140–141
   as an unattainable goal, 194
   and Egyptian patriotism, 195
   see also 'comprehensive unity'
Arafat, Yasir, 54
Aref, President Abd al-Salam, 24, 25, 26, 28, 42, 142, 143, 149, 155
Aref, President Abd al-Rahman, 56
al-Asad, President Hafiz, 196, 199
Aswan High Dam, 14–15
Authoritarian System
   definition, 98
   Egypt as, 103–7, 121–2
   and the personality variable, 107
al-Azhar, Sheikh of, 90, 189
al-Azhar, University of, 90
Azm, Khaled al, 18

Baath Party (Iraq), 56
   and unity with Egypt, 41–2
Baath Party (Syria)
   and unity with Egypt, 19–20, 30, 41–2
Badran, Shams al-Din, 116–17
Baghdad Pact, 12–16, 103, 129, 130, 149, 161, 171
Bandung Conference, 12
Bandwagon, propaganda technique of
   definition of, 170
al-Bitar, Salah al-Din, 19, 29, 41, 136
Bourguiba, President Habib (of Tunisia), 25, 45, 169
Britain, 9
   occupation of Egypt, 3–4
   policies in the Middle East, 126

Cabinet, *see* Egyptian Cabinet
Cairo, Arab summit conference in (1964), 43–4, 149
Capability
   definition of, 70, 95–6
Chamoun, President Camille (of Lebanon), 17, 22, 25, 142, 168, 169
Charisma
   definition of, 102

229